ANITA RODDICK

BODY AND SOUL

Profits with Principles—

*The Amazing
Success Story of
Anita Roddick
&
The Body Shop*

CROWN PUBLISHERS, INC.
New York

Published by Crown Publishers, Inc.,
201 East 50th Street, New York, New York 10022.
Member of the Crown Publishing Group.

Published in Great Britain by
Ebury Press in 1991.

CROWN is a trademark of Crown Publishers, Inc.

Manufactured in Great Britain

Library of Congress Cataloging-in-Publication Data
Roddick, Anita
Body & soul / by Anita Roddick.
p.   cm.
1. Body Shop (Firm)—History.   2. Cosmetics industry—
Great Britain—History.   3. Roddick, Anita, 1942-   .
4. Women in business—Great Britain—Biography.   I. Title.
II. Title: Body and soul.
HD9970.5.C674B637   1991   91-12772
338.4'766855'0941—dc20   CIP
ISBN 0-517-58542-1

10   9   8   7   6   5   4   3   2   1

First American Edition

CONTENTS

A girl whose cheeks are covered with paint Has an advantage with me over one whose ain't.

Ogden Nash

There are quantities of human beings, but there are many more faces, for each person has several.

Rainer Maria Rilke

The world is a looking-glass and gives back to every man the reflection of his own face.

William Makepeace Thackeray

To all those customers
in the first years
who brought their bottles
back for a refill

I am donating all my royalties from this book to the entrepreneurial, spirited people and organizations working to right social wrongs. They will include UNPO, the Unrepresented Nations and Peoples' Organization, a self-governing, self-help organization made up of the world's 'voiceless' people: the Kurds, the American Indians, the Tibetans and others learning from each other's experiences and providing legal, media and other professional services. Also The Medical Foundation, a team of doctors who provide physical and psychological help to victims of torture; and people like Nicu Stancesceau, a prisoner of conscience and a torture victim himself, who is setting up a printing press to disseminate information, free from state censorship, to the people of Romania.

INTRODUCTION

When I opened the first Body Shop in Brighton in 1976 I knew nothing about business; my sole object was simply to survive, to earn enough to feed my kids. If it hadn't worked, I would have found something else to do.

But it did work. And I'm glad. Today The Body Shop is an international company rapidly expanding around the world and in those intervening years I have learned a lot.

Much of what I have learned will be found in this book, for I believe that we, as a company, have something worthwhile to say about how to run a successful business without losing your soul.

This is not a conventional autobiography nor is this a conventional business book. But there is a lot of my life in this book because it is, after all, the story of a personal vision. A vision is something you see and others don't. Some people would say that's a pocket definition of lunacy. But it also defines entrepreneurial spirit. Yet entrepreneurs need to be driven. If I had to nominate a driving force in my life, I'd plump for passion every time. My passionate belief is that business can be fun, it can be conducted with love and a powerful force for good.

In business, as in life, I need to be entertained, to have a sense of family, to be part of a community, to feel constantly the thrill of the unexpected. I have always wanted the people who work for The Body Shop to share those feelings.

Now this book extends the 'family' even further, out into the public arena. I'd like to think there are no limits to our family, no limits to what can be achieved. I find that an inspiring thought. I hope you do, too.

I AM STILL LOOKING FOR THE MODERN-DAY EQUIVALENT OF THOSE QUAKERS WHO RAN SUCCESSFUL BUSINESSES, MADE MONEY BECAUSE THEY OFFERED HONEST PRODUCTS AND TREATED THEIR PEOPLE DECENTLY, WORKED HARD, SPENT HONESTLY, SAVED HONESTLY, GAVE HONEST VALUE FOR MONEY, PUT BACK MORE THAN THEY TOOK OUT AND TOLD NO LIES. THIS BUSINESS CREED, SADLY, SEEMS LONG FORGOTTEN.

1

NASTY BUSINESS

I hate the beauty business. It is a monster industry selling unattainable dreams. It lies. It cheats. It exploits women. Its major product lines are packaging and garbage. It is no wonder that Elizabeth Arden once said that the cosmetics business was the 'nastiest in the world'.

To me, the whole notion of a 'beauty' business is profoundly disturbing. What is beauty? I believe beauty is about vivaciousness and energy and commitment and self-esteem, rather than some ideal arrangement of limbs or facial features as celebrated in fashion magazines and beauty pageants. Yet the beauty business is what the cosmetics industry is all about.

In my view the cosmetics industry should be promoting health and wellbeing; instead it hypes an outdated notion of glamour and sells false hopes and fantasy. With the muscle of multi-million dollar advertising budgets, the major cosmetics houses seek to persuade women that they can help them look younger and more 'beautiful'. Yet they know that such claims are nonsense.

What is even worse is that the industry seems to have absolutely no sense of social responsibility; and in its desperate need to chase profits in an area that has been experiencing, at best, sluggish growth for years, it is moving into territory where it should have no place. It is producing lipstick and eye shadow for children in a society where the spread of child pornography is causing increasing concern. It has even launched expensive perfumes for babies and toddlers – how decadent can you get?

While totally frivolous and worthless products proliferate, the industry is signally failing to take account of real needs. Look at the demographic change in Western society. We now have an ageing population, with 12 per cent over the age of sixty-five. As you get older your skin and body change and your requirement for cosmetics also changes. A major thrust of The Body Shop research is devoted to the needs of the elderly. But is the rest of the industry coming up with products for older people? Only those which purport to sell youth. There is not a single cosmetics company addressing their demands. Why not? Because they are too busy creating products that no one needs, too busy trying to persuade women that they need not grow old.

Inside the Dream Machine

The essential dilemma for the cosmetics industry can be easily explained. The big growth area is not in fragrance or make-up, but in skin care products, yet the simple truth is that such products can do nothing more than cleanse, polish and protect the skin and hair. That's it. Amen. End of story. There are no magic potions, no miracle cures, no rejuvenating creams. That is all hype and lies.

The skin is made up of three layers – under the outer (the stratum corneum) is the epidermis and under that lies the dermis, largely made up of collagen fibres, a fibrous protein which gives it support. When you age, these fibres are not replaced as rapidly and become damaged by the cumulative effect of sunlight, pollution and an assortment of urban and environmental stresses. As a result, the dermis gets thinner and so the outer skin sags and wrinkles appear – in other words, you start to age visibly. Some cosmetics companies endeavour to persuade you that they manufacture products that can supplement your skin's natural collagen supply, thus hitting the ageing process where it hurts. No such luck. Like the camel trying to squeeze through the eye of a needle, collagen molecules are simply too big to penetrate the outer layers of the skin. Therefore they can't supplement your own collagen reserves, which are generated deep down in the dermis. The plain truth is that no cosmetic product can prevent the ageing process. Nor, indeed, would one even be allowed under existing consumer legislation. Any product that could do that would not be a cosmetic, it would be a drug.

It seems that no one in the 'beauty business' wants to face up to this fundamental fact (at least in public), just as no ones wants to admit, for example, that every moisture cream can work. It does not matter if it is in a plastic pot and costs £2 a litre or if it is in a cut-glass designer jar with a solid gold stopper and costs £200 per gram. The net result is essentially the same. All moisture creams, whatever fancy names they may have, work on the principle of encouraging the skin to absorb moisture and retain it. That's all.

The industry clearly has a vested interest in concealing this information from the customer. So, to camouflage the truth and confuse the consumer, cosmetics companies are rewriting the book on dirty tricks in advertising, from spurious 'promises' which can never be fulfilled ('We promise you'll look and feel years younger') to mystification with pseudo-scientific, hi-tech jargon ('Contains DNA22-b, the astonishing new formula!'). It is all part of their effort to invest a product with qualities which will somehow make it appear better than its competitors.

So we have sales assistants at cosmetics counters in department stores dressed up in white coats like laboratory assistants. I am intrigued by those who buy 'cosmeceutical' products, like moisturizers with 'anti-time' devices 'tested by NASA', and the 'Time Complex Capsules' to turn old skin into young skin. We have creams 'synchronized to your skin's natural rhythm'. We have liposomes and niosomes and all the other hype-osomes.

And we have an entire industry that, in order to justify its own spurious existence, must believe that the world is filled with women desperate to cling to their fading youth, eager to believe nonsense dreamed up by cynical advertising copywriters and willing to pay ever bigger prices for ever smaller portions of lotions not much more effective than any old grease you care to think of.

Fact or Fancy

Perhaps it is just too much to expect a cosmetics house to tell the unvarnished truth: 'Ladies, this cream is no better and no worse than any other cream on the market but we are asking you to pay a lot of money for it because it is in a very fancy bottle and a very nice box.' If they did that, where would the cosmetics industry be then? Instead of the truth, we are offered fantasies packaged by the advertising industry: stunning pictures of ravishing 'super-models' lounging on the deck of a yacht in the Caribbean, or descending a sweeping staircase in a ballgown, or flirting with an impossibly handsome companion at a pavement café in Paris. The implication is all too clear: use this product to become youthful, glamorous and desired.

Thus are women enslaved by the images of beauty and glamour gazing out at them from every advertising hoarding, every glossy magazine and every television commercial, enslaved to a never-ending struggle to attain some unattainable standard of perfection. By preying on women's fears – of lost youth, diminishing appeal and fading beauty – the false hopes offered by the cosmetics industry can only result in misery, demoralization and a deep-rooted sense of inadequacy.

The worldwide cosmetics and toiletries market has a turnover in excess of $80 billion, with the biggest profits generated at the 'prestige' end of the market, dominated by giants like Procter and Gamble, Unilever, Shiseido, L'Oreal, Avon and Revlon. The doyenne is Estée Lauder, one of the new family firms still in business, nowadays it is run by Leonard Lauder, Estée's son, who was once memorably quoted as saying that he aimed to cater for the 'kept woman mentality'.

All these companies spend millions on research and development – usually between 2 and 3 per cent of their turnover – not so much in any realistic hope of finding a miracle cure to the problem of ageing, but to produce creams and potions that seem like miracle cures. Most skin-care treatments simply make the skin absorb and retain more water resulting in a smoother surface and a plumping up of the skin. They might temporarily seem to reduce wrinkles, but they are in no sense anti-ageing. Yet skin care is the big growth area in the market, largely because women seem willing to pay increasingly higher prices for increasingly smaller pots of cream, if they can be convinced that the stuff will prevent or remove wrinkles. It is in the convincing – the marketing – that the real science lies, and it is there that the budgets are fattest. The multinationals think nothing of spending $10 million on the promotion of a new product.

Even more obscene sums are spent on promoting and advertising perfumes. It said that the average cost of launching an up-market fragrance is now over £5 million: Calvin Klein spent £17 million in a single year promoting Obsession. If you hit the jackpot with a new fragrance it is like having an oil well in your back yard, since you can charge up to £100 a gram for a product that might cost no more than £1 to manufacture. Advertising and packaging account for nearly half the retail price of a bottle of perfume. Designing the purple bottle for Poison – the greatest European scent success of the eighties – was said to have cost Dior £1 million. Why worry? The biggest-selling top-price perfumes – like Chanel No.5, L'Air du Temps, Giorgio, Elizabeth Taylor's 'signature' fragrance, Passion, and Poison itself – probably accrue around £50 million a year each. Some 30 per cent is profit, split between the retailer and manufacturer.

Part of the problem is that the industry is now controlled by men, even though, ironically, it was founded by a handful of powerful women.

As an example of even more ludicrous extravagance, the recent launch of Chanel's new men's fragrance, L'Egoiste, takes some beating. Chanel hired a French art director, Jean-Paul Goude, to produce a thirty-second television commercial which consisted of a surreal montage of models appearing at windows flying open and slamming shut. The original idea was to use the façade of the Carlton Hotel in Cannes, but Goude decided the light was not right on the French Riviera. Where was the light right? Brazil.

One hundred and fifty workmen were employed for a month and a half to reconstruct the façade of the Carlton Hotel, turrets and all, in Brazil. No fewer than forty-seven models and actresses were required for the shooting, which took ten days. It is said that Goude wanted to hire Jack Nicholson to play the role of the Egoist, but he turned out to be too expensive, even for Chanel. No one will admit how much it cost to make this commercial, but it must have taken the lion's share of L'Egoiste's £1.3 million launch budget. Who pays for this extravagance? The consumer, of course.

Cosmetics Kings Rule

Unquestionably, part of the problem is that the industry is now controlled by men, even though, ironically, it was founded by a handful of powerful women – Helena Rubenstein, Elizabeth Arden, Coco Chanel and Estée Lauder. Most of the cosmetics houses they set up are now no more than baubles in a string of multinational companies. The businessmen who run them betray little grasp of the fact that the notions they are trading in – age, beauty, self-esteem – are more often than not an emotional powder keg for their customers. Instead, they exhibit a blind faith in the efficacies of technology or, worse still, they dive for the bottom line. Corporate raider Ronald Perelman has talked about using the profits generated by Revlon as a 'funding vehicle for our other investments'. But there is only one way for a cosmetics company to become a cash cow for a multi-billion-dollar holding company – and that is by putting a fuse to that powder keg.

I remember reading a remark by Charles Revlon, the founder of Revlon, who said: 'In the factory we make cosmetics; in the store we sell hope.' Well, hope is fine, but where is the evidence that the industry has ever been capable of fulfilling hopes? One of the cosmetics trade associations recently claimed, with apparent pride, that the industry created 'hopes and dreams'. I think the essential truth of this statement (although personally I have never met a woman who bought a moisturizer to fulfil her hopes and dreams) was entirely unintentional.

If in fact the cosmetics industry was nothing more than a dream machine, that perhaps would not be too bad. But the truth is that instead of creating hopes and dreams the men running the industry are actually creating false needs and unnecessary fears. Why? So they can market a product to meet those illusory needs or alleviate those illusory fears. (The vaginal deodorant was a classic example.) Their objective is simple: survival in the corporate jungle. It is a grotesque business charade which, in the end, demoralizes women.

I have never met someone from the cosmetics industry who doesn't know – with absolute certainty – that nothing they produce can do anything more than cleanse, polish and protect the skin and hair. But do they care? Of course they don't.

Having decided which insecurity they intend to capitalize on, they must then find an antidote, preferably some 'scientific' or 'revolutionary' formula about which they can make extragavant claims. It does not really matter much what it is, since it is not going to work anyway. If it looks good, feels good and smells good, the cosmetics captains can rely on the power of advertising to persuade women it is doing them good.

It is immoral to trade on fear. It is immoral constantly to make women feel dissatisfied with their bodies. It is immoral to deceive a customer by making miracle claims for a product. It is immoral to use a photograph of a glowing sixteen-year-old to sell a cream aimed at preventing wrinkles in a forty-year-old.

Obviously, they will want to ensure it is perfectly safe, so for them that means testing it extensively on animals. (In fact can we be sure that cosmetics companies which test their products on animals are motivated by concern for the wellbeing of their customers; or really more worried by the prospect of a crippling lawsuit?)

Next come the all-important decisions about packaging and presentation. Hours of time, endless agonizing and thousands of pounds will be devoted to getting the presentation right. The cosmetics captains will agonize over the shape of the bottle, the type of stopper, the colour of the ribbon round the neck, the design of the label, the size of the box. And what about the name? Should it be folksy or exotic? Sexy or sensible? Armies of market researchers will be despatched onto the streets to gauge public reaction to a range of test names.

When all the decisions about presentation have been made, then comes the ticklish problem of fixing the price. It could well be that the ingredients which make up the product do not cost more than a few pence, but this is irrelevant. First the consumer has to pay for all the expensive packaging, but in any case the cosmetics captains believe, truly believe, that if a product is marketed too cheaply then no one will believe it is any good. So they ponder the question of the price from the opposite perspective: not 'what is the least we can charge?', but 'what is the most we can get away with charging?' So a secretary has to work three or four hours to make the after-tax cash necessary to buy herself a lipstick.

I believe this to be immoral. It is immoral to trade on fear. It is immoral constantly to make women feel dissatisfied with their bodies. It is immoral to deceive a customer by making miracle claims for a product. It is immoral to use a photograph of a glowing sixteen-year-old to sell a cream aimed at preventing wrinkles in a forty-year-old.

That's Business?

It is immoral, but it slots perfectly well into the context of a general business environment in which greed has become respectable and worth is measured by what you accumulate rather than what you contribute; into an environment of insider trading and backhanders; into an environment in which bosses award themselves exorbitant pay rises while they are sacking hundreds of their employees. It is immoral, but certainly no more so than Milken and Boesky and their insider trading, or the million-pound fees paid for advice in the City fraud trials. If someone offered me £1000 for advice I would be surprised. If someone offered me £100,000 I would be deeply suspicious. If someone offered me £3 million – for *advice*, for Christ's sake – I'd run a mile!

I am mystified by the fact that the business world is apparently proud to be seen as hard and uncaring and detached from human values. Why is altruism in business seen as alien to the point where anyone claiming to be motivated by it is considered suspect? I personally don't know how the hell anybody can survive running a successful business in the nineties without caring. I don't know how they keep their role within the community. I don't know how they keep their soul intact. There is not even any humanity in business language; indeed it is conspicuous by its absence. John Harvey-Jones, the brilliant former head of ICI, once said that the word 'love' was as threatening in business as talking about a loss on the balance sheet. Perhaps that is why using words like 'love' and 'care' is so difficult in today's extraordinarily macho business world. No one seems to know how to put the concept into practice. Instead, the chauvinist City encourages the idea that there is some mystique about business, using alienating jargon to prevent ordinary people from understanding what is going on. It has been made into a science, which it is not: it is just trade.

I think all business practices would improve immeasurably if they were guided by 'feminine' principles – qualities like love and care and intuition. Women, too, would understand the need for an ethical philosophy to guide international business. Today's corporations have global responsibilities because their decisions affect world problems concerning economics, poverty, security and the environment. Yet while global business binds the planet in a common fate, there is no international code of practice, no agreement on mutual responsibilities. And so much *could* be done.

> **I think all business practices would improve immeasurably if they were guided by 'feminine' principles – qualities like love and care and intuition.**

'Business is a combination of human energy and money and to me that equals power. I would go so far as to say that business is the most powerful force in society today and it is a force that ought to be harnessed to effect social change, to improve the quality of life in those societies around the world where basic needs are not being met.' This is a quote from an American friend, Ben Cohen, co-founder of Ben and Jerry's Ice Cream Company of Vermont, which is like a brother company to The Body Shop. I completely agree with Ben, and further believe that business not only bears a responsibility to effect change, but ought to be the instigator of that change.

The trouble is that the business world is too conservative and fearful of change. All this talk about free enterprise, innovation, entrepreneurship, individuality...it's nothing but hot air. High street giants, business empires everywhere, worship mediocrity. In their love affair with giantism they pay public lip service to the need for change, but I believe that unofficially they fear it.

It baffles me why these giant corporations do not occasionally pause and spend some time in their archives, investigating the soul of the company – how it got started, what it has achieved. The shared heritage of company and community should be emphasized; conversation should be generated with the consumer. Then, perhaps, instead of these huge corporations getting bigger and bigger and more and more faceless, someone might think about turning them into something more personal for their customers.

In the old days, the great British retailers may well have been driven by the profit motive but they were also great philanthropists, functioning pillars of society and builders of the community. Their monuments were museums and cultural foundations. Now what is the retailing industry building? Shopping malls! Monuments of non-communication and schools for alienation, which dull the mind with their uniformity. Is any retailer thinking about how to make a shopping mall function socially as an arena of human contact or centre for useful, social information, like a village well in traditional societies? I doubt it.

I started with a kind of grace which clung to the notion that in business you didn't tell lies.

For me there are no modern-day heroes in the business world. I have heard of no multinational company which genuinely incorporates the pursuit of profit with social awareness, which provides any kind of vision for its workers, which accepts that commercial success and social responsibility are entirely compatible. I have met no captain of industry who made my blood surge. I have met no corporate executive who values labour and who exhibits a sense of joy, magic or theatre – qualities which I think are essential in business.

In the fifteen years I have been involved in the world of business it has taught me nothing. There is so much ignorance in top management and boards of directors: all the big companies seem to be led by accountants and lawyers and become moribund carbon-copy versions of each other. If there is excitement and adventure in their lives, it is contained in the figures on the profit and loss sheet. What an indictment!

I am still looking for the modern-day equivalent of those Quakers who ran successful businesses, made money because they offered honest products and treated their people decently, worked hard themselves, spent honestly, saved honestly, gave honest value for money, put back more than they took out and told no lies. The business creed, sadly, seems long forgotten.

Born Innocent

I didn't know anything about business when I opened the first Body Shop in Brighton in 1976. The vocabulary of business was part of a language I did not speak. And I certainly had no ambitions to start a big international company. I didn't want to change the world; I just wanted to survive and be able to feed my kids. The extent of my business acumen went no further than the grim knowledge that I would have to take in £300 a week to stay open. But I did know how to trade.

I started with a kind of grace which clung to the notion that in business you didn't tell lies. I didn't think of myself as an entrepreneur. My motivation for going into the cosmetics business was irritation: I was annoyed by the fact that you couldn't buy small sizes of everyday cosmetics and angry with myself that I was always too intimidated to go back and exchange something if I didn't like it. I also recognized that a lot of the money I was paying for a product was being spent on fancy packaging which I didn't want. So I opened a small shop to sell a small range of cosmetics made from natural ingredients in five different sizes in the cheapest possible plastic containers.

I did not deliberately set out to buck the trend – how would I even know what the trend was? – but it turned out that my instinctive trading values were diametrically opposed to the business practices of the cosmetics industry in just about every area:

- They were prepared to sell false hopes and unattainable dreams; I was not. From the start, we explained to customers in simple language everyone could understand exactly what a product would do and what it wouldn't do.
- They sold through hype; I was so innocent I didn't even know what hype was.
- They thought packaging was important; I thought it was totally irrelevant. We happily filled old lemonade bottles with our products if a customer asked.
- They tested on animals; I was repulsed by the practice and made it clear that I would never sell a product that had been tested on animals.
- They spent millions on market research; we simply said to our customers, 'Tell us what you want and we will try and get it for you.'
- They all had huge marketing departments; I never fully understood what marketing was.
- They had enormous advertising budgets; we have never spent a cent on advertising. At the beginning we couldn't afford it, and by the time we could afford it we had got to the point where I would be too embarrassed to do it.
- They talked about beauty products; I banished the word 'beauty'.
- They worshipped profits; we didn't. In all the time I have been in business we have never had a meeting to discuss profits – we wouldn't know how to do it.
- Finally, and most importantly, they thought it was not the business of business to get involved in wider issues, in the protection of the environment or involvement with the community; I thought there was nothing more important.

I honestly believe I would not have succeeded if I had been *taught* about business.

Challenging the Status Quo

A great advantage I had when I started The Body Shop was that I had never been to business school. As I didn't know how things were supposed to be done, I didn't know the rules and I didn't know the risks. As far as I was concerned there were no rules, and so I just went my own merry way working from gut instinct. I honestly believe I would not have succeeded if I had been *taught* about business. I would, for example, have learned to kow-tow to people who are usually irrelevant to enterprise thinking, like bank managers. I found that a bank manager is the last person to ask for business advice because he is only a house-keeper of money. For him it is always a question of percentages and break-even points, profit and loss; he rarely gets to grips with an *idea* and how to promote and manage it. That's not business, that's just housekeeping.

Unfortunately, in Britain the two are confused and so no one is nurturing new talent and bright ideas. At a dinner I once sat next to a bank manager who was at pains to justify turning down loans because of the number of new businesses which failed. He baffled me. All I could say to him was: 'Do you realize how many great opportunities you've lost?'

There is no real culture for ideas here. In the United States getting start-up money is easy – at least it was before the recent Savings and Loans crashes when the banks lost their credibility almost overnight. You could get money for starting a dogs' funeral service if you wanted to. Here, it is so much more difficult because we British don't have that culture of enterprise. We have too much respect for 'business' as perceived by 'businessmen' – which seems to mean just money, or the City, or banks – and there's very little willingness to put money into innovation.

To me, what is wonderful about The Body Shop is that we still don't know the rules. Instead, we have a basic understanding that to run this business you don't have to know anything. Skill is not the answer, neither is money. What you need is optimism, humanism, enthusiasm, intuition, curiosity, love, humour, magic and fun and that secret ingredient – euphoria. None of this appears on the curriculum of any business school.

The status quo says that the business of business is to make profits. We have always challenged that. For us the business of business is to keep the company alive and breathlessly excited, to protect the workforce, to be a force for good in our society and then, after all that, to think of the speculators. I have never kow-towed to the speculators or considered them to be my first responsibility. They play the market without much concern for the company or its values. Most are only interested in the short term and quick profit; they don't come to our Annual General Meeting and they don't respond to our communications. As far as I am concerned, I have no obligations to these people at all.

How do you ennoble the spirit when you are selling something as inconsequential as a cosmetic cream?

I believe that if companies are in business solely to make money, you can't fully trust whatever else they do or say. They may create jobs, pay taxes, contribute to charity and provide an array of goods and services, but all that is incidental to their real purpose, which is to make profits for their shareholders.

I don't understand why anyone would want to run a business like that. The whole sense of fun is lost, the whole sense of play, of derring-do, of 'Oh God we screwed that one up.' I see business as a Renaissance concept, where the human spirit comes into play. It does not have to be drudgery; it does not have to be the science of making money. It can be something that people genuinely feel good about, but only if it remains a human enterprise.

How do you ennoble the spirit when you are selling something as inconsequential as a cosmetic cream? You do it by creating a sense of holism, of spiritual development, of feeling connected to the workplace, the environment and relationships with one another. It's how to make Monday to Friday a sense of being alive rather than slow death. How do you give people a chance to do a good job? By making them feel good about what they are doing. The spirit soars when you are satisfying your own basic material needs in such a way that you are also serving the needs of others honourably and humanely. Under these circumstances, I can even feel great about a moisturizer.

Today The Body Shop is a global business with more than six hundred shops trading in eighteen different languages in thirty seven countries around the world, in locations ranging from the Arctic Circle to Bondi Beach. It is a business unlike any other: we have no marketing department and no advertising department. We operate according to criteria which place more emphasis on human values than on strictly commercial considerations.

Keeping Our Soul Intact

Social and environmental dimensions are woven into the fabric of the company itself. They are neither first nor last among our objectives, but an ongoing part of everything we do. They make our lives infinitely more difficult and challenging, yet richer in every human sense.

Not a single decision is ever taken in The Body Shop without first considering environmental and social issues. We do not, for example, sell any products which consume a disproportionate amount of energy during their manufacture or disposal, cause unnecessary waste, use ingredients derived from threatened species or threatened environments, or adversely affect other countries, particularly in the Third World. We have an Environmental Projects Department which monitors the company's practices and products to ensure they are environmentally sound and up-to-date, organizes campaigns, coordinates global projects, gives guidance and support to local activities and liaises with other pressure groups. We have a vigorous 'Trade Not Aid' policy, encouraging local communities in the Third World to utilize their resources and trade with us to help alleviate poverty. We use our shops worldwide as 'arenas of education' to proselytize among staff, customers and passers-by on issues as diverse as the destruction of the rainforests and the spread of Aids. Every shop has its own local community project run by volunteers from the staff.

As a result of what we have learned during the last fifteen years, we have evolved a simple credo. It goes like this: you can run a business differently from the way most businesses are run; you can share your prosperity with your employees and empower them without being in fear of them; you can rewrite the book in terms of how a company interacts with the community; you can rewrite the book on Third World trade and global responsibility and on the role of educating the company, customers and shareholders; finally, you can do all this and still play the game according to the City, still raise money, delight the institutions and give shareholders a wondrous return on their investment.

The dilemmas we had to resolve early on were fundamental to developing our ideas. How do you cope with the creation of wealth, not only for yourself but also for your franchisees, without corroding the spirit? How do you stay successful and still keep your soul and your sense of fun, and remain human in a business environment that alienates humanity in every way?

We dealt with these dilemmas by coming out of the closet and declaring publicly that we intended to be a force for social change. We believed that it was possible to shift from a value system of ever-increasing profits to one in which core values were concerned with human and social issues and were founded on feminine values like love and care. We all shared an extraordinary level of optimism and a determination that our resources, plus the audience of millions passing by on the pavement and through the shops, could combine to raise consciousness, encourage debate and lead to action.

What we embarked upon was nothing less than an experiment founded on principles totally alien to mainstream business. Since 1984, the year The Body Shop went public, as far as I am concerned the business has existed for one reason only – to allow us to use our success to act as a force for social change, to continue the education and consciousness-raising of our staff, to assist development in the Third World and, above all, to help protect the environment. What we are trying to do is to create a new business paradigm, simply showing that business can have a human face and a social conscience.

What the financial community finds fairly perplexing is how we can adopt these attitudes and still be so highly rated on the stock market. And I keep telling them that there is no great mystery. All we are trying to do is create a business environment in which people are happy and fulfilled, so that they feel good about what they are doing and good about themselves.

We communicate with passion – and passion persuades.

Fundamental to this approach is our obsession with education, motivation and communication. We communicate with passion – and passion persuades. We preach and teach; we educate and inform. We do not, for example, train our staff to sell; I hate high-pressure sales techniques. The idea that everyone should walk out of our shops having bought something is anathema to me. We prefer to give staff information about the products, anecdotes about the history and derivation of the ingredients, and any funny stories about how they came on to Body Shop shelves. We want to spark conversations with our customers, not browbeat them to buy.

I spend about four months every year travelling the world looking for new products, and I make sure everyone knows where I have been, whom I have met and what ideas have surfaced, whether it is paper-making in Nepal, finding a use for brazil nuts in the Amazon, or how we might be able to adapt an old Japanese skin-care treatment made from nightingale droppings (we can't). In this way we involve our staff in everything that is going on. Mostly under thirty, mostly female, for them work is about a search for daily meaning as well as daily bread, for recognition as well as cash, for stimulation rather than torpor. They don't want to escape responsibility; they understand that responsibility enhances the quality of their existence. They are saying, 'I want a society and a job that values me more than the gross national product. I want work that engages the heart as well as the mind and body. I want a government that fosters friendship and nourishes the earth. I want something in my life not just to invest in, but to believe in.' In short, they simply want the chance to dream of noble causes – and that is not easy when you are selling a moisture cream. The way we can make the dream come true is to encourage them to campaign on environmental

and social issues, to let them see that the organization for which they are working has decent human values.

During the late eighties and early nineties The Body Shop has combined with Friends of the Earth, Survival International and Greenpeace to run joint campaigns on acid rain, recycling, the vanishing countryside, the ozone layer, the green consumer and the genocide of indigenous tribes. Our staff achieved what no other environmental group internationally has ever achieved: in less than a month they collected more than one million signatures to protest against the burning of the rain forests. All we did was bring the issue to the marketplace and use our shops as a campaign platform. We donated window displays and provided posters and leaflets, and our staff and customers did the rest.

Obviously, at The Body Shop we want to keep the flag of social change flying and the ideas flowing. I anticipate it will be harder to remain radical as the years go by, but I am determined that we will become more radical, not less so.

It helped, I think, that we did not market our products as if they were the body and blood of Jesus Christ.

Sometimes when I look back on the last fifteen years I can't believe how easy it has been. Essentially all we did was address a whole group of women that the cosmetics industry had previously ignored – women like myself, who are not stupid and don't want to pay a fortune for a moisture cream which is nothing more than an oil and water emulsion. Why should it be as expensive as gold? These women wanted products with benign ingredients produced by a company run by women and with an understanding of women. If your products fulfil a need, are good value, effective and visually exciting; are presented in a stimulating but non-threatening retail environment; and you have an enthusiastic and well-educated staff, there is no great problem selling them.

It helped, I think, that we did not market our products as if they were the body and blood of Jesus Christ. We did not think it was necessary to take a moisture cream too seriously. The trouble with marketing is that consumers are hyped out. The din of advertising and promotion has grown so loud that they can no longer tell one pitch from another and they are becoming cynical about the whole process. They have heard too many lies. What we have tried to do is establish credibility by educating our customers, giving them intelligent information about where ingredients come from, how they are tested and what they can be used for. It humanizes the company, making customers feel they are buying from people whose business practices they know and trust.

What I cannot understand is why people often seem to think The Body Shop is extraordinary. It does not seem to me that we have been doing anything particularly revolutionary; I think of it as basic common sense and common decency. Business is, after all, just another form of human enterprise, so why should we expect less from it, in terms of social ethics, than we do from ourselves and our neighbours? Why is a company that is not greedy thought to be remarkable – or, more commonly, suspect?

Fortunately, attitudes are changing. The marketplace is now more human-oriented, more issue-oriented. People are saying they don't want to work for a, for example, chemical company that's screwing up the environment. Today there are even 'ethical' investment funds operating – and not before time. Increasing numbers are becoming committed to a more holistic, human way of trading, and I feel these people will be prime movers in a groundswell of change. I still believe that enlightened capitalism is the best way of changing society for the better. And I think that by the year 2000 any company that does not operate like The Body Shop will have a hard time operating at all.

One thing I have learned is that you have to be true to yourself. At The Body Shop we've done it our way. Our success has been a combination of happy accidents, the right people, good products, an honest approach – and, of course, the right values. Obviously we screw up occasionally; I don't claim to know what I'm doing all the time – even half the time. Beware of those who do. Those who are unquestioningly, 100 per cent sure that they know what they're doing you have to watch out for – they're the dangerous ones.

Credibility

IT WAS A BRUTAL CRASH COURSE IN INJUSTICE. IF A SLUMBERING SOCIAL CONSCIENCE NEEDS A KICK START TO GET GOING, THEN DATE MY AWAKENING TO THE DAY I PICKED UP THAT BOOK, BECAUSE AFTER THAT I WOULD DRIVE MY MOTHER MAD PESTERING HER TO SUBSCRIPTIONS TO WHATEVER GOOD CAUSE I MIGHT HAVE STUMBLED ACROSS.

2

PASTA AND CHIPS

My mother's name is Gilda Perella. She was born in a small village near Cassino in central Italy, and came to England as a nanny when she was fifteen. She still lives in the terraced house in Littlehampton, Sussex, where I was born in 1942. It is called 'Atina', after her village, and has bright red window frames. Inside, it is equally colourful: the front room is stuffed with kitsch knick-knacks, little glass and gilt ornaments, painted figurines, vases of all shapes and sizes; in her bedroom there are silk drapes everywhere. My mother has turned bad taste into an art form. In the garden she grows hundreds of plants in plastic pots and old drain pipes – it's like a wilderness. I think she is absolutely wonderful.

Gilda Pirella aka my mum

When I was eighteen something happened which made me realize that she is also one of the most courageous and romantic women I will ever know. I was a student teacher at the time, and at college we had been researching the influence of heredity. We were all looking back into our families to see how they had affected our characters.

One day I was standing by the electric fire in the front room, brushing my hair in the mirror; I was always brushing my hair at that time – I was obsessed by it. My mother was cooking in the kitchen and I called out to her: 'Isn't it sad that you and Henry didn't have any children?' Henry was my stepfather, who died when I was ten.

My mother didn't reply for a second, then I heard her say: 'I did.'

I was amazed. I thought, *My God, I've got some half brothers or sisters somewhere!* I said, 'Where are they, then?'

She came into the room, wiping her hands on her apron, and just said: 'It's you and Bruno.' Bruno is my younger brother.

I will never forget the absolute joy of that moment when I learned that the man who I had always thought was my stepfather – and whom I adored – was actually my real father. Everything seemed to fall into

'I'll never forget the joy of the moment when I discovered my stepfather Henry was my real father'

place, and it made perfect sense to me. It was as if an enormous weight of guilt had been lifted off my shoulders because I had never been able to identify with the man I thought was my father; I just didn't like him, didn't like anything about him. I didn't feel, intuitively, that he had anything to do with me. It gave me a lot of confidence in gut feelings – taught me to trust my instincts above everything else, and stood me in very good stead when I came to open my first shop.

Something else happened on that day – a boundless faith in the ideal of romantic love was planted in me forever.

Later my mother told me the whole amazing story. Her first marriage was more or less arranged within the family. It was understood that when she got to England she would marry Donny Perella, whose family was also from Atina. That was the way things were done in Italian families in those days, but a few months before the marriage my mother fell hopelessly in love with Donny's cousin, Henry, and Henry fell hopelessly in love with her. There was absolutely nothing they could do about it so Henry went off to America, broken-hearted, and my mother married Donny. They opened a club on the south coast, in Worthing.

Her first child died of meningitis, but by the outbreak of the Second World War she had two small daughters. Lydia and Velia. Throughout this time she had never forgotten Henry and corresponded with him frequently. During the war he suddenly turned up in Littlehampton, where Donny had bought a café, and they began a passionate affair in secret. My mother said she begged him to give her children and she was soon pregnant with me. Two years later Bruno was born.

Donny knew nothing of the affair, and my mother was able to pass off both children as his. How she did it – how a naïve Italian woman could manage such duplicity – I will never know. Henry desperately wanted to marry my mother, but at first she could not face up to the prospect of a divorce. So he went back to America, swearing he would never return unless she divorced Donny.

To big Italian Catholic families like the Perellas divorce was a mortal sin, but my mother eventually plucked up enough courage, helped by the fact that Donny had never bothered to conceal the fact that he had a mistress. It was an almighty scandal: she had to argue with the priest and the family and the grandparents, but she did it – all for love. In 1950 Henry returned from America and married my mother, but he had contracted tuberculosis and was already a sick man. They only had eighteen months together before he died, of a heart attack. He was only thirty-nine. Her epic romance turned into an almost unbearable tragedy.

She lived with her secret for almost another ten years before she judged the time was right to tell me the truth. At last the instinctive sense of continuity I'd felt with Henry's family made sense. And something else happened on that day – a boundless faith in the ideal of romantic love was planted in me forever.

What Made Me?

My early childhood memories are intertwined with the small Italian community in Littlehampton, the Perellas and the Perillis, most of whom I was related to, and my parents' café, the Clifton. I have no idea how or why a handful of Italian families came to settle in a small English seaside town. They just did, and they owned most of the cafés.

The Clifton Café, Littlehampton

Littlehampton had been a popular resort in Victorian times, but its grandeur was distinctly faded by the forties and it survived largely on day-trippers in 'Kiss Me Quick' hats. The Clifton Café was a converted Methodist chapel in the centre of a terrace of three cafés directly opposite the railway station. The Station Café, on our left, was owned by Henry's brother; while Dora's Café, on the right, was owned by another member of the family. The Clifton opened at 5 a.m. to provide breakfast for the local fishermen and stayed open through the day, serving non-stop plates of egg and chips and pie and chips and sausage and chips and fish and chips, until there were no more customers. At weekends we did a good trade with the hordes of trippers that poured out of London with their buckets and spades for a day out at the seaside.

My mother was the cook and my grandmother peeled potatoes in the garden out the back. As soon as we were old enough, all of us children

1945.
My father
with me

1947.
The Perilla Family with a cousin
on the left. Baby Bruno, Lidia,
me looking shy (HA!) and Velia

1972.
Sam & Anita
in the garden of
Woodlands Hotel

1952.
Me, about 10 years old.
How I hated
my curly hair!

1990.
The Roddicks, with
Sam always playing the fool.
The Lonnach Games, Scotland

We did love to be
beside the seaside. . .

were expected to help in the café after school and at weekends, taking orders, clearing tables, washing up, buttering endless slices of bread, operating the till. The work ethic, the idea of service, was second nature to us – perhaps because we were immigrants, I don't know. It was just what we did. What I do know is that those few cafés in the town which were owned by local people opened at nine and closed at five on the dot; those owned by the Italians were open all hours.

Even when I was small I realized we were different from English families. We were noisy, always screaming and shouting, we played music loudly, ate pasta and smelled of garlic. My grandmother would sit outside on the front doorstep doing crochet; my grandfather made ice cream in a garage at the back of his house. I never thought we were poor, but I never thought we were rich. To me, wealthy people had pelmets over their curtains – I was always amazed by pelmets – and went on holiday together. We never had family holidays.

At home we all slept in one room and rented off the other bedrooms to make money. Lydia and Velia shared one bed, my mother and I shared another, and my father slept in a third bed behind a curtained partition.

We had some good times in that room. My older sisters were wonderful storytellers and some nights we would turn the lights out and sit in the dark, with just the street light coming in through the window, while they told spooky stories. That light was the inspiration for a thousand escapist fantasies. Even now, the glow of a projector in a dark movie theatre or a shaft of sunlight in a shadowy room will send me spinning back in time to that front bedroom in Littlehampton.

I did not get to know Uncle Henry when I was little because he was away in America, but his sister, my Aunt Mary, lived in the house opposite us. She was a free spirit and had a real sense of mischief that struck chords in me. My own mother was so overburdened by work that I used to fantasize that there had been a mistake and that perhaps Aunt Mary was my mother. Curiously, I discovered much later that Aunt Mary was the only other person in the family who knew the truth about Bruno and me.

When I was five my mother took all of us – the children, that is – on a trip by train back to her village in Italy. We were all very surprised to find, when we arrived, that Uncle Henry was there. I had no idea of the significance of this, but he made a big impression on all of us. I remember him playing the mandolin in the moonlight, while pigs snuffled around in the courtyard outside.

Back in Littlehampton the divorce proceedings must have started, but I was not really aware of what was going on except that grown-ups would stop talking the minute I walked into the room.

Style Hits Littlehampton

Things began to change when Uncle Henry bought Donny out of the Clifton Café and transformed it into an American-style diner with a long aluminium bar and high stools. He put in pinball machines and a jukebox – the first in Littlehampton – and instead of the unremitting chips-with-everything menu he offered exotic ice-cream sundaes with knickerbocker glories and a little known American drink called Coca-Cola. Almost overnight the Clifton Café became the most popular hang-out in town, especially for young people.

The transformation of the Clifton was my first lesson in marketing aesthetics and the importance of theatre in creating atmosphere. I remember being dazzled by the Americana, by the Vargas girls on the Coca-Cola promo cards, by the brilliant colours on the jukebox and the style of everything. I absorbed it all.

None of us children knew that our mother had married Uncle Henry until after they came back from the registry office and gave us the news. I was very happy about it. Every morning I would watch him shaving at the kitchen sink, studying every movement he made. I wanted to be like him because to me he was a great romantic. He loved the arts and the theatre and encouraged me to read widely, way beyond my age group – he introduced me to Eugene O'Neill and John Steinbeck. One day he was reading Henry Miller's *Tropic of Capricorn* and I asked if I could read it too, but he said it was too soon. I was not able to read it until ten years later, when I was living in Paris.

At that time I was at a Roman Catholic school, St Catherine's Convent. Three memories stand out from those days: a

The Perella Sisters, 1945

J. White & Son, Littlehampton

It's great to "go steady"

You like it...; it likes you!

HOT DOGS

DRINK Coca-Cola

ICE COLD

"fresh

COOL OFF...HAVE FUN...GO BOWLING!

talk we had on Canada, the pet parrot that one of the teachers kept in her classroom, and the comics and bubble gum I used to trade. Uncle Henry had brought a lot back from America with him and the comics were the most prized commodity imaginable, especially in a Catholic convent school.

I may not have learned much at St Catherine's, but I certainly learned how to trade. I had the monopoly on American comics and bubble gum in Littlehampton and I knew how to use it. Boys were nice to me for the first time, instead of pulling my hair and calling me 'Bubbles'; even 'big' boys of twelve or thirteen deigned to talk to me. I had the leverage and power to swap my precious commodities for whole collections of cigarette cards and movie albums (never dolls). Although I had all the comics already at home, I pretended they were arriving in small batches week by week so I did not flood the market. I would whet my customers' appetites by promising them that there was an incredible Batman or Captain Marvel coming in. It was an interesting discipline.

The fact that I can remember little else about St Catherine's is mute testimony to the abysmal education we received. I seemed to spend much of the day trying to look up the nuns' wimples to see if they shaved their heads. But I fell heavily for all the religious ritual. As an early introduction to theatricality, the Catholic Church wasn't half bad.

One nun I particularly liked, Sister Immaculata, always seemed to champion the underdog. She referred to tramps as 'Knights of the Road' and talked about the under-privileged in society and how they should be given more consideration. I was so carried away by her innate goodness that I gave my new school uniform to another girl from a very poor family whose own was very old and tattered. We changed in the cloakrooms; my mother was hopping mad when I got home but secretly proud of what I had done. Even to this day she talks about it.

One day as I was walking home from school I was passing Aunt Margie's café when someone ran out, very white-faced, and said to me, 'Don't go into the Clifton – your Uncle Henry's not well.' Of course I went straight there. A group of people were in the garden clustered around Uncle Henry, who had collapsed. I just knew he was dead.

I said nothing. In a daze, I just walked out. I didn't know what I was supposed to do. I thought I would walk down towards Butlin's amusement park to see if I could find my sisters or Bruno. On the way I passed my mother, still in her apron, running towards the Clifton. I said nothing to her, but I just kept walking – I think I walked around like a zombie telling everyone I knew that my Uncle Henry was dead. The last thing I can remember that day was being put to bed by my mother. As she climbed up on to the dressing table to close the curtains I thought: 'Nothing is ever going to be the same again in this house.'

My mother spent the next few days cleaning the house from top to bottom; it was the only way she could deal with her anger and grief. (I'm the same way now – whenever I'm angry or depressed I start cleaning.) I was sitting on the stairs talking to her while she was scrubbing the lino in the hall when there was a knock at the door. It was the local priest, who wanted to talk about the funeral. I don't quite know what happened, but somehow they started arguing and then my mother suddenly picked up the bucket of dirty water and threw the lot all over the priest as he stood there on the doorstep, then she slammed the door. I was speechless – sacrilege on that scale well and truly slaughters any sacred cows you might otherwise revere later in life.

My mother did not want me to go to the funeral, but I sneaked into the church and then hid in some trees and watched as my Uncle Henry was buried. I still could not believe that he was gone; in fact it was a good three or four months before I began to experience a real sense of loss. It was then that I became aware of the strength of the bond I had had with him. All those discussions we would never have, all those lost conversations... I could hardly bear to think about it.

Change and More Change

My mother took over the running of the Clifton Café full-time and our lives subtly changed. Before, we children had just 'helped out' in the café; now we were working, really working, to make ends meet. We knew what we had to do to survive. My mother was tough with all of us. If she sent me to the butcher's to get some meat and she did not like the look of the joint I brought back, I would have to go back and change it. It was not an easy thing to do when you were ten years old.

Maybe it was the family upheavals that paved the way for another experience that devastated – and changed – me at this time. At home one day I picked up a paperback on the Holocaust. There were six pages of photographs from Auschwitz and they made such an impression on me that I can describe every one of them today. Riveted, stunned, I sat on a little stool near the electric fire trying to comprehend how man could wreak such havoc on man. It was a brutal crash course in injustice. If a slumbering social conscience needs a kick start to get it going, then I date my awakening to the day I picked up that book, because after that I would drive my mother mad pestering her for subscriptions to whatever good cause I might have stumbled across.

At school I managed to fail my eleven-plus exam, but there was not a great drama about it because I honestly don't think my mother understood the difference between a grammar school and a secondary modern. She was still very *paysanne* in many ways. I had my nose in a book at every opportunity and she used to say to me: 'You shouldn't read so much, you'll-a hurt your brain.'

I went to the Maude Allen Secondary Modern School for Girls, where I was a deeply unpromising pupil for the first year. Then, in my second year, one of the teachers broke through my indifference and managed to capture my imagination. It was like a light bulb suddenly switching on in my head. The more enthusiastic I became the more the teachers responded, and as my interest soared so did my ability. School became a joyous passage in my life and I became an absolute pain in the neck to all the other pupils because I was so much in love with learning. I can remember leaving school every Friday absolutely exulting in all that I had learned during the week. The burden of it was so fabulous, I felt so powerful knowing so much more each week.

My teachers were exceptional. They encouraged me, indulged me, let me get away with murder and didn't try to stamp on my personality. They recognized that I was different and let me be so. It was like *The Prime of Miss Jean Brodie* – they made me feel special, creative, original, inspired me to write, inspired me to act, supported me in everything I wanted to do and treated me like a young adult. Those teachers are indelibly printed on my memory – I can clearly remember Mrs Kirk, who introduced me to the '1812' Overture, and Miss Springham, who advised me to read Dylan Thomas and John Steinbeck, Miss Springham had bright orange hair and iridescent blue eye shadow, a bit like Bette Midler. She used to swear in front of us – describe some book as being 'bloody awful' – and we would feel terrifically grown up and mature and privileged to hear her views expressed so bluntly.

James Dean Lives!

In a fit of predictable teenage passion, I became obsessed with James Dean. *Really* obsessed, as if I wanted to be him. I was at a point in my life when I was hungry for mentors. I was a sponge for experience, driven by an immense curiosity about the lives of others. That's why I loved the cinema so much. With my own sense of theatres, I would wear someone else's reality the way my schoolfriends would sport a new cardigan. I wanted – *needed* – to be different. It was all to do with my private concept of immortality. To me, anonymity was a kind of death, and my worship of James Dean was a rejection of the anonymity in the little seaside town I had somehow landed in. His influences were mine. Everything Jimmy read, I read.

That is how I came to the poetry of Walt Whitman. *Leaves of Grass* celebrated the purely sensual in a way that knocked me sideways. It didn't make literal sense, but it made perfect poetic sense. Brecht, Strindberg, Dostoevsky, Faulkner – all of them offered valuable lessons in the ways in which aesthetics could be shaped by a social conscience. The 'College of One' that F. Scott Fitzgerald created to enlighten his lover Sheilah Graham sounded ideal to me.

Under the influence of Dean, I decided to perform a soliloquy in the 'Method' style of Stanislavsky for the school talent competition. My Mum, sitting in the front row, probably expected me to come out and do a song and dance number. Instead the curtains opened to a totally black stage with me in the middle dressed in filthy rags and bound with chains. I began the soliloquy with a blood-curdling scream that almost gave my Mum a heart attack; she could never understand how I won the competition.

I became obsessed with James Dean. Really obsessed, as if I wanted to be him.

Words of Wisdom

When I was in trouble I always managed to get out of it. My Mum was fostering a boy called Chips who had been abandoned by his mother. I didn't much like him and when I went on holiday with a girlfriend to the Isle of Wight I brought back presents for everyone in the family except Chips. As a typically selfish teenager I was expecting to be welcomed home like a conquering hero, but the only one who greeted me with any warmth was Chips. I was so ashamed not to have a present for him that I decided to get him something special. I worked out a way of getting school dinners, without paying for them, and for several months I pocketed the money my Mum gave me every morning. Everything would have been fine if I had resisted the temptation to brag about my scheme, but I didn't. A prefect overheard me and reported me to the headmistress. I was certain I would get the slipper for such a serious offence, but when the headmistress asked me why I had done it I told her the truth about Chips. She was so touched that she telephoned my mother and said: 'This child is special. Give her more pocket money.' My mother was furious. In lieu of more pocket money, she gave me a good hiding!

I was also regularly in trouble, one way or another, over boys. Although we had to work in the café after school and at weekends, there was still time to enjoy ourselves and Littlehampton was a good place to grow up in the fifties. It was colourful and fun and there was a lot going on, especially in the summer. There was the Top Hat ballroom and Butlin's amusement park, there were carnivals and beach outings and parties and lots of opportunities to meet boys. Hundreds of sailors and airmen from a nearby naval air base would descend on Littlehampton on a Saturday night, to the uncontained delight of all the local girls.

I loved the boys and I was very inventive with the truth in order to arrange dates without my Mum knowing. One day she caught me playing hookey from school to meet a boy in town and gave me a terrific hiding, because she thought she would have to go to prison if it was discovered. I think my Mum was tough with me because I was unquestionably a pain in the neck – I always argued with her, always answered back. But being slapped never bothered me much, and I never stopped loving her for one moment. She taught me two fundamental truths that played a big role in shaping the rest of my life. The first was the importance of a work ethic; the second was the incredible power of love as a life force.

I knew, of course, that my mother loved all of her children, but I definitely sensed that Bruno and I were somehow special. In those days I never guessed the truth about my Uncle Henry, although in hindsight I can see she gave me plenty of clues. She would often say I was like Henry in one way or another – just little things like the way I ate an apple or sat in a chair. She told me that Uncle Henry always reassured her about me, tell her that there was 'something crazy' in me but that I would go great things. I think my mother believed that, too. She wanted me to be different. 'Be special,' she would say, 'be anything but mediocre.' I think she must have been echoing Henry's words, for her English was far from perfect.

'Be special', she would say, 'be anything but mediocre.'

At the same time as offering me the wisdom of her years, she had little idea about formal education. I sailed through my GCE's, but she did not really know if that was good or bad. I wanted to be an actress and was offered a place at the Guildhall School of Music and Drama, but my mother had other ideas after talking to my headmistress. She said acting would not be a suitable career for me and suggested teaching.

I was not too disappointed, and the more I thought about teaching the more I liked the idea: I could continue learning, which I loved, and the classroom could be my theatre. My qualifications to become a student teacher were not exactly impressive, but I managed to get an interview at Newton Park College of Education at Bath. I bought a new suit and a new pair of shoes – I looked like a middle-aged matron – and my Mum and my current boyfriend came to see me off on the train. It seemed such a long journey at the time. It was pouring with rain when I arrived in Bath and Newton College turned out to be a big Georgian mansion at

Newton Park College: 'I looked like a middle-aged matron. . .

the end of a long sweeping drive. As I walked up towards the house I caught my foot in a cattle grid and broke the heel off my shoe.

Lord only knows what they thought when they opened the door. There was this lop-sided eighteen-year-old dressed up like someone three times her age, soaking wet, with thick black hair in rats' tails, carrying a high heel. I can't remember much about the interview but I am sure I laid it on thick about being from a poor immigrant family and not having a father and longing to teach. Later I discovered they had grave reservations about taking me; they thought I would probably not toe the line. Nevertheless they decided to take a risk. I was in.

Opening Doors, Opening Minds

For the next three years I led a charmed life. I moved from an over-crowded terraced house in Littlehampton into a huge manor house with an orangery and Adam fireplace and Wedgwood ceilings, standing in grounds which looked as if they had been designed by Capability Brown. To sit reading quietly in the sun-soaked common room, surrounded by bookshelves, was to me a great luxury as I was completely unaccustomed to that kind of quiet, middle-class life. At home there were always people rushing in and out and there was not a bookcase in the house. Just having so many books around was bliss.

I was reading history and education but the college had a strong bias towards art, music and drama, which suited me fine. It was at Newton that I learned about aesthetics. There was a course on the subject run by Miss Elizabeth Newman, an extraordinary woman who lived in a crescent in Bath and drove around in an old lavender-coloured Morris Minor. She gave everyone on the course a precious object, like a carved wooden box or an Indian bracelet, and we had to look at these objects in a special way – to examine their history, how they were made, who made them and why. More than anyone else, she really showed me how to understand and appreciate art and design. It was through her that I developed an 'eye', an instinctive appreciation of aesthetics.

Miss Newman treated her class as if we were girls at an exclusive finishing school, and invited us to dinner parties at her house. I had never seen anything like it. Georgian chairs round a Georgian table in a

Georgian house. Sparkling silverware lined up at each place setting, crystal glasses, the finest food and wine. It was certainly a bit different from wolfing chips in the Clifton Café.

I took charge of the entertainment during my first year and arranged for all the boys from the local art college to come to our dances. Soon we had a pretty lively social life, but it was all very chaste. I thought it was bad enough having to deal with a Tampax, let alone dating boys. I was very aware of growing up, of maturing both emotionally and intellectually, but for me college still meant enjoying everything I had missed in Littlehampton – the comforts of a middle-class life, going to the theatre, learning to appreciate classical music. The only music I had listened to up until then had come out of a jukebox.

In my second year another teacher arrived who would have a profound effect on me. Mr Wainwright was a quiet academic from a working class background in a Northern mining village. I thought of him as a kind of D. H. Lawrence figure and worshipped him: he made history come alive for me in a way that no other teacher had managed to do. We have stayed in touch over the years – in fact he is now a Body Shop shareholder – and he tells a very funny story of his first lecture at Newton College. He says he had just got the class quiet when he heard footsteps coming up the stairs. Suddenly the door opened and this apparition with wild hair all over the place burst in, flung her coat on a chair, said 'Oh, fuck!', and stamped out again, muttering something about dropping a book at the bottom of the stairs. That was me.

Around this time I began to get neurotic about the fact that I did not have a proper boyfriend. Everyone was talking about the sixties being the decade of sexual liberation, the Pill was coming in and a lot of my friends were already living with their boyfriends. In short, it seemed that everyone was enjoying sex except me. I decided I had to do something about finding a boyfriend, and an excellent opportunity seemed to present itself at Bristol University's Rag Week dance.

Now one problem was that university students were all beatniks, incredibly hip and cool, whereas college students like me dressed like members of the Women's Institute. So I turned up at the dance looking like some cute kid on her way to church – but I was not going to let that hold me back. I stood on the edge of the dance floor and spotted a guy who was an absolutely brilliant dancer. I thought, 'Right, that's the one.' I took a deep breath, went straight up to him and started dancing like mad right in front of him. He looked at me as if I'd just been dragged in by the cat, put his hands on his hips and said 'What's the matter with you? Got St Vitus' Dance or something?'

The floor did not collapse and swallow me up, as I fervently prayed it would, and I went home convinced that I would remain a spinster all my life. Not long afterwards, however, I met a really nice guy, a beatnik type who was ten years older than me and not part of the college scene, and we had a little romance. We went to Cornwall on his Lambretta and slept in a loft in Newquay; and I stopped being neurotic.

Here Comes the Night: El Cubana!

During my final year at Newton College my mother sold the Clifton Café to one of my uncles, who promptly resold it for development at a fat profit. My mother was a great trader, like me, but had no business acumen at all. Things like that did not bother her, and anyway she was completely engrossed in her new venture – she was planning to open her own night club above a dry cleaner's and a butcher's shop in the centre of Littlehampton. She called it the El Cubana, if you please. Why she could not have had an Italian night club, I don't know. But it had to be Spanish, with castanets and straw hats hanging all over the place.

The El Cubana was the best thing to happen to Littlehampton – and the best thing to happen to my mother – for years. It had a jukebox and a little dance floor, but most of all it had my mother, absolutely queening it, sitting behind the bar in a cocktail dress holding court and cracking jokes in her thick Italian accent. She even learned to smoke. She had never smoked in her life, but she thought a night-club owner ought to smoke, so she would sit there puffing away and trying not to cough.

The members adored her because she was so full of life and fun. She has never really got a grasp of the English language and her malapropisms are legendary in the family. One day I was window shopping with her in Littlehampton and she saw a silver lurex dress in the window that she thought would be right to wear in the El Cubana. She marched in and said: 'I wanna try on the dress you got in the window. See, there! The durex one.' About this time she also bought herself a little car, but she was a terrible driver. She would get quite upset if I suggested she should perhaps indicate before she was going to turn. 'What for I need to indicate?' she would say. 'I know where I'm going.'

Gilda, the Queen of the El Cubana

The El Cubana was a further lesson for me about the importance of creating a style. My mother made the place look like a bar in Torremolinos, with a pretend-tile roof over the bar, rough-cast plaster and beamed walls and appalling tin trays with matadors and *señoritas* on them. It wasn't my style by any means, but it worked. The customers liked its eccentric exoticism and cheerful shabbiness. That was another lesson: one of the big mistakes in retailing is to make your shop so beautiful that it overwhelms the product. When we open a new shop I always try to mess it up a bit, to make it look more human.

The other thing I learned from the El Cubana was the power of music, the fact that it was able to speak personally to you. The club came alive the minute the music went on, and it is the same with shops. I don't think you want terrible musak churning out all the time and boring everyone to death; you need sounds to enliven and surprise. It is not easy to get it right and to this day we haven't really cracked it, but we are experimenting in our Body Shops all the time. In the United States we are trying out joyous gospel music interspersed with snippets of Martin Luther King speeches to celebrate Martin Luther King Day, and elsewhere we are playing around with environmental sounds so that customers will come into a shop in the middle of summer and find a tropical thunderstorm going on. Why? Oh, just for fun and surprise.

Soon I started teaching practice and was completely absorbed by it. Oh, how I loved teaching, loved making it into theatre, loved being on stage – although I had a little difficulty with mathematics and remember once having a whole class of eleven-year-olds trying to teach me where to put the bloody decimal point.

The Magic of Words

Being me, I was determined to do things differently. In one secondary modern school I decided to introduce a group of sixteen-year-olds to the magic of words, so I started the lesson by asking them to consider the difference between the words 'love' and 'fuck'. As a format to get their attention it certainly worked. We had a terrific discussion, with everyone animated and wanting to contribute, exploring why some words provoked such strong emotions. Unfortunately the headmistress came in, found 'FUCK' written in big letters on the blackboard and was not too pleased. I got an official warning from the head of Newton College.

Not long afterwards I learned that I had won a scholarship to study in Israel for three months in order to complete my theses. My educational thesis was on 'The Children of the Kibbutz' and my historical one 'The British Mandate in Palestine'.

That trip to Israel in 1962 was a seminal experience, one of the best things that ever happened to me. My mother always said there was Jewish blood in the family and I felt a romantic empathy with Israel as a nation that had suffered, had faith in its history and had survived. I was an Israeli-Jewish groupie, wanting to learn more and understand more.

The first thing I did was to work in a kibbutz on the shores of Lake Tiberias. We worked in the fields one week and with the fishing fleet the next. It was very physical, but there was a joy about getting up at three in the morning and working until eleven, when it was too hot to continue and you were completely exhausted anyway. I learned that it was a noble experience to be physically exhausted by honest labour, and I learned there was nothing more important to life than love and work. I learned the role the kibbutz played as the backbone of Israel's agriculture and why the most important rooms were the cultural hall, the children's dormitory and the cowshed. It all made a lot of sense to me.

Ours was more of a political kibbutz than a religious one, although the older folk were religious and I am afraid I forgot this last fact when I decided to play a little joke on the children. There was an English medical student working in the kibbutz who had a beard and long flowing hair and looked a lot like Jesus Christ. We two used to give lessons to the children in the afternoons and became great friends.

The lake was very shallow at the edge and one day I suggested a great wheeze. If we put little piles of rocks into the lake just under the surface of the water, he could walked out on them and pretend to the kids that he was walking on the water like... well, you know who. He thought it was a terrific idea. That night when the kids were asleep we measured out a path into the lake and scurried backwards and forwards placing our rocks in position. When we had finished you could not see anything of what we had been up to.

I learned there was nothing more important to life than love and work.

Next day after school we were playing around with the kids when my friend suddenly stood up with this strange, ethereal look on his face and began walking toward the water. No one but I knew what was going to happen, and as he started walking out across the lake, I shouted, 'My God, look! He's walking on water. It's the second coming!'

The children started screaming with excitement and calling for other people to come and see. I thought he looked wonderful out there, but then the older folks started turning up and they absolutely freaked out. They didn't think it was in the least funny and asked us both to leave next morning.

I spent the next two months hitch-hiking around Israel, immersing myself in the history and ideology that lay all around me. Sometimes I travelled with people I met on the road, sometimes alone. I slept wherever I could and took terrific risks. To protect myself from unwelcome attention at night I carried a pot of pepper and a big pin, but I usually found that being terribly English, terribly outraged, worked best. If anyone tried a quiet grope in the night I would sit up and say in a loud voice: 'How *dare* you!'

A Backpack is a Girl's Best Friend

While I was in Israel I had my first experience of drugs. I had got as far as the Dead Sea and was camping in a house owned by an American construction worker. One night he produced some marijuana and told me it would change my life, alter my state of consciousness. Not me, I thought. I had a few whiffs, got a bit giggly and quite enjoyed it, but that was about it. Amen. Another disappointment.

Israel changed me. When I got home I wanted to convert to Judaism and had to be talked out of it by a Rabbi who quickly recognized that I was more of a romantic than a serious candidate. He told me I only wanted to become a Jew because I wanted to identify with their persecution. Frustrated by his discouragement I immediately fell in love with his son, but that did not last long either.

More importantly, the months I spent hitching around Israel taught me that I was brave and that I could travel alone anywhere I liked. And I had seen the start of what would become known as the hippy trail – young people, free, enjoying a camaraderie, meeting up and separating, always on the move, exploring the world and their own abilities. I'd met Australian kids who had hitched halfway across the world to get to Israel and who had been to places I had never even heard of. Whatever was going on out there was exciting and it all seemed more enticing than nine-to-five in a classroom, no matter how much I enjoyed teaching.

Restless Spirit

At first I ignored the emotions churning away inside me, although I already knew in my heart that for me teaching was not going to be

enough. I graduated from Newton College and applied for a job in a junior school. I got it. A friend from Israel wrote and asked me to meet him in Paris. I was not due to start work for several weeks, so I went. He had already left by the time I arrived. Alone in Paris, I sat down and wrote a letter to my new school to say that I was very sorry but I was pregnant and therefore I would not be able to start work next term. I was not pregnant: I was *free* and I was in Paris.

I had wanted to visit Paris because I was fascinated by its artistic and literary reputation. I knew that *The Black Book* by Lawrence Durrell, one of my favourite authors, had been banned in England and published in Paris, and I almost fainted when, during my first few days there, I saw Durrell in the Olympia bookshop in La Cité. In the evenings I would hang around the Left Bank jazz clubs where

'. . . the months I spent hitching around Israel taught me that I could travel alone anywhere I liked'

people like Miles Davis and Thelonius Monk were playing. I found a job working in the library of the *International Herald Tribune* and stayed for nearly a year.

When I went home to Littlehampton, I found that little had changed. My mother was still running the El Cubana; my sisters were married – Velia had gone off to Canada – and Bruno was studying astrophysics at Imperial College in London. It seemed to me that I was the only member of the family completely adrift, and I thought again about teaching.

The only job I could get, part-time, was back at my old school – the Maude Allen Secondary Modern School for Girls. It was wonderful to be back there, but I knew it was only temporary and after two terms I found a permanent job teaching a bunch of spotty-nosed under-achievers at a comprehensive school in Bitterne, near Southampton. I took one look at my class and said to myself: 'Right, this is going to be fun!'.

I set out to make my classroom the most enthralling place in the world. I spent hours preparing each lesson, incorporating drama and music wherever I could. We acted significant moments in history. When we were studying the Reformation, I would play Georgian chants; for the Tudor period, Elizabethan songs. When we were doing the First World War I took them to the Somme so they could see what remained of the trenches. We actually found an old Woodbine packet in a field, and then we put on our own production of *Oh, What a Lovely War!*

I changed the classroom around almost every day. I would move all the desk and chairs into the centre, put up brilliant graphics all round the walls and invite the kids to walk around and make notes. It took me months to get it right, but it was stunning. In one incredible lesson I blacked out the entire classroom, cut a slit in a black cloth and asked them to look through a green wine bottle and write their own poems while psychedelic 'Tangerine Dream'-type music played in the background.

The only rule in my classroom was that no one should be bored, and at the end of a year the lethargic, dull-eyed kids that I had started with were unrecognizable. They were proud of themselves, and proud of what they had achieved. I got them to lay out their best work on big boards, each drawing or poem or essay beautifully framed and separated by ribbons. It looked magnificent and I arranged to have it put on display at Southampton Art Gallery, where everyone could see what creative achievements these children were capable of.

Following the Hippy Trail

I enjoyed teaching, but I still had itchy feet and yearned to join all those other young people I had seen on the hippy trail. I hitched to Greece for a holiday that summer and returned via Geneva, where I decided to try and find a job. All the young women in Geneva either wanted to work for the financier Bernie Cornfeld, because he paid a lot and threw great parties, or the United Nations, because you did not have to pay any tax. I had no qualifications that would have been of any interest to the UN, but a great deal of confidence in my ability to sell myself. I knew that if I wrote in no one would take a blind bit of notice, so I just turned up and asked to see someone in the Personnel Department. They were a bit taken aback, but eventually I got to see someone who asked me if I could do shorthand. I said no, but I had longhand and a good memory. They asked me if I could type and again I said no, but wasn't it just hit and miss and a good rubber? Before they could show me the door I said: 'Listen, I'm the most diligent and tenacious worker you'll ever get. I love to work. I'm a great researcher...' I went on like that and literally talked myself into a job. Enthusiasm and energy either daunts people or it seduces them. Luckily for me, it seduced them.

Job-hunting in Geneva: passion persuades prospective employers

I worked in the department of women's rights at the International Labour Organization, gathering information about women in the Third World and organizing seminars and conferences. I learned from the UN the extraordinary power of networking, but I was appalled by the money that was squandered on red tape and all the wining and dining that was going on with no apparent check on expenses. I found it offensive to see all those fat cats discussing problems in the Third World over four-course lunches at the United Nations Club.

The best thing about Geneva was that it was in the centre of Europe. I liked being able to move so quickly from one culture and language to another, and I travelled a lot, but after a year I had run out of places to go and things to see and decided it was time to move on. Baudelaire called fear of home and hearth '*la grande maladie*' and I was beginning to recognize that I had a full dose.

Baudelaire called fear of home and hearth '*la grande maladie*' and I was beginning to recognize that I had a full dose

I took the savings I had accumulated during my year at the UN and caught a train to Southampton, where I boarded a boat bound for Tahiti. What I was looking for was an adventure, and it seemed to me that Tahiti was a sufficiently exotic place to find one. I sweltered all the way through the Panama Canal to Tahiti, spent a wonderful month there and then went on to Australia, via the New Hebrides and New Caledonia.

In Australia I needed to earn some money to continue my trip. I first tried to get a job teaching, then writing for children's television, but I ended up selling weatherboarding in Sydney. I can sell anything to anyone and I made enough to be able to continue on through Réunion, Madagascar and Mauritius on my way to South Africa. Everywhere I went I did my best to get to know the local people, to talk to them and eat with them and learn about their lives.

In Johannesburg I got into trouble by going to a club on the wrong night. It was one of those places which had alternate nights for different races, but I didn't want to hear black jazz with a lot of white racists, so I went on a 'black night'. Of course I was picked up almost immediately by the police and given twenty-four hours to get out of the country.

I had got just enough money left for a ticket back to England, and I decided it was time to go home. I felt at that stage that I had learned so much from my experiences, from all the people I had met, that I wanted to return and take stock of my life. When I turned up on my mother's doorstep in Littlehampton next day she gave a shriek of joy. I began to tell her everything that had happened to me, but she had some news of her own that couldn't wait. 'I've got a wonderful man for you to meet,' she said. 'He comes into the El Cubana and he's so like Henry it's unbelievable. I've been showing him all your letters so he can read about you. His name is Gordon. Gordon Roddick.'

THAT IS HOW THE FAMOUS BODY SHOP STYLE DEVELOPED – OUT OF A SECOND WORLD WAR MENTALITY (SHORTAGES, UTILITY GOODS, RATIONING) IMPOSED BY SHEER NECESSITY AND THE FACT THAT I HAD NO MONEY. BUT I HAD A VERY CLEAR IMAGE IN MY MIND OF THE KIND OF STYLE I WANTED TO CREATE: I WANTED IT TO LOOK A BIT LIKE A COUNTRY STORE IN A SPAGHETTI WESTERN.

3

TRADESWOMAN'S ENTRANCE

The moment I set eyes on Gordon Roddick in the El Cubana I knew that I wanted him to be the father of my children. I didn't want to marry him, didn't even want to live with him. I just wanted his children. I was Italian: I loved babies, I was genetically programmed to have babies, it was my destiny to have babies. And I was nearly twenty-six years old.

Gordon had trained as a farmer, but his real interests were writing — mainly poetry and short stories — and travel. He was then twenty-six and had already worked his way round the world: tin mining in Africa, sailing down the Amazon in a canoe, sheep farming in Australia.

While I was travelling in Africa, Gordon had suddenly turned up in Littlehampton and taken to spending his evenings in the bizarre intimacy of the El Cubana, which he found preferable to the beery *bonhomie* of the local pubs. He was tall, thin and quiet, and my mother was immediately drawn to him because he reminded her so much of Henry. She found out he was working on a nearby farm and was soon mothering him like mad, mending holes in his trousers, sewing his buttons on and cooking him great steaming plates of pasta to fatten him up.

My old man

Being my mother she also regaled him with lengthy stories about her daughter Anita who was a teacher and who was travelling the world. Every one of my postcards was pinned up behind the bar, between the castanets and the sombreros, and every time a letter arrived from me she would make poor Gordon sit down and read every word. After six months of this, he thought he knew me pretty well.

It was strange when I walked into the club, that day I got back from Africa, and saw him sitting there. We had an instant rapport, even though our only shared experience was that we both spent quite a bit of time travelling the world. We discovered we had lived on the same street in Sydney and had met a lot of the same people. That's how it was on the hippy trail in the sixties – you'd move from place to place, but constantly see familiar faces and meet friends of friends. These tenuous connections of kinship spread round the world, linking and interlinking armies of young people on the move in their rootless search for some kind of nirvana. Gordon's path and mine must have nearly crossed so many times in faraway places – yet here we were, finally meeting at the El Cubana in Littlehampton! I'm still astonished how two people, out of billions in the world, can meet and make a connection.

Gordon says I pursued him relentlessly, and I suppose I did. That's the way I am. I think Gordon was rather overwhelmed by me: I was as loud and brash as he was quiet and introspective. He told me later that when he went home that night he had a 'sinking feeling' that his 'fate was sealed'. He should have been walking on air!

My first march, 1965

In fact we did not have a courtship so much as an intensive investigation of each other, of our lives and hopes and dreams. Our personalities were very different, but we shared a great deal in terms of values. We both espoused vaguely left-wing radical politics. We were both members of CND and had tramped the streets on Ban the Bomb marches. We both had well-developed social consciences, instinctively supported the underdog, worked for what we believed were good causes, and raised funds for charities like War on Want and Freedom from Hunger.

For an intense four days we walked around Littlehampton talking, talking, talking. It was autumn. The candyfloss stalls and amusement arcades were shuttered; the shore was deserted except for wheeling seagulls. Muffled in coats and scarves, we tramped for miles back and forth along the beach, sat on park benches in the public gardens and stopped in occasional cafés to warm up over mugs of coffee. At the end of those four days I packed my bags and moved out of my mother's terraced house into Gordon's one-room flat a few streets away.

We had such a great time in that little flat. One weekend when Gordon was away I redecorated the entire place and painted huge black footsteps up one wall, across the ceiling and down the opposite wall. On another wall I wrote 'YIPPEE' in six-foot-high letters and painted two big ears on each side of the window, as we had a friend who was always trying to snoop on us and see what we were doing.

I still did not feel I was making any great commitment other than wanting to get pregnant, although at some point early on I did have a moment of serious doubt about the wisdom of what I was doing. I knew I wanted to have a baby, but I did not know anything about Gordon's finances and I began to worry about money. Supposing he could not support us? It was worry that drove me to do, sneakily, what I did. Gordon was going off to Edinburgh Festival, where he was submitting some poetry, and while he was away I went through his drawers and found some share certificates. I hadn't a clue what they were worth – I am not even sure I knew precisely what a share certificate was – but their existence

YIPPEE!!

was enough to convince me that my baby wouldn't starve. I didn't tell Gordon what I had done for ages.

I was still loudly claiming that I had no plans to live with Gordon permanently; but what happened, of course, was that by living together we learned to love each other. Certainly, as soon as I became pregnant my great need to be independent began to diminish. Pregnancy also put paid to our plans to travel overland to Australia to start a pineapple plantation, which we had talked about a lot.

Gordon was trying to earn some money writing children's stories and I had a job teaching at a junior school in Worthing. I had never taught juniors before and really loved it, but they soon worked out that their Miss Perella was in a condition that no unmarried lady ought to be in. I had a craving for cream buns and kept rushing to the cupboard where I kept my supply, and all the kids would nudge and wink and give each other knowing looks.

The school was run by two delightful old spinsters. All my life I have never wanted anyone to be disappointed in me, and I knew these two old dears would be deeply disappointed to discover I was pregnant – because I was, of course, unmarried. I did not have the heart to tell them the truth, so I said that I was ill and that I would have to leave at the end of the term.

And Then There Were Three...

In August 1969 I gave birth to a baby girl whom we named Justine, after the heroine in Lawrence Durrell's *Alexandria Quartet*. Considering she had just come from my womb, I was surprised how little I

loved her at first. I think the myths of motherhood lead you to expect so much about giving birth, whereas the reality is that you are just exhausted. I had to learn to love her, but it took just two or three weeks and then we loved her with the selfless, overwhelming passion that can only exist between parents and children.

We moved into a slightly bigger flat and Gordon got a job as a labourer to earn more money. We were happy, no doubt about that, but we were also adrift, not knowing quite what to do with our lives. Gordon was not making much progress as a writer and we talked again about going to Australia, or about starting our own business here in England, but we could never seem to make a decision about anything.

Mother and baby, 1969

Justine was only fifteen months old when I found I was pregnant again. Before I got to look too much like a barrel, we decided to take a trip to the United States to visit friends in San Francisco. We justified the expense by telling ourselves that we would look out for 'business opportunities', but in truth we were much more interested in taking a look at Haight-Ashbury, then the heart of the flower children's dream community engaged in a joyous celebration of the human spirit (and other things).

We took Justine with us in a back harness and had a really great time travelling around with our friends, half-heartedly looking for 'business opportunities' and whole-heartedly enjoying ourselves. One day we drove out to Lake Tahoe in Nevada and when we got there we decided, for no particularly reason, to continue to Reno, which was only about thirty miles further north. As we were driving into the city along a highway lined on both sides with wonderfully tacky, neon-lit marriage parlours we decided, on the spur of the moment, to get married.

It was as much as lark as anything else. We didn't partic-ularly approve of the institution of marriage, so we thought if we were going to do it we might as well do it in as ridicu-lous a place as possible. We pulled into the parking lot of a place called something like the Silver Horseshoes Wedding Chapel. Gordon rushed inside and discovered they charged $50, which cooled his ardour a bit, but he also somehow discovered that we could get it done cheaper at the town hall.

I didn't have my passport or my birth certificate with me and I thought there was no way they would marry us with-out some kind of documentation. How wrong I was. When we got into the town hall I explained to a girl at the desk that I didn't have any identification.'That don't matter none, honey,' she drawled. 'All you need is twenty-five dollars. Take the door on the right at the top of the stairs.'

'Don't worry, sweetheart. If you stay three weeks you can get divorced'

Upstairs we discovered there were two octogenarians and a couple of gays in the queue ahead of us, and by this time I was starting to get very nervous and grumpy. Eventually we were ushered into a kind of courtroom and pronounced man and wife in about ten seconds flat. The registrar shook Gordon's hand and kissed me on the cheek. I must have looked shell-shocked, because he whispered in my ear, 'Don't worry, sweetheart. If you stay three weeks you can get divorced.'

That was our wedding day. My wedding outfit comprised a pair of tattered corduroys bulging at the waist and a red rain slicker, worn with sneakers and a howling baby in a harness on my back. We had to bor-row a ring from David and Alma, our friends. Even in a place like

Reno there can have been few marriages contracted in such haste and probably fewer still that have lasted as long as ours. Actually, I am not at all sure if it is considered a legal marriage in Britain.

Afterwards we sent a telegram to my Mum to tell her what we had done, then we sat on the sidewalk and celebrated with a bottle of cheap Californian wine. Our honeymoon night was spent in a seedy motel room which we shared not only with Justine, but with David and Alma, too. We didn't have enough money for separate rooms and the four of us spent the evening baby-sitting Justine and playing snap.

We never managed to put together any kind of business deal while we were in California, although we did think about trying to import 'Baby Buggies', those amazing collapsible pushchairs which were then new on the market. Everyone was raving about them in the United States and we began making enquiries about importing them into Britain, but we discovered that someone had obtained an import licence just a month earlier.

Back home in Littlehampton our second daughter, Samantha, was born in July 1971. It was a very difficult forceps delivery that left me weak and exhausted. By then Gordon had started a little picture-framing business, but he had become bored by it and we were having a struggle to make ends meet; and it would be worse now that we had two small children. We needed a bigger place to live and we really wanted a business we could run together – and I was hopeless at picture-framing. A potential solution to all these problems eventually presented itself in the unlovely shape of the St Winifred's Hotel, Littlehampton, outside which a 'For Sale' sign had appeared.

Life at St Winifred's

St Winifred's was a former residential hotel which had fallen on hard times. It was a between-the-wars, red-brick large family house, with its front door set squarely in the middle (I've never owned a house with its door in the middle since – though I've always wanted to: it has such a reassuring, comfortable feel). It had eight bedrooms, although you would not have wanted to sleep in any of them, and the whole place was extremely run down, but to us it had the potential for being turned into the most fantastic little bed and breakfast place in town. Gordon scraped together what remained of his savings and made a silly offer which, to our amazement, was accepted. In what seemed an alarmingly short space of time we were the new proprietors.

We set to work immediately organizing essential repairs and renovations, cleaning it from top to bottom, painting, decorating and stamping our personality on the place. We worked on it all through the winter and spring of 1971 to be ready in time for the summer season, and we made it as stylish as we could within our limited budget. I remember we painted the dining room dark brown; we couldn't afford pictures so we hung big blown-up photographs of Littlehampton on the walls.

On the very day when we moved the furniture in, a couple asked if we were open for bed and breakfast. We put them in a bedroom, rushed around the corner to the local shop to buy some eggs, bacon and tomatoes and cooked it for them the next morning. They wanted to stay for a second day and paid us five quid. Boy, we thought, this is easy.

It got a little less easy when we were cooking twenty breakfasts every morning, but it was still a lot of fun and it was a buzz having people around. It seemed ideal. Gordon and I had always wanted to find a way in which we could work together, and making our home into our business meant we could even divide up domestic responsibilities like looking after the children. And we shared everything – from nappy changing to getting up in the night when one child or the other called.

Everything was going fine until the summer season ended. Suddenly there were no bed and breakfast customers any more. It was as if they had disappeared from the face of the earth. Littlehampton was still attracting visitors, but they were day trippers who headed home in the evening and had no interest in a bed, let alone breakfast, at the St Winifred's. We were marooned in this huge house with its eight empty bedrooms and horrendous maintenance costs and we were going to be bankrupt unless we did something – quickly.

What we did was turn half of St Winifred's back into a residential hotel, so that we would have a regular income coming in every week. It was an important lesson for us – to confront the fact that we had made a mistake and to take immediate steps to change course.

There was no shortage of would-be residents, so I don't know how it happened that we managed to attract the kind of guests that made St Winifred's a role model for Fawlty Towers. Most of them were eccentric, and some were completely loopy. There was one old dear, a former headmistress, who thought every day was Tuesday, called me 'hostess', thought Gordon was the plumber, walked around with an alarm clock and asked for breakfast every evening at eight o'clock. At Justine's third birthday party, another guest walked into the room in a silk housecoat and threw a bucket of water over the assembled mothers. Then there was Mr Wilson, a lovely old man who used to write for BBC radio and had been a prisoner in Greece during the war. He was a fascinating character, but ran up against my mother's strong views about male grooming. My mother was baby-sitting for us one night and when we got home we found her sitting in the kitchen with Mr Wilson, who looked rather strange.

'What's happened to you, Mr Wilson?' I said, 'You look different.'

Before he had a chance to reply my mother said: 'Look at his eyebrows. I cut 'em off. They were disgusting.'

Luckily my mother did not assault all our guests, and St Winifred's began making a modest – very modest – profit. Once the hotel was running smoothly there was not really enough to do to keep Gordon and me fully occupied and so we began to think about starting up a second business. As I knew a little about the catering business from working in the Clifton Café we plumped for a restaurant – though without any real idea of what it would entail. Full of confidence, we found suitable premises in the centre of Littlehampton, borrowed £10,000 from the bank to buy a lease and set about planning the grand opening of the new Roddick enterprise, which we decided to call Paddington's Restaurant.

Paddingtons ... wrong street, wrong time, wrong town: "Wossa kwitch?"

Cooking for the Masses?

It was a very stylish place for the time – bentwood furniture, potted palms and old photographs of Littlehampton (removed from St Winifred's) on the walls. Our idea was to offer health food dishes with an Italian flavour – things like lasagne and spaghetti and vegetarian quiches and home-made soups with garlic bread. In the early eighties dozens of restaurants succeeded with just such menus, but in the early seventies, in a place like Littlehampton, it flopped.

For three weeks we sat in an empty restaurant. Those few customers who ventured in would stare at the menu with glazed eyes and eventually look up and say, 'Wos lazagney?' or 'Wossa kwitch?' Most of them ended up having spaghetti, because they had had it on toast out of a tin, and then they would discover they had no idea how to get the real stuff into their mouths. It would have been funny if it had not been evident to both of us that we were, once again, going broke.

What saved us, once again, was our willingness to recognize that we were wrong and our ability to move swiftly on to the next idea.

The reason was quite simple – we had done everything wrong. It was the wrong kind of restaurant in the wrong street in the wrong town, launched at the wrong time – in the middle of the Tories' 'three-day week' crisis. We were young, we thought we knew it all and we had certainly not bothered to take any advice. We thought we could impose our will on our customers and sell gourmet health food in an egg-and-chips town.

What saved us, once again, was our willingness to recognize that we were wrong and our ability to move swiftly on to the next idea. 'We've got to face up to the fact that this is not working,' Gordon said after another depressing evening looking over a sea of empty tables. 'We're going to have to change the menu completely. Let's get in a char-griller and a chip fryer and do the best steaks and hamburgers in town.'

The effect was miraculous. American-style hamburger restaurants were already very popular in London, and a lot had been written in the newspapers about the extraordinary phenomenon of almost permanent queues outside places like the Great American Disaster and the Hard Rock Café. So Littlehampton's swinging set, such as it was, was happy to find a similar restaurant on its own doorstep.

Paddington's suddenly became the most popular place in town, particularly on a Saturday night when there was never a spare table. We deliberately set out to create a kind of campus style and lively atmosphere: we played loud rock music all the time and had cheerful, good-looking waiters wearing jeans and our own Paddington's Restaurant T-shirts; Gordon would write political messages attacking the council on the top of the blackboard menu. This was a foretaste of our belief that business should have a social conscience. When a local businessman came into the restaurant and boasted that he had just secured an order to supply the local council with net curtains at full retail price, Gordon was outraged and immediately scribbled a message on the blackboard asking why the council should waste our money like that.

We both needed to be there all the time. I was usually out front taking orders and chatting up the customers; Gordon ran the kitchen. At the beginning we had planned it the other way round, since I was the one who could cook, but it didn't work out like that. After I had been in the kitchen for a couple of days it looked like a bomb had hit it, and Gordon had managed to drive away half our customers with his somewhat brusque manner. When someone complained that the cream was not fresh, for example, Gordon called him 'white trash' and threw him out.

When we changed roles it worked very well, just as it does now. I am good out front, dealing with the public and the customers, and Gordon is a fantastic behind-the-scenes organizer. His strengths are my weaknesses, and vice versa; that is why we are a good partnership. I think we are able to work together successfully because we do not interfere with each other and we have confidence in each other's abilities.

Learning

Running a successful restaurant is one of the most exhausting and time-consuming occupations in the world. Sir Terence Conran, who also started out in business running a restaurant, says it is the best possible training ground for learning about service and for prospering in the retail trade. He is convinced that one of the real reasons The Body Shop is a success is because of what we learned when we were running Paddington's.

At the beginning I certainly found it a lot of fun and I was constantly astonished to discover how bizarre people were, particularly in a quiet little place like Littlehampton. Every Saturday night, for example, some ordinary-looking bloke would pass by on the other side of the street and as he got opposite the restaurant he would drop his trousers and waggle his bum in our direction.

This was nothing compared to the behaviour of some of our customers. One evening very early, before any other customers had arrived, a couple came in and ordered two coffees. Fine, we gave them two coffees. Then they picked up the shaker filled with parmesan cheese for pasta and began pouring it into their coffee, which they proceeded to drink, smacking their lips. I could not take my eyes off them, and I watched in fascination as the woman wriggled down in her seat and began doing something under the table. I couldn't make out what was going on until she straightened up again with her tights in one hand. She smoothed them out, wrapped them around her neck under her hair and tied a big bow on top of her head.

I realized I was going to have to get them out before other customers arrived, so I bustled out of the kitchen, looked at my watch and called to one of the waiters. 'My goodness, it's late! We should have closed half an hour ago.' He looked at me as if I had gone mad, especially when I started noisily putting chairs up on to the tables. Eventually he got the message and we managed to hustle the odd couple out.

Another night some day-tripper got mugged just round the corner and staggered into the restaurant to ask if he could use the telephone to contact the police. Unfortunately, the minute he opened the door a fight broke out between two tables, and as the chairs started to get smashed Gordon came rushing out of the kitchen waving a meat cleaver. The poor guy had to seek shelter behind the hat stand. Afterwards he told me he could not believe he was still in Littlehampton – he thought he had wandered into some saloon in the Wild West.

Gordon and I had virtually no social or family life while we were running Paddington's. The only cultural input into our lives came from our involvement in radical politics: we started Littlehampton's first

Hotelier and happy customer, 1972

Shelter group, and the occupation of Centre Point – a huge empty office block in the centre of London – to protest about the plight of the homeless was planned in the front room of our hotel. There were a lot of empty council-owned properties in Littlehampton and we thought it was outrageous that they should remain empty while there were so many people homeless.

When Paddington's had been open a year, my mother decided she had had enough of being the Régine of Littlehampton and so she sold the El Cubana. Being a doting Italian grandmother, she immediately took over looking after Justine and Samantha in the evenings while we were at the restaurant. Justine was then four and Samantha two, and they had both suffered to some extent not just from working parents, but from having parents who worked every waking hour. We could always rely on the family network to help out when necessary, but for the children it was obviously second best. When Sam started going to a day nursery we nicknamed her Bruiser because she was always bashing the other kids; I think it was probably because we had not given her as much attention as we had given Justine. It was something I often felt guilty about.

All my life I had been drilled to observe a strict work ethic; Gordon, too, enjoyed work. But after three years of running the hotel part-time and the restaurant full-time we were literally worn out. We were rarely home before one o'clock in the morning and were often so tired we could hardly drag ourselves up the stairs to bed. Sometimes we would wake next day with our muscles aching so much that we could hardly get up.

We did not even have time for each other and our marriage was beginning to suffer as a result, exacerbated by the fact that we had no privacy – being at St Winifred's was like living in a commune with a lot of elderly people. And despite all the leisure time we had sacrificed, we were not even making much money. All we were doing was surviving.

One night when we crawled into bed Gordon voiced what I had been thinking for some time. 'This is killing us,' he said. 'I can't cope with it any more. Let's pack it in.'

Dreaming and Doing

Gordon is a very unusual man. Although he would be the very last one to admit it, he is at heart an adventurer and a dreamer. I knew that well, so it was not too much of a shock when, after we had sold Paddington's, he announced that he wanted to take off for two years to fulfil a childhood ambition. The shock came when I learned what that ambition was – he wanted to ride a horse from Buenos Aires to New York.

I don't know many men who would contemplate undertaking such an expedition – a daunting 5,300-mile horseback trek, much of it through remote and dangerous territory – completely alone. It had been his dream to attempt the trip ever since reading *Tschiffley's Ride*, an account of a similar trip by the Swiss explorer and writer Aimé Tschiffley in the thirties. "If I don't do it now, while I am still young and fit," he explained, "I never will."

I can't pretend I was thrilled at the prospect of him going off for two years and leaving the children and me, but at the same time I could not help but admire him. It was such a romantic and brave thing to do that it was impossible to be resentful about it. I have always admired people who want to be remarkable, who follow their beliefs and passions, who make grand gestures. I had dreamed that we would giggle our way round the world together at some time, but I simply did not have the courage to contemplate doing what he was about to do, even if I didn't have the kids to worry about.

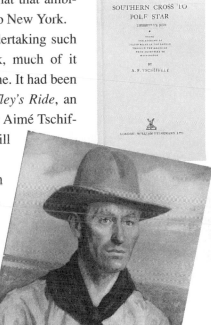

Gordon's guide

Some of our friends found the whole thing a bit bizarre; they probably thought our marriage was on the rocks. Actually I thought the fact that Gordon could confidently contemplate such a trip was an indication of the strength of our marriage, rather than the reverse. We had never been possessive of each other and there was a strong streak of independence in both of us.

We talked a lot about what I was going to do and how we were going to organize things while he was away. Once we had got rid of the restaurant we realized just how much it had drained us, physically and emotionally, and we did not want to go back to anything like that. Most importantly, I wanted to have a home life, which we had never had before, and I wanted to be able to spend some time with the children, who were then six and four. They had virtually been brought up by their grandmother, and I was concerned that they were growing closer to my mother than they were to me. But I also needed some income, because Gordon would obviously not be contributing anything while he was away and the hotel did not make enough to keep us. We had not sold the hotel along with the restaurant, for we thought of it as our home.

What I would like, I said to Gordon, was a small business that was controllable and only occupied my time from nine to five. The answer, clearly was a shop. So it was agreed. While Gordon researched and planned his expedition – he was already spending a lot of time at the Royal Geographical Society and had tracked down Tschiffley's wife in London – I would look around for a little shop.

'Just a Little Shop'

I already had an idea of what kind of shop I would like. It seemed ridiculous to me that you go into a sweet shop and ask for an ounce of jelly babies and you could go into the grocers' and ask for two ounces of cheese, but when you wanted to buy a body lotion you had to go into Boots and lay out five quid for a bloody great bottle of the stuff. Then, if you didn't like it, you were stuck with it.

One of the great challenges for entrepreneurs is to identify a simple need. People tend not to trust their gut instincts enough, especially about those things that irritate them, but the fact is that if something irritates you it is a pretty good indication that there are other people who feel the same. Irritation is a great source of energy and creativity. It leads to dissatisfaction and prompts people like me to ask questions. Why couldn't I buy cosmetics by weight or bulk, like I could if I wanted groceries or vegetables? Why couldn't I buy a small size of a cream or lotion, so I could try it out before buying a big bottle? These were simple enough questions, but at the time there were no sensible answers, although it did not take a brilliant business brain to work out that bigger profits accrued from selling bigger bottles.

It was also obvious to anyone who thought about it that a lot of the cost of cosmetics was down to fancy packaging. That was another source of deep irritation to me. When I bought perfume all I cared about was what it smelled like. I didn't give a damn about what the bottle looked like, and furthermore I did not know any women who did! We all suspected we were being conned, but there was precious little we could do about it.

I sat down and discussed it with Gordon, telling him the kind of shop I was thinking of opening was one that sold cosmetics products in different sizes and in cheap containers. It made perfect sense to him. (I always think it is odd when I look back on it. The idea for the shop was so simple that it hardly merits being described as an 'idea' at all.) For our experience in the hotel and the restaurant we also knew that we could be fast on our feet, and if my idea did not work we would be able to change it or keep tweaking it until it did work. If we couldn't sell creams and shampoos, we would chuck them out and sell something else.

Doing It Naturally

The other half of the equation was that I wanted to try to find products made from natural ingredients. At that time, no one was talking much about the advantages or potential of natural products — the green movement had yet to get started – but I knew that for centuries women in 'under-developed' areas of the world had been using organic potions to care for their skin with extraordinary success. I knew this to be true because I had seen it with my own eyes, initially in the Polynesian islands.

When I had arrived in Tahiti the first thing that struck me was the women. I was mesmerized by them. They were straight out of a Gauguin painting, with a wonderfully liquid quality. They had absolutely terrible teeth because they chewed sugar cane all the time, but their skin was like silk. It did not make any sense to me. I imagined that, with all the exposure to the sun and the  In Tahiti, 1967

rigours of their lives, their skin would soon become dry and crepey, but even the elderly women had soft, smooth and elastic skin.

One of the wonderful things about women, which I don't think many social anthropologists have fully understood, is that we are bonded by shared experiences – by babies and the rituals and problems of our bodies. Men need gambits to open conversations with other men. Women don't, because a sense of camaraderie and mutual interest already exists between us. All women are interested in looking after their skin, for example, and that is why one women can go up to another, without any hesitation, and ask, 'How come your skin's so soft?'

When I put that question to women in Tahiti they showed me what looked like a lump of cold lard. It was, in fact, cocoa butter, extracted from cocoa pods, which they rubbed on to their skins just as they had

Our cocoa butter poster, 1991

been taught by their mothers, and just as their mothers had been taught by their grandmothers. It was not only a wonderful conditioner, but it also stopped them getting stretch marks when they were pregnant and soothed skin disorders like eczema. You would often see a group of women sitting around talking and rubbing cocoa butter on to each other's bodies. Naturally I tried it myself – I found it was marvellous, although it smelled bizarre.

Later on my travels I kept coming across further examples of women using local natural ingredients for skin and hair care. I loved to watch the native women's beauty and bathing rituals: I was fascinated by their ingenuity, and made it my business to talk to women wherever I went to find out what they used on their bodies. I saw women using as a shampoo, a kind of green mud which worked wonderfully. I saw women eating pineapple, then rubbing the inside of the skin on to their faces.

Whenever I could I adopted local practices – caring for my body and hair in the same way as the native women, and using the same ingredients. All the conventions I had learned about looking after my body were slowly broken down. It was a revelation to realize that there were women all over the world caring for their bodies perfectly well without ever buying a single cosmetic. These women were doing exactly what we were doing in the west in the way of polishing, protecting and cleansing their skin and hair, but they were doing it with traditional natural substances instead of formulated ingredients. What amazed me was that these raw ingredients which hadn't been processed in any way, were doing a damn good job.

It was a revelation to realize that there were women all over the world caring for their bodies perfectly well without ever buying a single cosmetic.

So when I started to look for products for my shop I already knew of about twelve natural ingredients that I had seen working in various areas of the world and which I thought I might be able to use. I make no claim to prescience, to any intuition about the rise of the green movement. At the forefront of my mind at that time there was really only one thought – survival. My husband was going off for two years riding a horse across the Americas, and I knew I had to survive and look after my kids while he was away.

By then I also had a name for my embryonic business – The Body Shop. It was not original: I had seen it in the United States where dents were banged out of cars in garage 'body shops' everywhere. I must have stored it away in my subconscious memory, and I certainly thought my use of the name was a lot more appropriate. I found out later there were already other stores in the USA which had made the same connection.

Hell-raising, Hair-raising, Money-raising

Before I could make any further progress I needed to raise some money. Gordon and I had calculated I would need about £4,000 to get the business started, but I thought that as we could use the hotel for collateral there would be no problem. Unfortunately, I went about it in entirely the wrong way. I made an appointment to see the bank manager and turned up wearing a Bob Dylan T-shirt with Samantha on my hip and Justine clinging on to my jeans. It just did not occur to me that I should be anything other than my normal self. I was enthusiastic and I gabbled on about my great idea, flinging out all this information about how I had I discoverd these natural ingredients when I was travelling, and I'd got this great name, The Body Shop, and all I needed was £4,000 to get it started. I got quite carried away in my excitement, but I was on my own. I discovered that you don't go to a bank manager with enthusiasm – that is the last thing he cares about. When I had finished, he leaned back in his chair and said that he wasn't going to lend me any money because we were too much in debt already. I was stunned.

I went home to Gordon absolutely crushed. 'That's it,' I said. 'It's hopeless. The bank won't give me any money.' I was ready to give up, but Gordon is much more tenacious than I am. 'We will get the money,' he said, 'But we are going to have to play them at their own game.' He told me to go out and buy a business suit, and got an accountant friend to draw up an impressive-looking 'business plan', with projected profit and loss figures and a lot of gobbledegook, all bound in a plastic folder.

A week later we went back to the same bank for an interview with the same manager. This time I left the children behind and Gordon came with me. We were both dressed in suits. Gordon handed over our little presentation, the bank manager flipped through it for a couple of minutes and then authorized a loan of £4,000, just like that, using the hotel as collateral. I was relieved – but I was angry, too, that I had been turned down the first time. After all, I was the same person with the same idea. It was clear to me that bank managers did not want to deal with mothers with babies. When we went back the second time I might just as well not have been there, because the manager only talked to Gordon anyway. I was cast in the role of the little woman who just happened to be along.

I did not realize then the importance of anonymity. There are times when you need to be as anonymous as the people who work in banks, and to play the game entirely by their rules. If they want loan applicants to come in with shaven heads, you shave your head. And, sadly, you will never get a loan if you don't have collateral. There is not a bank manager in the country prepared to take a chance on any venture, no matter how brilliant the idea, without collateral. If we had not had the hotel to offer as collateral, The Body Shop would never have come into being. I often wonder how many fantastic ideas never came to fruition because of the lack of imagination of those people who sit behind desks in banks all over the country and who are too frightened to take a gamble. There are only two ways of raising money: the hard way and the very hard way!

Making It Up

Once I had got the finance, I had to find out who could make up the products. I had been doing a lot of research on do-it-yourself cosmetics in Worthing public library and mixing ingredients in the kitchen, but I wasn't getting on too well and every time Gordon went into the kitchen he slipped on the floor and nearly broke his neck. We were having a lot of trouble getting our mixtures stable, although we had some good ingredients.

Finally I thought, *This is ridiculous, I'm not a cosmetics chemist or a pharmacist*, so I approached a couple of the big cosmetics manufacturers, including Boots, to ask if they would make products for me. First, they were not the slightest bit interested in manufacturing the small quantities I needed, and second, they thought the ingredients I wanted to use were ridiculous. They had never heard of Rhassoul mud, they thought cocoa butter was something to do with chocolate, and they were indifferent to aloe vera. I think they thought I was completely mad.

In the end I went through the Yellow Pages and found, under 'Herbalists', a small manufacturing chemist's not far from Littlehampton who said they might be able to help me. I got in my little green van, drove straight over there and met this young man who had just taken over running the company. He was very nervous but very nice; I told him what I wanted, and we drew up a list of twenty-five possible products using those natural ingredients that were readily available – things like cocoa butter, jojoba oil, almond oil and aloe vera. I only wanted small quantities of each product and he wanted his money in advance – £700. That was the entire sum I had budgeted for product development. I *had* done a budget, of sorts. I'd allowed a certain amount for the overheads of the shop; some for rent and rates; some for 'shop fitting' – some basic pine furniture; and some for products.

All this time I had been looking for a suitable site. I did not think Littlehampton was ready for the kind of shop I envisaged, and decided that the most sensible place to open would probably be Brighton, which was only twenty miles from Littlehampton and had a strong student culture supporting a number of thriving 'alternative' businesses. With its elegant Regency terraces Brighton was everything that Littlehampton was not – fashionable, up-market and expensive, yet popular with hippies, artists and the liberal intelligentsia.

After traipsing the streets for what seemed like an eternity I finally found a small, scruffy, empty shop in a pedestrian precinct called Kensington Gardens, close to the centre of the town. I did not pay too much attention to its condition because I knew it was in a good position, so I happily paid six months' rent in advance.

Throughout this period Gordon was making preparations for his expedition. I was staggered at how little he was planning to take with him – he was relying on virtually nothing but an Ordnance Survey map to find his way across some of the most remote parts of South America. When he wasn't poring over maps at the Royal Geographical society he helped me with the setting up of the shop. One evening we sat down and went through all the figures. Gordon worked out that I would need to make £300 a week to survive.

'What happens if I don't?' I asked.

'Give it six months,' he replied breezily, 'then pack it in and meet me with the kids in Peru.'

The shop was in a truly terrible state when I took it over – it had water running down the walls. I painted the whole place dark green, not because I wanted to make any environmental statement but because it was the only colour that would cover up all the damp patches. Then I hung larchlap garden fencing on the walls to hide the dripping water.

Necessity Is the Mother

That is how the famous Body Shop style developed – out of a Second World War mentality (shortages, utility goods, rationing) imposed by sheer necessity and the simple fact that I had no money. But I had a very clear image in my mind of the kind of style I wanted to create: I wanted it to look a bit like a country store in a Spaghetti Western.

It is curious, looking back on it, how necessity accorded with philos-

Our first shop. Brighton, March 1976

ophy. Even if I had had unlimited funds, for example, I would never have wasted money on expensive packaging – the garbage of conventional cosmetics. And although I had set out to sell my products in a range of different sizes, I also needed to do so aesthetically, in order to make it appear as if the shelves were filled. With only twenty-five products on offer, the shop would have looked pathetic if there was just a single size of each, but with five sizes I could at least make sure that I filled a wall with bottles.

The cheapest containers I could find were the plastic bottles used by hospitals to collect urine samples, but I could not afford to buy enough. I thought I would get round the problem by offering to refill empty containers or to fill customers' own bottles. In this way we started recycling and reusing materials long before it became ecologically fashionable, but again it was born out of economic necessity rather than a concern for the environment.

Everything was done on a shoestring. I hired a designer to come up with the shop's logo for £25, and I got friends round to help with filling the bottles and hand-writing all the labels. I certainly couldn't afford to have the labels printed, and anyway I thought they looked nicer handwritten. We did all the filling in the kitchen of the St Winifred's Hotel, decanting the stuff into jugs and then pouring it into bottles.

Some of the products were pretty bizzare at the time, so I wrote postcards explaining exactly what was in each bottle, where the ingredients came from and what they would do. Offering customers honest information would later become a cornerstone of our trading philosophy.

What started as economic necessity became a point of principle

A week before the shop was due to open I had the fright of my life when I got a letter from a solicitor threatening to sue unless I changed the name of the shop. It was incredible. There were apparently two funeral parlours in Kensington Gardens who claimed their business would be affected, that the bereaved would not want to hire a funeral director whose premises were close to a 'Body Shop'. (There was also a betting shop nearby which was taking bets on how long we would be able to stay in business).

All my life I have been intimidated by headmasters and solicitors, and at first I simply did not know what to do. But then it occurred to me I might be able to get some free publicity out of it. I made an anonymous telephone call to the local newspaper, the Brighton *Evening Argus*, and poured out a colourful story to a reporter about a 'mafia' of undertakers ganging up on some poor defenceless woman who was only trying to open her own business while her husband was planning to go off and ride a horse across South America. The *Argus* took the bait and published a centre-page spread. I never heard any more from the solicitors and what I learned then was that there was no need, ever, to pay for advertising.

At nine o'clock on Saturday, 27 March 1976, the first Body Shop opened its doors for business at 22 Kensington Gardens, Brighton. By lunchtime I was so busy that I had to telephone Gordon to ask him to come and help. At six o'clock we closed the doors, sat down and counted the takings I had stuffed into the front pocket of my dungarees. I was thrilled: we had taken exactly £130.

There was a wonderful sunset as we drove home that night in our little green van. I was not just happy – I was euphoric.

Many people perceive The Body Shop as a one-woman business. That's so far from the truth! It didn't even start that way – Gordon has always been involved from the very beginning. We wouldn't have got the initial funding from the bank if he hadn't come up with the simple but effective strategy of playing by their rules. Gordon and I operate on the partnership principle – he does his bit, and I do mine, but we do it together, with a common purpose....

TO ME THE DESIRE TO CREATE AND TO
HAVE CONTROL OVER YOUR OWN LIFE,
IRRESPECTIVE OF THE POLITICS OF THE
TIME OR THE SOCIAL STRUCTURES, WAS
VERY MUCH PART OF THE HUMAN SPIRIT.
WHAT I DID NOT FULLY REALIZE WAS
THAT WORK COULD OPEN THE DOORS TO
MY HEART.

4

GOING TO MARKET

Brighton shopkeepers opening up for business in the spring of 1976 occasionally had cause to sniff the air, then pause and scratch their heads at the curious sight of this odd woman in dungarees with unruly dark hair walking down the street intently spraying strawberry essence on to the pavement. It was not a madwoman – it was me, laying a scented trail to the door of The Body Shop in the hope that potential customers would follow it.

Believe me, I was prepared to try anything in those early days to get customers into my shop. I wanted to get passers-by to stop, so I put big, old-fashioned sandwich boards outside and got local art students to make posters promoting one or another of the products. I drenched the front of the shop in the most exotic perfume oils so that it always smelled wonderful as you approached; inside I hung huge branches of dried flowers from the ceiling, and there was fragrant pot-pourri everywhere.

Once I had got people inside, it was all down to me. I never *sold* anything to anyone, at least not in the way that selling was then understood; it was not my style to be a pushy saleswoman. In the retail trade, sales staff tend to use counters as a refuge to avoid making contact with customers. That was not me: I was never behind the counter. I would be tidying a shelf next to someone and I would dab something like the Glycerine and Rosewater Lotion on the back of my hand and say: 'Umm, I love the smell of this. Here, try it. What do you think?'

'I was prepared to try anything in those early days . . .'

The only time I was uncomfortable with this new trade of mine was if I thought whoever was buying could not really afford it. Then I tried to encourage them to take the smallest size or to bring in their own bottle for a squirt of something at ten pence. Otherwise I adored the whole process of trading, of watching someone come into the shop and looking along the shelves. Sometimes I found myself literally holding my breath, waiting for the moment when they would reach out and choose something. I thought it was wonderful to have a shop full of products that people actually wanted. (It still is!)

A Small Shopkeeper

Without my entirely understanding it, and certainly without my planning it, the shop seemed to appeal to lots of different kinds of customers – to students, young mothers, day trippers, foreign visitors. Even guys liked to come in and look around. Women of my Mum's age liked the notion of returnable bottles, perhaps because it reminded them of those thrifty days during and after the war. It was classless, friendly and stylish; people felt comfortable even if they were only browsing.

Being in the shop every day was also an education for me, because I realized that some people came in just to have someone to talk to. It was a shock to discover that there was a lot of loneliness out there, loneliness that could be temporarily alleviated by simple gestures, by talking, touching and bonding.

Talking about the products was never a chore. Passion persuades, and by God I was passionate about what I was selling. I loved to tell people where the ingredients had come from, how they were used in their original state and what they could do. The names of the products themselves generated endless questions – Honey and Oatmeal Scrub Mask, Cucumber Cleansing Milk, Seaweed and Birch Shampoo, Avocado Moisture Cream, Hawthorn Hand Cream, Cocoa Butter Body Lotion....

I never wanted to be in a position where I was made to look a fool by someone who knew more than I did, so I read everything I could lay my hands on about the use of natural ingredients for skin and hair care and how to make up your own products. I think I probably got every book ever published on the subject and I experimented at home all the

No interior design
awards this year.

time, using vodka as an alternative for pure alcohol and mixing it with natural oils to see what I could come up with.

Passion persuades, and by God I was passionate about what I was selling.

The best times were when the shop was full of people and I was run off my feet. The worst times were when there was no one to talk to, the days when no one came into the shop at all. I paid, I expiated my sins, on those days, staring out into the street and praying for someone, anyone to come in. Working alone in 300 square feet of retail space can be the most frustrating experience in the world. I would try to keep busy by housekeeping, or rearranging a display, or bottling at the back of the shop, but in the end you are left with absolutely nothing to do... except stand there and worry and get varicose veins.

People who start small retail businesses with very little money take tremendous risks and rarely succeed. Without adequate funding you often cannot get the best location – which is crucial – and you are at the mercy of inflexible suppliers demanding payment within thirty days. I'm amazed that people open shops without any real knowledge of the product, without knowing how to sell and without first evaluating the competition. If I was to start a skincare company now, I would make damn sure to do something completely new and not just imitate The Body Shop.

In many ways I should not have succeeded because I didn't have a clue about business. The extent of my business acumen was that Gordon said I had to take £300 a week to survive. There were many weeks when I was well short. I tried opening on Sundays and going out in the evenings, with a selection of products loaded in my van, to talk to schools or evening institutes or anyone who would have me. Still, some weeks I was lucky if I made £150.

My interest in financial matters did not extend much beyond making enough money to keep going; if I was short of cash to pay a bill. I simply kept the shop open later. I only had the vaguest idea how to keep accounts; aesthetics were far more important to me than accounts.

Aesthetics ruled everything. When I was a teacher I was obsessed with the style and detail in my classroom; now it was the same with my shop. I wanted to create the right atmosphere and sense of style. I made up my mind that I didn't want one of those ghastly modern tills, so I used to stuff the money into the pockets of my dungarees (silver in one pocket, coppers in another, with notes in the front bib) and count out the change like a barrow boy.

It was clearly evident to everyone that The Body Shop was a hick little cottage industry, and therein, I think, lay a lot of its attraction. But it also created problems. I was very pleased with the folksy, hand-written labels on the bottles, for example, but we used the wrong ink. People who left my products in steamy bathrooms – and most did – soon discovered that the ink began to run. After a few days the label was completely illegible, so they couldn't see what they had bought. Customers started bringing containers back and asking me If I could tell them what was inside, although there was never any bad feeling.

The perfume bar: 'a combination of playtime, theatre and a bit of fun.'

I could not afford to put perfumes in the products because they cost such a lot of money, so I set up a little 'perfume bar'. I filled a typesetter's tray with a selection of perfume oils – musk, apple blossom, frangipani, honeysuckle, patchouli, jasmine, and so on – and let customers choose their own fragrance to mix with whatever products they were buying. If they wanted to make their own eau de toilette, I told them to mix it with vodka. It all added to the wonderful smell in the shop and gave people the opportunity to experiment and create their own individual products. No one had ever done that before, and it was enormously popular: it was a combination of playtime, theatre and a bit of fun.

Bottling It Up

The hardest job, in terms of physical labour, was the bottling. Gordon had left for Buenos Aires about two months after the shop opened, so I did not have him to help me any more. I was not earning enough to get a contractor to do it, so I collected the products myself in bloody great five-gallon containers which I had to lug into an area at the back of the shop. Then I would decant the stuff into whatever size bottles I needed on the shelves. I did not want to waste anything so when the container seemed empty I cut it in half with a bread knife so that I could scrape out every last drop.

I could never have coped in those early days if it had not been for my mother. Every female entrepreneur with children knows that her kids are the weak link in the chain of juggling work and family. For me, that weak link was removed by the constant presence of my mother, who was always available to look after Justine and Sam. I had imagined that with a shop I would be able to devote much more time to the children, particularly after the exhausting years of running the restaurant, but I had not counted on working on Sundays, or going out in the evenings to peddle my wares from my van, or spending hours in the garage bottling up the products. I had also not counted on how disturbed the children would be by Gordon's absence.

Bottling: the hardest job

Every female entrepreneur with children knows that kids are the weak link in the chain of juggling work and family.

I have to confess I was so involved with the shop that I did not miss Gordon as much as I thought I would, but Justine and Samantha took it very hard – particularly Justine, who was then six. They had been used to us both working – that was a constant – but one parent suddenly disappearing was too much for her and she became very unsettled and stressed. I pinned up enormous maps all round the kitchen walls with pictures of Gordon on a horse, so that they could both get an idea where he was, but Justine would cry and cry every day when I left home to open the shop.

I certainly couldn't afford a nanny or an au pair, so looking after the children devolved on my Mum and our wonderfully extended Italian family. Justine and Samantha really grew up in her house in Littlehampton, where I too had grown up. I usually took them to school in

Gilda, a working mother's godsend

the mornings and went straight off to open up the shop. My Mum looked after them after school and kept them until I finished work. If I was going out in the evening they stayed overnight with my Mum and I would go and have breakfast with them next morning. That's how working mothers survive.

Gordon was held up in Buenos Aires for a month or so at the start of his trip and I heard from him regularly during that period. But when he actually set off he could only post letters from mission stations on his route and there were sometimes long gaps which would make me very nervous, although I was certainly getting a vicarious thrill out of his determined flight from anonymity. After living and working with him so closely for seven years I found it odd to be mistress of my own space, time and energy. But I also learned a lot about how to tackle the everyday tasks that women are so often conditioned by our society to think they need not worry about.

The Body Shop Hots Up

The summer of 1976 was one of the hottest on record, and Brighton – only an hour from London by train – was enjoying its best season for years, with tourists and holidaymakers arriving in droves. As one magical sunny day followed another, more and more people began coming into the shop. The simple fact was that girls were wearing fewer clothes and showing more flesh, and they were using more of the kind of skin products that I was selling. The notoriously fickle British climate did me a big favour that year. I felt wonderfully independent and proud. My husband was away doing his own thing, something exciting and adventurous. I had my babies. I had a lot of friends. I had my own business. Life was good.

I was usually able to run the shop alone on weekdays, but on Saturdays a friend, Aidre, came in to help, and before that summer was over I was already beginning to discuss with her the possibility of opening a second shop. It was crazy, of course. The Body Shop was not nearly well enough established to think about expansion: it had only been trading for a few months. Obviously the sensible, pragmatic thing would be to wait for a few years to see how it worked out.

I knew all that – but I wasn't the sensible, pragmatic type. I could have stayed with just one shop, but I didn't want to. That is the difference between an entrepreneur and a non-entrepreneur. It was nothing to do with making a lot of money or speculating how big the business would be in ten years' time; I don't believe entrepreneurs think like that. Entrepreneurs are doers as well as dreamers – they want to find the best way of pushing an idea along and use money to oil the wheels. And that is what intrigued me – to try and discover how far I could push my idea, my vision. I just thought: *Wouldn't it be great, wouldn't it be cheeky, if I could replicate the Brighton shop somewhere else?*

That somewhere else, I decided, would be Chichester, which was about the same distance from Littlehampton as Brighton, but to the west. Chichester was different from Brighton but had some of the same advantages for a business like mine – it was a yachting resort and a pleasant cathedral city, with well-preserved Georgian architecture and a theatre which attracted plenty of visitors.

I looked around for a site and found a very nice shop in a side street. It was bigger than the one in Brighton and a very unusual shape which I could immediately see had potential. I thought: *Yummy, this is it!*

When I went back to the bank to raise the money. I got the same brusque treatment as before. I only wanted to borrow £4000, but the answer was no. I had no track record. I had only been trading for a few months and was not making all that much money. Another shop was not viable. I should wait for at least another year.

Before . . .

A *year*? A year was an eternity to me, and I had no intention of waiting that long before I opened a second shop. I had to find someone willing to invest in me – someone who would realize I didn't do things by halves, that I had energy and a total commitment to what I was doing.

It was Aidre who came up with the solution. Her boyfriend Ian McGlinn, owned a

local garage and had some spare cash. He said he would lend me £4000 in return for a half share of the business. It seemed a pretty good deal to me. In truth there wasn't much of a business to split, and I was only really interested in getting together the finance for a second shop. I wrote and told Gordon what I was going to do. He wrote back as soon as he could telling me not to do it, not to give away half the company. But it was too late – by the time his letter arrived I had already done it.

Ian McGlinn's £4000 investment in The Body Shop in 1976 was the best decision he ever made. When the company went public in 1984 his stake was worth £4 million; it is now worth in excess of £140 million. Giving away half the business is considered by many as the biggest mistake I have ever made, but I don't resent it. I needed the money, I needed it quickly, and Ian was the only one then who would give it to me. £4000 was quite a sum in those days, and it was not unreasonable of him to expect something back in return – a 50 per cent stake in two small shops was hardly a fortune. I think he believed that if he eventually got eight grand back it would have been a terrific investment; in fact it was like winning the football pools over and over again.

To succeed you have to believe in something with such a passion that it becomes a reality.

... and after. Our second shop. Chichester, September 1976

People are often surprised at the situation, but our attitude is very straightforward – we don't need the money, so why should we worry about it or begrudge Ian his good luck? We're relaxed about it. Certainly neither Gordon nor I envy him in the least; our pleasure and fulfilment are obtained from running the business, not from the money it makes.

The Chichester shop opened in September, with Aidre in charge. Once again, we did most of it ourselves, working in the evenings with hammer and nails, fixing up the same larchlap garden fencing we had in Brighton. A lovely old friend of mine, a sergeant-major type who had done some work at the hotel, did the painting and we had a young hippy kid helping to put up the shelves, but everything else was down to us.

As the shop was bigger than Brighton it was a little bit more difficult to fill the space, so we bought jewellery, multi-coloured scarves, cards and books – anything, in fact, that we thought we could sell. When people started asking where we found the typesetter's trays that we used for the perfume I went out and bought fifty straight away. We eventually sold hundreds and hundreds of them – everyone wanted one to hang on the wall and put their little knick-knackeries in it.

We were still fighting for survival, so I would sell anything. If they wanted the shirt I was wearing, I'd sell it. We devised little uniforms for ourselves and for the girls who helped out on Saturdays: baggy, collarless grandfather shirts with The Body Shop logo screen-printed on the back. We wore them with rolled-up dungarees and espadrilles and thought we looked great.

Even then we would reuse or recycle everything we could. For Christmas we bought a job lot of little wicker baskets, packed them with the straw that came from the perfume canisters, filled them with small bottles and stuck dried flowers in the top to sell as gift packs. I will never forget the day when both shops each took £100. We celebrated with a bottle of Algerian wine. It tasted like dry-cleaning fluid, but nothing could dampen my excitement. I had never, ever, thought that we would be able to notch up such figures. It was wonderful to have such a positive indication that I had got it right, that I was right to trust my gut instinct, that we were providing products that people wanted and charging a price they were willing to pay and still enable us to make a profit. To me, that was bliss.

Early Secrets of Success

The Body Shop succeeded for two principal reasons. First of all, I simply had to survive while Gordon was away. The underlying drive that kept me going was that I had to eat and the kids had to be fed and clothed. It was pure survival: I knew that somehow or other I would have to find the reserves of energy to overcome whatever problems arose.

Second, to succeed you have to believe in something with such a passion that it becomes a reality. I had total faith in the idea of the shop and I had a zest for trading. That's not something you can learn. It's either in you or it's not. I loved to trade, and I knew the idea of selling skin and hair care products made from natural ingredients, and selling them in different sizes, was a good one. And when enough people tell you what a good idea it is it helps build your confidence, which is another vital ingredient of success.

It was nothing to do with luck. The only place where luck comes before work is in the dictionary. Granted, the timing was right. I don't think it could have happened in the forties. People in the seventies were beginning to be more receptive to products and remedies that had proved themselves over the centuries. But someone else might have conceptualized what I did and got it very wrong. I worked at it and got it right.

There were still plenty of problems, of course, and one of them was that the Chichester shop did not have a direct road access. To deliver the five-gallon containers I had to park my van some distance away, then hump each container on a trolley up to the shop. It was very heavy work for a woman, and one day while I was making a delivery I got a parking ticket. I was furious and refused to pay. When a summons arrived to appear in court I took one of the containers with me, along with an impassioned speech and a plea for leniency. 'How are businesses to survive,' I asked the court in my best Perry Mason style, 'if you are not prepared to show any flexibility? Surely it's better that I am trying to run my own business than being on the dole? You tell me how I can carry this container into my shop in less than twenty minutes and I'll do it.' The magistrates were sympathetic, but not so much so that they waived the fine. Reluctantly, I paid up.

Early in 1977 I got a telephone call from a young herbalist called Mark Constantine. He had written a book about herbal cosmetics and was trying, without a lot of success, to market his own herbal shampoos. He wanted to know if The Body Shop would be interested. I remember he was calling from a payphone and had to keep feeding coins into it. I was having trouble finding cocoa butter at the time, and I asked him if he made anything that used it. He said he did – his uncle worked at a chocolate factory and could get all the cocoa butter he needed. I was keen to extend our range of products, so I asked him to come and see me at the Chichester shop.

Mark turned out to be as manic a herbalist as I was a trader. He was tall, dark, a kind of hippy character, and we hit it off immediately. He told me he'd had a row with his parents and had been living in a wood somewhere: I was very impressed by that. He was studying trichology at night and spend-

Mark Constantine: tall, dark herbalist

ing his days dreaming up wonderful herbal products that he could not sell because they looked so bloody awful. He made a henna cream shampoo, for example, that looked liked sludge and smelled like horse-shit. There was also a lettuce lotion with little bits of lettuce floating around in it, and a honey and beeswax cleanser with black specks caused by bees returning to their hives with dirty feet!

I thought we could overcome the problem with cards explaining what the products contained and why they looked the way they did, so I swallowed hard and gave him an order worth £1000. It was a record for both of us – the biggest order I had ever placed and the biggest, by far, that he had ever received. (I later learned that he had been as terrified as I was – could he fulfil the order? Could I sell it? We both had a lot of chutzpah in those days.) At the time he was living on £30 a week and mixing up his products in his kitchen, I had quite a few sleepless nights worrying about that order and whether or not the stuff would sell. In fact it all went in less than a month and I gave him an even bigger repeat order. His creative contribution to our product range since then has been immense – his company has grown with us and is The Body Shop's major supplier.

Return of the Traveller

In April, I heard that Gordon was coming home. We had made tentative plans to meet in Lima in February, but I was so busy with the shops that it was impossible. The idea was that we would have a holiday and Gordon would decide at that time whether or not to continue with his journey. I think if I had gone out to meet him and told him how upset the children were by his absence he would probably have abandoned the trip there and then. But I did not go, and he continued on through Peru. He had covered 2000 miles and was in Bolivia when one of his horses slipped, fell down a precipice and was killed. He did not have the heart to carry on after that and headed for home.

It was strange, at first, having this tall, sun-bronzed stranger invading our space. He had been away for more than a year and the children hardly recognized him. They were certainly nervous of him, and very, very shy; and I have to confess that even I found it odd having a husband again, having the rhythm of my life disrupted. It was difficult for Gordon, too. He had grown used to being independent. I think what had happened was that we had both grown incurably selfish, the way people do when they are alone. If Gordon had completed his trip he

might have been away so long that we would have become irredeemably estranged.

Luckily, we managed to solve the problems by taking a holiday with the kids. We rented a motor home and all went off to France together. It was the best thing in the world we could have done – we went away as strangers and came back as a family.

When things had settled down a bit we

The homecoming: Gordon and girls

started working together again. I was very pleased and proud to see that Gordon was impressed with the shops, and when he said: 'OK, what can I do to help?' I just said: 'Bottling.' That was the most time-consuming and exhausting of all the jobs, and I was more than happy to hand it over. Gordon moved the whole bottling and labelling operation into our garage and took over delivering supplies to both shops as they were needed, paying the wages and keeping the books. It made things a lot easier for me; once again we slipped naturally into complementary roles in which neither of us felt obscured or threatened by the other.

The hotel was still functioning, just about, with six elderly residents; but now that Gordon was home and the shops were doing reasonably well we thought we deserved some privacy as a family. So we put the hotel on the market and found an idyllic little thatched cottage in Rustington, a village near Littlehampton. Box Tree Cottage – had an inglenook fireplace, a little well and gnomes in the garden. I could not have been happier when we moved in.

Expansion the Organic Way

Gordon's return was providential, because after a year's absence he brought back with him fresh vision. He saw the potential of the business and found a way for us to expand, even though we had no more money and the banks wouldn't lend us any more.

It started with Max Bygraves' daughter, Chris Green, who wanted to open her own shop in Hove. We thought it was a great idea – we agreed that she could call it The Body Shop and that we would supply all the products she needed. The shop was entirely hers – our only interest was in selling more products. It was a completely informal arrangement – we didn't bother with a contract or anything like that, and we certainly didn't think of charging a fee. Then Aidre said she would like to open a Body Shop in Bognor Regis with her parents and so we did the same deal with her. It seemed like the most natural thing in the world; we were simply grateful that other people wanted to have a shop like ours and were willing to sell our products in it.

In fact people were coming into the Brighton shop all the time saying how much they loved it and how much they wanted to have a shop just like it. When I talked about it with Gordon he saw it as the perfect way to grow without having to raise a lot more finance. He called it 'self-financing' – what is now called franchising, although we had never heard of the word at that time.

Gordon's theory was that if hopeful shop owners financed their own shops, we could simply say, 'Fine, go ahead' to those who wanted to open a Body Shop. We also thought that with increased volume of sales we could buy things more cheaply and so increase our profitability. Gordon went off to see our lawyer, a man with the wonderful name of Mr Careless, and worked out a simple supply and distribution agreement which would require franchise holders to sell our products.

In 1978 the first informal franchises began operating and the first Body Shop franchise opened outside the UK (actually, it was not so much a shop as a cupboard) in a kiosk in Brussels. It was financed by a businessman as a present for his wife, but it was so tiny that their first order was for only £300.

We developed a simple formula that seemed to work. In return for the franchisee putting up the money to open a shop, we provided a licence to use the Body Shop name and the products to sell. We also offered all our expertise and experience to help run it, and as often as not Gordon and I would put on our overalls and do as much as we could to get it ready for opening.

Getting Off the Ground

Deb McCormick, who now has five Body Shops in the south-west of England, was typical of the bright young women who were coming to us and asking to open a shop. After taking her finals at London University she was vaguely considering careers in journalism or politics until she discovered that Aidre's Body Shop had opened up in her home town of Bognor Regis. She says the moment she walked into the shop she thought, 'This is it!' She telephoned Gordon straight away and he invited her to come and see us. We still had the hotel then, and when Deb arrived she found Justine and Sam holding a sale of toys and books outside. She wasn't allowed in until she parted with 30 pence for a book on nomadic furniture (yes, there is such a thing).

She was tremendously enthusiastic and had already decided that Bath was the town where she would like to live, so we simply told her to go off and find a site. She hit a snag immediately: because she was so young she found that the estate agents in Bath would not take her seriously. She solved the problem by camping on the doorstep of the leading estate agent at a quarter to nine every morning; she was such a pest that he became quite keen to find her something to get her off his back.

When she had found a shop, we told her how to get the money from the bank. By then we knew a lot about banks and we literally rehearsed her interview, telling her what to wear and what to say, she got the loan and Gordon delivered 70 gallons of products to her mother's home in

Bognor Regis so that they could start bottling. Then Gordon and I drove down to Bath to help get the shop ready. Deb took £60 on her first day and was euphoric. Two months later Gordon got a call from her asking if he could explain how to use a calculator; we knew then she must be doing all right.

Meanwhile, we had somehow persuaded the bank to stump up enough for us to open another shop of our own, in Reading, before the end of 1977. My God, I worked my buns off getting the Reading shop opened, although we were never totally exhausted like we were when we had the restaurant. It was partly to do with the fact that after a day in the shop you would come out smelling like a bed of roses, instead of stinking of chip fat. No one can tell me that aromatherapy doesn't work.

It was two hours' drive each way from Littlehampton to Reading. I lost count of the number of times the van broke down or ran out of petrol and I had to hitch-hike. And I was still going out in the evenings to talk about the products to any organization that would have me. Sometimes I would not pick up more than thirty quid, but I always thought it was worth it. Even if I did not sell much during the course of the evening, I balanced that fact with the hope that some of the people I talked to would be persuaded to come into the shop.

By the end of that year Gordon had moved the bottling operation into an old furniture depository he had found near my Mum's home in Littlehampton, and Mark Constantine was running short courses to teach staff about the products and how to advise customers on skin and hair care. Even in those days we knew the importance of educating and involving the people who worked for us, even if they were only there on Saturdays. I wanted to make sure that our staff knew more about our products than anyone else and that they had ready answers to all the questions they hoped they would never be asked.

Until you have traded for more than a year you can't really see how things are building up. You survive for the first year with little break-throughs, indications that you are doing OK. I can remember, for example, the first week the Brighton shop took £500, and then the first week that both shops together took £1000. In the second year you are able to compare your figures each month with the previous year and get a clearer indication of what progress you are making. Figures never really meant much to me, but Gordon was very good at making projections about how fast we should be expanding. And it was obvious to him that we were doing all right, even though the general business climate was depressed, with a recession and high unemployment.

For the first couple of years we more or less opened wherever anyone asked if they could open a shop. I don't think we said 'No' to anybody – now we have to say 'No' to nearly everybody. It *was* a ludicrous way of doing things, but it didn't really cause us any headaches. Our attitude was that if they could find what they thought was the right site, then it was the right site – nobody was going to set up shop in too rotten a position. In 1979 Sweden's first Body Shop opened in Stockholm, and another started up in Athens.

Trusting to Instinct

I had always trusted my instinct about people, even though I had a tendency to be impressed by absolutely stupid things. I can clearly remember offering the first franchise in North America to a Dutch-Canadian woman for no other reason than that she was not wearing a bra. She came down to see us at the warehouse in Littlehampton, and when she walked in I gasped: 'My God, you're not wearing a bra!' No

'My God, you're not wearing a bra.'

one was walking around Littlehampton in those days wearing a tight T-shirt and no bra, and I thought this woman was great. She was short, like me, and an immigrant, like me. She had actually come over from Canada with the intention of copying The Body Shop operation but when she realized how big it had grown she settled for a franchise instead. She stayed with us that night and we got pissed on cherry brandy, which was the only thing in the house we ever seemed to have to drink.

All the early franchisees were women, and that pleased me – I was comfortable with that. I could see that men were good at the science and vocabulary business, at talking about economic theory and profit and loss figures (some women are, too, of course). But I could also see that women were better at dealing with people, caring and being passionate about what they were doing. In my experience, women were also less likely than men to believe that the joy of business was contained in the bottom line.

With managers in place running the shops, I wanted to know more about the industry. I thought I could learn from the big boys in the business, so I bought all the trade magazines and started going to conferences and presentations given by people like Revlon and Estée Lauder, always sitting at the back in the hope that I would not be noticed. But what they were selling and the way they were selling it was the antithesis of my own beliefs, and it did not take them long to realize that I was an alien. I did not speak the same language as these people, I did not even look like them – all the other women were in silk and furs, while I was in jeans. All I learned was how to be uncomfortable.

I did not speak the same language as these people, I did not even look like them.

It seemed to me there was not a single truly creative spark to be found in the cosmetics industry and that the real creativity came from the perfume houses. They were the gentlemen of the industry; the others were the cowboys who simply provided the vehicles to sell the perfumes. So I switched my curiosity, visiting the perfume houses, whenever I could, talking to the perfumiers – wonderful old gentlemen in white hats – and learning from them. I loved the fact that many of them were small family businesses with a long history and their own culture, and that the skill of testing fragrances through smell had been handed down through the generations.

They treated me very well and with respect, perhaps because they were curious about me. They could not understand how I was able to sell perfume as a simple raw ingredient in plastic bottles. It broke all the rules. Where was the so-called romance, the art, the design, the hype, the language – the top, middle and bottom notes, and all that?

There I was, telling my customers to do what they liked with it – mix it with anything they fancied, pour it in the washing-up water if they liked, stick it in their ears for all I cared. I think the perfume houses were embarrassed by the basic way I was going about it, but they were also intrigued because I was selling a lot. A kilo of perfume oil makes an awful lot of eau de toilette which takes a long time to shift. The Body Shops were getting through a kilo of perfume oil in a couple of days.

For me, in those days everything was a learning process. I scoured shops similar to mine to see what our people were doing. My very favourite shop was Culpeper's, the herbalists. I thought their stores were dreamy, with a wonderful sense of style, a great smell and terrific presentation. The Body Shops were ragbags by comparison; we didn't look as if we knew one herb from another. I also envied the fact that Culpeper's had the best sites in every town.

I think what really separated us from stores like Culpeper's during our gestation period was our burning enthusiasm. There was a tangible sense of euphoria in every Body Shop. Maybe we were amateurs and, maybe we didn't look serious, but we were mad keen and excited by what was going on and we were changing constantly – we just loved change.

Developing a Style

It took time for us to develop a distinctive style and identity: we weren't even sure if we would end up selling skin and hair care products. It was certainly what we wanted to do, but on some trading days as much as 60 per cent of our turnover came from sundries and knick-knacks. The certainty and confidence that we could survive by selling only our own products came later.

In the seventies there was not yet much general interest in natural products. None of the big stores stocked them, and the cosmetics industry was relying on its usual daft gimmicks, such as 'hidden ingredients' and 'Factor X' to persuade women to buy their products. Their marketing technique was blatantly immoral – they created fears and anxieties and then offered products intended to allay those fears.

We operated from an entirely different perspective: we *responded* to needs rather than creating them. When the London Marathon started, many of the runners complained about their sore feet; Katie, my first employee at Chichester, pointed out that we did not have a foot lotion in our range. We did some research and discovered one very old remedy using oil pressed from peppermint leaves and another which was a herbal infusion of the flowers of arnica, a mountain plant. I rang Mark Constantine and asked him if he could produce something similar and he came up with a wonderful lotion made from peppermint, menthol and arnica, with almond oil, cocoa butter and lanolin. It not only soothed tired feet and softened hard skin, it also helped inhibit foot odour.

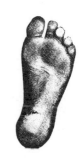

By then I had hired a public relations person, Janis Raven, and she dreamed up a wonderful stunt to promote the product. She contacted the organizers of the next London Marathon and got permission for us to stand along the route and hand out free samples to all the competitors. It was a cute little story that made many of the newspapers next day, and Peppermint Foot Lotion became one of our best-selling products.

Janis had an important role in the early development of the company because we could not see any point in paying to advertise if we could get free publicity through editorial coverage in newspapers and magazines – although in truth we did not get much attention in the press until our first London shops opened, in Portobello Road and Covent Garden. The two young women who opened the Covent Garden shop were selling Guatemalan rugs and army surplus clothes from a market stall in Camden Lock when they contacted us and asked about a franchise. Their parents put up their homes as collateral for a bank loan, and we let them have the products on an interest-free loan for six months to get them started. Today they have six shops in central London with a massive turnover.

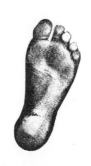

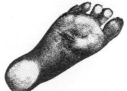

Look, Here We Are

I think the media considered The Body Shop too parochial to bother with before we arrived in London. But soon after the Covent Garden shop opened *Cosmopolitan* magazine published a feature about us, and that was a kind of launching pad for media interest that continues to this day. I have always enjoyed being interviewed, talking about the company and putting forward our ideas; it helps, I suppose, that I have the reputation of being Ms Mega-mouth.

For a while I found I was in great demand to appear on women's magazine programmes on afternoon television. But all they wanted me to talk about were things like how to make a face mask with boiled lettuce and blended avocado, or how you could remove the odour from your husband's socks by stewing them with nettles. I'd be in the studio with great piles of natural ingredients demonstrating how to make all this stuff in the kitchen like a latter-day green Fanny Cradock. I used to get so frustrated because I had to do so much homework and preparation and it was nothing to do with selling Body Shop products. However, there was some spin-off as I made sure I was introduced as 'Anita Roddick of The Body Shop', and I always put in a plug for the shops if I possibly could.

Although both Gordon and I were working long hours, we still functioned perfectly well as a family. I don't think the children suffered at all; in fact their lives improved immeasurably because they were no longer living in a hotel with a lot of old people. They were at a school just down the road from the Box Tree Cottage, close enough for them to walk there and back, and we were usually around in the evenings to help them with their homework. On Saturdays they would occasionally help in one or other of the shops, filling shelves and jobs like that, but usually they preferred just to play with their friends. And we always took wonderful holidays together as a family; we never let the business interfere with things like that.

As the number of shops grew so did the demand for our products, but we rarely had any supply problems. Most of our manufacturers were small companies, like ourselves, and one of the things I had always been brought up to do was to pay bills promptly. I didn't know that it was standard business practice, even among big companies, to delay paying bills as long as possible, so we always paid on the nail. I expect most accountants would say it was stupid, but the result was that our suppliers looked after us and always gave us the very best service. It was yet another example of our naïveté turning, fortuitously, to our advantage.

Family Matters

From the start we ran the company in a very informal way, as if we were all one big extended family – and in many ways we were. The first managers' meeting was held in the front room of my mum's house and she cooked lasagne for everyone. We were very good at employing the right people, people who would fit in, and we fostered a kind of benevolent anarchism by encouraging everyone to question what they were doing and how they were doing it in the hope of finding better working methods. We always listened to suggestions from the staff, no matter how wacky, since we were very aware that we were all learning together how to run the business. Word apparently got around that we were an unusual company and a good employer. It was nice – and not unusual – to have people turn up at the warehouse out of the blue asking if they could work for us. One of them, Eric Helyer, is now on the main board.

By 1980 we badly needed to move to a new warehouse, as the old furniture depository was bursting at the seams. Gordon and I had a small office partitioned off in one corner and the rest of the building was used for storage, bottling, labelling, mixing and grinding up ingredients; but even so we simply did not have sufficient space to supply the number of shops that were now trading.

Gordon hoped to persuade the bank to lend us enough money to build a new warehouse and office complex on a site in Littlehampton, and he arranged for a meeting at our existing warehouse so he could demonstrate the problems we were having and put on a little presentation about the company. On the day of the meeting, the bank manager and two of his assistants were sitting with us around the single table in our office and Gordon was going through the figures when the door burst open and in walked my mum, heaving an enormous laundry basket. She banged it down on the table and proceeded to fold clothing in front of us loudly complaining about the state of Gordon's shirts and the number of buttons she now had to sew on. Gordon and I took one look at the faces of the bankers, which were frozen with embarrassment, and started to shriek with laughter. They could not understand what we found was so funny.

The bank's sense of humour may not have been particularly acute, but its attitude towards us was changing perceptibly. They could see the amount of work we were putting in and the way the company was growing, and although they were still cautious they were much more prepared to be cooperative. In fact, the last time the bank turned us down was when I asked for a loan to open a second shop in 1976. After that they gave us everything we wanted.

We moved into the new warehouse and offices in October 1982, at which time new shops were opening at the incredible rate of two a month; there were further shops in Iceland, Denmark, Finland, Holland and Eire. We were by then charging a £3000 premium for a franchise and exercising much stricter control over what could and could not be done in the shops. We had learned, from experience, that it was absolutely essential to maintain a strong identity.

The biggest mistake we ever made was at a get-together with the franchise holders when we offered them a choice of three shop styles – in dark green, dark mahogany stain or stripped pine. We kept our strong 'corporate aroma' through the products, so the shops always smelled fantastic, but when they began to look different I realized almost immediately that it was the wrong move.

We never had an authoritarian approach to running the business and we thought of all the franchise holders as our friends, so it was very difficult when we wanted all the shops changed back to dark green. Some of them were trading very well with dark stained wood or pine interiors, and it took a lot of argument to get them to change. I was sympathetic. I knew how hard they were working and I knew what some of them had risked to open a Body Shop, but I also knew, with absolute certainty, that we had to hold on to our original image and style.

The Body Shop today is distinctive because you can see the colour and recognize the style regardless of where the shop happens to be. We have more than six hundred shops around the world and there is no dilution of the image in any of them. The look has developed quite a lot since the early hippy 'crunchy Granola' feel; nevertheless we have managed to maintain a very strong visual corporate identity, and I believe it is a vital element of our success. A true key to success is knowing what features set you apart from the competition: you must emphasize them, constantly restate them, and never be seduced into watering them down. It is a myth to think that the bigger a company grows, the harder it becomes to cling to its original style.

A true key to success is knowing what features set you apart from the competition.

While we were trying to convince our franchise holders of the need to toe the same style line, we also began the process of encouraging them to throw out the knick-knackery and concentrate on selling just The Body Shop range of hair and skin products, which was expanding all the time. It was quite a battle, because some of them were earning more from sundries than they were from our products; but I had a very clear vision of what I wanted the shops to look like, and what I did *not* want them to look like was some messy market stall draped with gewgaws and woolly socks. The difficulty was that, having given the franchisees a certain amount of freedom about what they could sell, it all became a question of taste. It was hard to have to say you did not want them to sell something because you thought it was bad taste.

We had stuck closely to a policy of being open and honest about our products, and it was paying dividends among customers who were increasingly irritated by the patently dishonest advertising of the cosmetics industry. Women in the eighties were less and less inclined to fall for the 'buy this mixture of oil and water and you will be a movie star' pitch dreamed up in the expensive offices of advertising agencies.

When we made mistakes, we always admitted it. We had a 'nourishing cream', for example, until someone pointed out that only food and drink can actually nourish the body. So we took it out of the range and put little signs up explaining the reason. In some cases our honesty was our undoing: we had a shampoo for greasy hair which we called, simply, a 'de-greasant'. It sounded like something you used to clean out an engine and was a complete failure. We even had a 'hormone cream' for a while; I can hardly believe it now.

The biggest flop in those early years was our attempt to launch a 'mother and baby' range. It was a perfectly good idea and there was nothing wrong with the products, but they did not sell because we had no real credibility at that time. What mother wanted to buy a cream to put on her baby from some hick little shop, without really knowing whether it had been properly tested and analysed? Now that we have the reputation and authority we have a fantastically successful mother and baby range, but then it was different. I think my mum is still using up some of the creams from that first range.

Fortunately our product failures were not disasters because, unlike all other cosmetics companies, we had invested no money in the packaging and promotion. All our bottles were standardized, so if a product did not sell we had lost nothing but the raw materials. It gave us wonderful freedom to experiment.

Mama toto – a collection for mother and baby

Formulas and Fanatics

I was constantly on the lookout for new ideas and new products, no matter how quirky they seemed at first. One day a wonderful Jewish lady from Vienna turned up at our warehouse with an amazing story and a bag full of what looked like granules of lime and gypsum. She explained, in lengthy and colourful detail, that the granules were a secret skin-care treatment originally devised by her grandfather for the Archduke Ferdinand, and it was so effective that Helena Rubenstein had once tried to obtain the formula. I thought it was a great yarn, although I was less sure about the product. But we tested it and it actually worked; we bought it from her and added it to our range as Viennese Chalk Facial Wash. She took 10 per cent of what we sold and, back in Vienna, retired in some comfort.

Not all such approaches were so successful. I had a telephone call

one day from a woman who said she had the most wonderful idea for a
Body Shop product – but she could not discuss it over the telephone,
she had to see me in person. We arranged to meet, like a couple of spies
in a John Le Carré movie, in the back room of the King's Road shop. I
was waiting for her when there was a knock on the door and a very fat
woman walked in. I had to suppress a giggle because she looked like a
caricature from a Beryl Cook painting: she had a hairnet tied over her
blue rinse and carried an enormous black plastic bag.

First of all she took out a grubby scrap of paper which she asked me
to sign. It was an agreement that I would never divulge what she was
about to show me. I signed it, and then she said I had to look her in the
eye and swear that I would never give away her secret. Still trying not
to laugh, I solemnly swore that her invention was safe with me.
Satisfied at last, she dug into her bag and produced a kind of wooden
fork with what looked like a Carmen roller fixed between the prongs
She proceeded to rub it up and down her face while explaining that it
removed all trace of wrinkles. By now I was absolutely convinced I
had been set up for *Candid Camera*, and I was looking round to see
where the television camera had been tucked away. But there was no
camera, and it seemed to take forever to convince her that I was unfortunately unable to market her invention. When you are at the mercy of
your curiosity, as I always was, you are also at the mercy of visiting idiots.

Throughout the first years of The Body Shop's development I don't
think there was ever any point at which Gordon and I sat back and
thought about how big the company had grown or about how successful it was. That realization was forced upon us when we had the first
approach, in 1981, to go on to the Unlisted Securities Market. It came
from a friend of a friend, a very established kind of guy with a plummy
public school accent, the kind that always makes me want to laugh.

I can remember it so well. We had recently moved from Box Tree
Cottage to a larger house in the village of Houghton, near Arundel, a
ten-minute drive from Littlehampton. He came to see us there, sat
down at our kitchen table and said in his fruity voice: 'Do you two
want to be millionaires?' Now that was a question we had *never* asked
ourselves. We just didn't know what to say. We were too embarrassed

to answer. Wanting to be a millionaire seemed to me to be a positively obscene ambition. We had not gone into business to get rich; we have never even *thought* about getting rich.

We told him we didn't think we were ready to go public just then, but it set Gordon thinking about a flotation some time in the future. There were a number of attractions. One was that we would be able to take some equity out of the business, pay off our mortgage and buy ourselves a degree of financial security. The other was that by putting some shares into public ownership we could ensure we retained control of the business. With Ian McGlinn owning 50 per cent of the company, we were increasingly worried that we had to get his approval for every major decision we wanted to make. In fact he wasn't interested in the business, but, even though he hadn't interferred, he always had the potential to if he so desired.

Another problem was that the retail boom was just beginning but The Body Shop was still not being taken seriously on the High Street. Retail trading is all about location, and we thought that if we were a public company we would be more respected and better placed to get the best locations. We were also very attracted to the idea of making all our staff shareholders, so that they could participate more directly in the success of the company. And we could not help but be intrigued by the prospect of being in the City, being up there with the big boys, even though we certainly had no love for the City's manners and morals.

Although we had been trading for five years we sometimes found it hard to believe what had happened in those years. Here we were, a poet and a teacher, running this international company that was growing at an unbelievable rate. Our turnover had grown from £278,000 in 1979 to £828,000 in 1981, although our after-tax profits were still miniscule – less than £20,000.

It had been damned hard work, but it had also, paradoxically, been ludicrously easy, and we were both enamoured with the notion of seeing how far we could push The Body Shop idea. We were still basically offering franchises to anyone who came knocking at our door – the only criterion was whether they had the money. It had never occurred to us to sit tight, to say to ourselves, 'OK, we're doing very nicely, thank you. Let's just carry on like this.' That was not the way either of us thought. So we finally decided that going public would be the next logical step.

Going Public

Gordon said he would need at least two years to prepare the company for flotation, to put our house in order and install a new accounting system. At that time our infrastructure was virtually non-existent: I handled all the product development, design and public relations; Gordon dealt with all the legal and financial matters – things like leases and franchise problems – with the help of a local solicitor and firm of accountants.

Gordon wanted to make quite sure he understood the nuances of going public and that there were no risks to our retaining control. He was under a lot of pressure to hurry – venture capitalists would have floated a wardrobe in those days if they thought they could make a few bob – but he absolutely refused to be rushed. Only when he was sure he knew as much about the flotation as anyone else in the great financial world did he give it the green light.

It was a great relief to me that Gordon handled all the negotiations and undertook all the reorganization that was needed to get the company ready. In many ways it was a very boring time for me, because I had to attend hundreds of meetings with guys in City suits using a lot of jargon I couldn't understand. Finance bored the pants off me; I fell asleep more times than not.

Businesswoman of the Year, 1986

The meeting I best remember is the one when someone from our stockbrokers, Capel Cure Myers, came down to Littlehampton to explain to the staff what going public would mean. It was a wonderful scene. All the staff, about forty of them, were sitting on chairs in the warehouse listening to a man in a pinstriped suit talking about the Unlisted Securities Market – I don't think a single person in the audience understood a word of what he was saying. Certainly my mum, who was sitting in the front row, had no idea what was going on. She kept mouthing at me, 'What's he talking about?' To this day we still haven't mastered the art of explaining the intricacies of share-owning even though everyone who's been with us for a year can become a shareholder.

I only really started to take an interest in the flotation when it came to aesthetics. They wanted the offer brochure to be very sedate and boring. I told them I wanted it very bright and colourful and different from anything that had been done before. In the end we did it ourselves; I was not going to compromise my aesthetic values for them.

What Price The Body Shop?

On the day before the flotation, in April 1984, there were lots of last-minute discussions about what the price should be. It seemed incredibly important to everyone, although I couldn't see why. The meetings went on until late at night. In the end it was decided to enter the market at 95p for a 5p ordinary share.

Gordon and I stayed in London overnight, and took a taxi to the Stock Exchange early next morning. I can remember standing there, behind the scenes, at nine o'clock as a huge clock went DOINNGGG and trading began. Four or five people began trading Body Shop shares immediately and we watched as the price went up from 95p, to £1, to £1.05, to £1.10.... I have to admit it was just thrilling. People were shouting and cheering and the whole thing was being filmed by BBC Television. I think it was the first time television cameras had been allowed into the Stock Exchange. In the end the price stopped at £1.65. Someone turned to me and said, 'The Body Shop is now worth £8 million, and you are worth £1.5 million.' I couldn't take it all in.

After the Stock Exchange closed I had to rush around to be interviewed on television and by the newspapers. The Body Shop was the day's 'good news' story – it was in the middle of the miners' strike – and I was presented as being one of 'Thatcher's children', which bugged me considerably; I didn't think our success had anything to do with Margaret Thatcher. That evening we went out with a lot of City types to a party at the Hippodrome.

Driving home late that night, Gordon and I talked about the day's events. What had happened was a benchmark, we both recognized that. We were now major shareholders in a public company which looked as if it was going to grow and grow. We were millionaires, but neither of us could really grasp that notion as being a measure of success.

Before the flotation, Gordon and I had been so busy just running the business day to day, helping to open shops, keeping them supplied and keeping pace with expansion, that we never really stopped to consider the wider implications of what we were doing. We never, for one moment, looked ahead and thought, *My God, maybe in ten years' time we'll have a thousand stores around the world and four thousand employees!* I am not sure how we would have reacted had we done so. We might have been scared stiff.

The beginnings of The Body Shop had been a balancing act – balancing time with the kids against time with the business, balancing taking risks against caution. I looked on the business as a kind of personal playground, as well as something that provided self-esteem and money for our survival.

To me the desire to create and to have control over your own life, irrespective of the politics of the time or the social structures, was very much part of the human spirit. What I did not fully realize was that work could open the doors to my heart.

IN A SOCIETY IN WHICH POLITICIANS NO LONGER LEAD BY EXAMPLE, ETHICAL CONDUCT IS UNFASHIONABLE, AND THE MEDIA DOES NOT GIVE PEOPLE REAL INFORMATION ON WHAT IS HAPPENING IN THE WORLD, WHAT FASCINATES ME IS THE CONCEPT OF TURNING OUR SHOPS INTO CENTRES OF EDUCATION.

5

ON THE CAMPAIGN TRAIL

A lot of people – those who did not know us very well – thought that after going public we would perhaps sell up and retire to a life of indolent luxury. Gordon and I never remotely considered doing such a thing. The Body Shop was too much our baby ever to let it go.

When we got home that night we sat in front of the fire and Gordon said, 'OK, what do we do now?' I knew he was not putting forward alternatives, like shall we sell up or shall we carry on. The unspoken implication of his question was crystal clear to me. We now had wealth and status in the business community. Wealth plus status equalled power. How were we going to use that power?

First, we both knew that the simple pursuit of ever-increasing profits was not going to be enough. We frankly were not that interested in money. However, we did recognize that a function of profits was to create jobs and provide security and prosperity for our employees. That was fine, but then what?

We accepted that it was our inherent responsibility to motivate and involve our staff and franchise holders, to try and make the working week a pleasure instead of a living death. How could we do that? In all kinds of ways. By education. By stretching their abilities and their imaginations. By involving them in issues of greater significance than selling a pot of skin cream.

And what were the social responsibilities of business? Should not a business that relied on the community for its success be prepared to give something back to the community? Should there not be a trade in goodwill as well as in commerce? All this, and much more, we talked about long into the night, and it began to dawn on us – no matter how trite it may now sound – that The Body Shop had both the potential, and the means at its disposal, to do good.

Soul Traders

For someone like myself, whose thinking was forged in the sixties, it was a magical prospect. The very notion of using a business as a crusader, of harnessing success to ideals, set my imagination on fire. From that moment The Body Shop ceased to exist, at least in my eyes, as just another trading business. It became a force for social change. It became a lobby group to campaign on environmental and human rights issues. It became a communicator and an educator.

In terms of our ability to effect change, we had a lot going for us. We were a slightly zany, fashionable enterprise with an eye-catching presence in the high street. Our customers and staff were mainly young, susceptible to new ideas, likely to be socially aware and terribly passionate.

We had at that time thirty-eight shops in the UK and fifty-two abroad, and there seemed to be no reason why the company should not continue to expand. Gordon had set a basic infrastructure in place when we were preparing to go public, and I still controlled all the product development. We were determined not to dilute our image – we were only interested in developing our original idea, and we felt we had a brilliant concept of organic growth. We were not tempted to play the game of diversification and acquisition; we wanted to stay with what we knew – selling our own products in our shops. And although there was clearly a limit to the number of Body Shops which would be able to trade profitably in each country, we had no idea what that limit was – only that we were a long way away from it, even in the UK.

We were proud of the fact that The Body Shop was a big company that traded like a little company. It still had a soul, a sense of values, a human face. But we were acutely aware that the bigger we grew the more those qualities were endangered. The environment of big business alienates humanity. We had a horror of becoming like the financial institutions with which we had been spending so much time during the two years in the run-up to the flotation. The last thing in the world we wanted was to become an amorphous multinational employing bored clock-watchers with little or no interest in what they were doing.

The problem was that working in a shop or warehouse was not the most stimulating or rewarding occupation. I knew that; I had done it long enough. Nevertheless, we believed that work could and should be a life-enhancing experience and that such a situation could be achieved by nurturing a sense of corporate idealism. Working for The Body Shop should be not just selling bars of soap, but working for the community, lobbying for social change, campaigning for the environment . . . working, in fact, for the greater good. To use the vernacular of the sixties, we wanted to get into the consciousness-raising business.

We had always campaigned vigorously against testing cosmetics products on animals because we thought it was totally unacceptable and downright repugnant that animals should suffer for the questionable ideals of female vanity. But there were also masses of other issues in which I felt we could become usefully and actively involved.

Making Connections

We made a small start in 1985, in our first year as a public company, by sponsoring posters for Greenpeace, which was lobbying against the dumping of hazardous waste in the North Sea. We paid for a hundred posters in prime city centre sites, showing the Greenpeace ship battling through a stormy sea with the slogan 'Thank God Somebody's Making Waves'. In the corner was a little flag saying 'You can join Greenpeace at The Body Shop', the only indication of our involvement. It was Greenpeace's first link with any commercial company.

In the following year we used the shops directly for the first time as a platform to protest against the slaughter of whales. The Save the Whale campaign, also in conjunction with Greenpeace, was a natural for The Body Shop. Quite a few of our products were based on jojoba oil, a wax derived from a desert plant which the American Indians had used for centuries on their bodies and hair. The interesting thing about jojoba oil was that it had almost identical properties to spermaceti, the oil from sperm whales, which was used by the cosmetics industry in many different creams.

Obviously substituting jojoba for spermaceti would have a direct impact on helping to save the sperm whales, which were facing extinction from over-fishing by Scandinavia and Japan.

I can't remember whether Greenpeace approached us or we approached them, but I loved the idea of campaigning jointly with them. It took me back to the days when I was a student and went on CND marches, or when I was a teacher and organized all the kids at school in Southampton on a march for Freedom from Hunger. I loved the collectivism of making a statement in that way.

Greenpeace designed the Save the Whale campaign because we didn't have any expertise in that area at that time. There were posters, collecting boxes, leaflets, membership application forms and Save the Whale stickers to put on all the bottles containing jojoba oil. We sent a whaling video to all the shops so that the staff knew what was going on. It was a very emotive subject and they loved being involved, although some of the franchise holders began to fret about us getting 'too political'. That was not an argument I was prepared to countenance.

It was an excellent campaign, very visual and exciting, which was good for Greenpeace as well as for The Body Shop. After all, we didn't have very interesting products to display – just those boring old bottles with green labels which all looked much the same – and I thought the big Save the Whale posters really brightened up the shops.

Unfortunately our first venture into environmental campaigning foundered on petty jealousies. We were very keen to put the campaign into our shops abroad, but we discovered we would have to get approval from separate foreign branches of Greenpeace, none of whom seemed to want to run with the idea. I was amazed that a non-governmental organization like Greenpeace could be so territorial and restrictive. We felt like poor little Bisto kids, only being allowed to sniff at a good idea.

I was very disillusioned and thought I wouldn't involve myself with these people again. The campaign had been successful in recruiting members for Greenpeace, but I considered it to be a failure since fewer than half our shops had been involved because of the problems with taking the campaign abroad. I still believed that The Body Shop could be a powerful environmental lobby, but we were lonely. We needed to be educated as a company, and we needed to find a buddy and a mentor who would trade knowledge and information in return for campaign support. I began shopping around for some other group that we could bond with and Friends of the Earth came top of the list, largely because I was very impressed with Jonathon Porritt, its then director. Greenpeace had worried about becoming linked with a commercial organization, but I don't think Friends of the Earth had too much trouble with that because they liked us – they could see our motives were honourable and that we really cared.

We learned from that experience, and we learned very quickly, that simple, emotive imagery was the key to getting a message across.

Our first campaign with Friends of the Earth – against acid rain – should have been our last, because we got it absolutely wrong. We were arrogant; we thought we knew how to do it. We hired a brilliant Polish instructor who produced an extraordinary surreal poster showing a dead tree sprouting from a decomposing human head against an industrial background of smoking chimneys. The quirky copyline said 'Acid Reign', which we thought was really clever. It was very, very sophisticated: the trouble was that our customers and the public hadn't got a clue what we were getting at. (In fact, someone came into one of our shops – I think it was in the Channel Islands – and asked if we were now selling LSD. I still don't know if it was a joke or not.) Ninety-eight posters went up in the UK shops and another 217 abroad, and all we achieved was to mystify everybody.

It was a terrible waste, because I insisted that our first FoE campaign went into the windows of every Body Shop. Our window displays were then generally pretty tedious and it seemed to me that visually striking campaign posters in the front windows of every Body Shop would make a big impact on the high street. Unfortunately, as no one knew what we were on about, the impact was more than muted.

We learned from that experience, and we learned very quickly, that simple, emotive imagery was the key to getting a message across. We learned that the first bite is taken with the eye and that something very graphic and very striking is needed to grab attention. We did better with the next FoE campaign, on the dangers to the ozone layer, with a poster showing a child in a huge desert landscape, dressed in aluminium like a spaceman and carrying an aluminium umbrella with holes. It bore the copyline 'Ozone or no Zone?' We had a quote from a Roger McGough poem to go with it: 'The way we mistreat the earth, Anyone would think we owned it.'

Our object was to try and reduce the use of CFCs in aerosols – at the same time we prudently made sure that we, as a company, did not use CFCs in any part of our operations. I didn't want anyone to be able to point a finger at us and accuse us of not practising what we preached. We had to have our own house in order. Actually, we had never sold any products in aerosol form because I had always considered them to be a grossly wasteful and unnecessary form of packaging.

The View from the City

Although at this time the financial cost of our environmental campaigning was small – certainly less than it would have cost to advertise in the Sunday colour magazines – I thought it was significant that none of the financial advisers or accountants ever asked what it had to do with the business of selling hair and skin products. It was quite evident that all they cared about was a six-monthly audit of our accounts and a healthy bottom line. On that score they had no worries: during our first year as a public company we opened nearly fifty new shops, and our profits more than doubled to £2.4 million.

Such figures got to mean less and less to me. I often wished that our success could be measured in quite different ways. How did we rate in terms of education and communication? How did we compare in caring for our staff? How did we make out in fulfilling our social responsibilities? Where did we stand on the quirkiness scale?

As far as I could make out, the City viewed The Body Shop with a sense of bemusement. We were passionate, quirky and breaking all the rules, and those pinstriped dinosaurs in Throgmorton Street could not pigeonhole us – could not understand how, despite all that, we had somehow managed to get it right.

You can be proud to work for The Body Shop – and, boy, does that have an effect on morale and motivation!

Yet no matter how nervous they were about what we were doing, they were anxious to court us because specialist retail outlets were starting to take off and 'niche markets' were the buzz words in retail trading. Businesses like ours were seen, at least in the City, as the good guys and the baddies were the big department stores, which were perceived to be cumbersome and tedious and not addressing the needs of the consumer. There was a great proliferation of Tie Rack and Sock Shop look-alikes and the City was positively orgasmic about the whole 'niche market' concept.

In fact if any grey suit had bothered to ask me the connection between protecting the ozone layer and selling moisture cream, I could have laid it out very clearly. First, our environmental campaigning raised the profile of the company considerably, attracted a great deal of media attention and brought more potential customers into our shops. On that basis alone it could be justified as a sensible commercial decision. And much more important, in my view, was the tremendous spin-off for our staff, enabling them to get involved in things that really matter – pushing for social change, improving the lot of the underprivileged, helping to save the world. You can be proud to work for The Body Shop – and, boy, does that have an effect on morale and motivation!

Then, of course, there was my own psyche. Gordon was happy with his role as the hands-on manager of the company. He enjoyed it and he was good at it; he had an innate ability to understand the business, to gauge its growth and to keep control, and he was happy to keep a low profile. Someone stopped him in the street one day and said, 'I hear your wife is doing very well. What are you doing these days?' He thought that was hilarious.

I was less sure of my role, and was beginning to feel more and more uncomfortable about being a part of the cosmetics industry. I felt a lot happier and a lot more excited mixing with environmentalists rather than financial analysts and stockbrokers. Whenever we had a franchise holders' meeting I always brought in an environmentalist to talk to the group, and I made sure that the tentacles of whatever campaign we were promoting spread right through the company. The posters were not just in the shops, they were all over the offices and warehouses, too.

Finding Fellow Travellers

I wanted Gordon to be involved in this side of The Body Shop, in this consciousness-raising process, and not just swamped in the business of running the company. It happened when I was put in touch with a group of American businesses called Social Venture Network. I was delighted to discover that we were not alone in our views and that there were other like-minded companies, albeit in the United States. There was Ben and Jerry's Ice Cream Company in Vermont, which allocated 7.5 per cent of its profits to a foundation providing grants for social programmes. There was Rhino Records, one of the largest independent record labels in the USA, which was working to preserve the recorded arts. There was Patagonia, a company producing wonderful outdoor clothing, which put 10 per cent of its profits into environmental campaigning.

Through Social Venture Network we became firm friends with Ben Cohen, co-founder of Ben and Jerry's. Ben is very hot on taking the drudgery out of work – they do zany things like declaring a 'moustache day', when everyone has to come to work wearing a false moustache – and he and Gordon hit it off immediately. Together they began working with Cultural Survival, an anthropological organization based in Boston, on the projects in Brazil to help the endangered indigenous tribes and to try to prevent the wholesale destruction of the rainforest. (As a result of their efforts Ben and Jerry's would eventually introduce a 'Rainforest Crunch' into their range of ice creams, and The Body

Shop developed a brazil nut conditioner.) Many of the Social Venture Network companies are now like family – we get together frequently to swap ideas, exchange personnel and share experiences. Ben and Jerry's is probably closest to us in terms of culture and also faces similar problems of accommodating growth without sacrificing values or changing style.

Soon Gordon got to know all the people with whom I had been campaigning – people whom I adored and who had only previously been names to him. We developed a wonderful communion and found we could discuss everything in shorthand, without tedious explanations.

I believe that service – whether it is serving the community or your family or the people you love or whatever – is fundamental to what life is about

It was brilliant to have Gordon's active support and blissful on a personal level, because it added another dimension to our relationship and our conversations – outside of the kids and our worries about the business. It was a spiritual dimension, although that was not a term we ever used, in that it was concerned with service and responsibility. I believe that service – whether it is serving the community or your family or the people you love or whatever – is fundamental to what life is about. It is difficult to talk about and difficult to define, but you know when it is lacking in your life.

Our conviction that education was a vital key to running a successful company prompted us to try and educate our shareholders, too. We never issued the kind of glossy annual reports that companies like to impress their shareholders with. We gave our boring-looking lists of figures on the simplest of recycled paper; but we also included a totally different, innovative, detailed profile of the company and our values, with sections on subjects like community care and global thinking, brilliantly designed and definitely not boring. By the standards of the City it was bizarre, but I don't think we ever had a shareholder complain.

Certainly none of them could ever complain that they did not know

'We never issued
the kind of glossy
annual reports that
companies like to
impress their
shareholders with.'

what kind of company we were, or that they did not know what they were letting themselves in for when they bought Body Shop shares. I had said publicly, time and time again, that I did not consider speculators to be my primary responsibility, or even one of my primary responsibilities. They were way down the list, as far as I was concerned, particularly since many of them only came in for the profits and did not give a damn about what we were doing.

Our Commitment Continues

In 1986 we set up our Environmental Projects Department, with a staff of four. Operating from our offices at Littlehampton, their function is:

- to oversee and coordinate our campaigning
- to ensure that the company's products and practices are environmentally sound
- to check that everything in our range fulfils our commitment to our customers that Body Shop products do not consume a disproportionate amount of energy during either manufacture or disposal and
- do not cause unnecessary waste
- do not use materials from threatened species or threatened environments
- do not involve cruelty to animals, and
- do not adversely affect other countries, particularly in the Third World.

In addition, the Environmental Projects Department established links with national and international environmental groups and gave guidance and support when shops wanted to organize local activities. I was very keen to encourage franchise holders and their staff to get actively involved, at a local level, in whatever we were doing.

After two years campaigning with Friends of the Earth I decided we were ready to go it alone. We certainly had the ability to reach people, since there were an estimated 2 million people going into our stores every week and another 10 million passing by our shop windows on some of the world's busiest shopping streets. We had run joint campaigns with FoE on acid rain, recycling, the vanishing countryside, the ozone layer and the green consumer. Our relationship was very amicable, but I felt hampered by all the meetings and decisions by committees and I was frustrated by the time everything took. There were no hard feelings and never have been – just great communication and shared learning. We had had a two-year relationship, and that is a long time. In those two years they had got to know us very well, and knew we would continue to refer to them and continue to seek their advice. In any case it would have been impossible for me completely to sever my contacts with Friends of the Earth, because by then Jonathon Porritt and I frequently appeared on the same platform together, talking about environmental and social issues. Jonathon would press for changes in government policy, while I looked for a change in business attitudes and philosophies. My only regret was that I had been unable to persuade Friends of the Earth to open their own Body Shop franchise. I thought it would be a great way for charities and pressure groups to benefit from business, but there were always too many problems.

Seize the Time

I particularly wanted to be free to take up issues in the news as they arose. But when you make decisions by committee, as we had had to with FoE, it is always painful and laborious and the whole process is maddeningly cumbersome. I wanted to be able to identify a cause, design a campaign and get it into the shops in a matter of days, and the only way I could do that was with my freedom. When there was that terrible gale in the south of England in October 1987, and 15 million trees were destroyed in a single night, we had collecting boxes for tree planting in every Body Shop within a couple of days – we could never have reacted so quickly if the decisions had been taken by committee.

We were also able to make an instant decision to support the launch of 'Mates', non-profit-making condoms designed to help prevent the spread of Aids. We already knew, from the suggestion boxes that were in every shop, that our customers would like to be able to buy condoms in The Body Shop – presumably because they would have felt more comfortable making such a purchase in one of our shops than they would in a chemist's. The alarming spread of Aids made it even more imperative that condoms should be widely available, and I felt that the retail industry could make a real contribution, in this respect, towards helping to fight the disease. All it required was cooperation and a sense of social responsibility. Richard Branson and I set up the Health Care Foundation to help bring this about.

What I momentarily forgot was that the retail world is deeply conservative and fearful of change, and that profit and image are more important than social responsibility. Some surprising excuses came in. Marks and Spencer's said selling condoms was not within their 'customer profile'. Burton's at first said they would, and then changed their minds, explaining that selling condoms was wrong for the 'Burton environment'. I expected Tie Rack and Sock Shop, as the cream of young retail entrepreneurs, to be with us, but they both said no. I was appalled. It was as if the retail industry had nothing to do with the community – a concept completely at odds with my own views.

Human Beings, Human Rights

We had more success when we joined with Amnesty International in a campaign to raise awareness of human rights violations around the world. Window posters and explanatory leaflets about Amnesty's work distributed in our UK shops resulted in more than a thousand new members for Amnesty. To me, there was nothing incongruous about a shop selling skin and hair products linking up with an organization like Amnesty International. As a business we valued people, we saw our customers as human beings, we operated in a wider context than that of the high street and we recognized that our freedom to operate was underpinned by other, more basic and more profound, freedoms – those fought for by organisations such as Amnesty. It seemed only right and proper that we should support them.

We soon settled comfortably into a routine of running shop-window campaigns for two-week periods throughout the year, with posters acting as the focal point. We returned to some issues very close to our hearts, like recycling and animal testing, time and again. We urged people to get involved, using simple facts and figures to push them into action: 'In one year an average UK family throws away 624 large plastic drink bottles, 600 cans and six trees' worth of paper, yet 80 per cent of household waste is reusable. Find out about recycling facilities in your area. If they don't exist: demand, campaign.' We were scrupulous in ensuring that our own business practices accorded with our principles. It was strict company policy, for example, to use recycled paper for everything from our letterhead to the warehouse lavatories. We collected the cardboard boxes that came into our warehouse, reused those that were still serviceable and batched the remainder for pulping. We tried to find uses for all the other containers of odd shapes and sizes – one shop on the south coast found that local fishermen could use our plastic drums as floats, and some metal containers made useful plant pots.

Reaching Out

On the subject of animal testing we produced a twelve-page educational leaflet, the first in a series called *Issues*, outlining the arguments for and against using animals to test cosmetics products and explaining our own unequivocal position – basically that it was cruel and unnecessary. Millions of them (printed on recycled paper, of course) were distributed through our shops worldwide, translated into other languages where necessary, and made available free for customers and the public. Avoiding all ingredients tested on animals had been a fundamental plank of our trading philosophy from the start; whenever testing was required, we tested on people – either volunteers from our own staff or Animal Aid volunteers at a clinic in Dorset with which we were associated. Since most of the ingredients in our products had been used by someone, somewhere, for hundreds of years, the risks to volunteers were minimal and the tests were positively benign compared with those undertaken on animals by the cosmetics industry – like force-feeding lipstick to rats and mice until they died to measure toxicity, or dropping shampoo into the eyes of a conscious rabbit restrained in stocks for seven days. The leaflet encouraged action – writing to cosmetics companies, writing to MPs and newspapers, getting the issue discussed. We listed other organizations that were against animal testing, and reminded consumers of their ultimate power: if enough people refused to buy products that had been tested on animals, testing would cease.

By and large, the franchise holders have been sympathetic to our business philosophy and have usually supported our campaigns enthusiastically. I only got into trouble once, when I committed The Body

I WILL
Executions
NO LONGER
Prison without trial
ALLOW
Torture
THIS
Disappearances
TO HAPPEN

Join Amnesty International

Shop to support FREEZE, the campaign against nuclear weapons. I got a strong message from the franchise holders that I had gone too far, that I should not be speaking for them on such issues. My first reaction was, 'If you support nuclear weapons, what the hell are you doing in one of my shops?' I could not understand how anyone could support weapons of mass destruction. But then I realized I did not necessarily have the right to speak for The Body Shop on every issue, and that there were times when I should speak only for myself. I accepted that principle – and completely ignored it. I have never been able to separate Body Shop values from my own personal values.

I have never been able to separate Body Shop values from my own personal values.

I also accepted that we should be prepared to put our money where our mouth was, particularly in the area of animal testing. We offered financial support to two important groups – the Fund for the Replacement of Animals in Medical Experiments (FRAME) and the Skin Treatment and Research Trust (START), which had made a major breakthrough by growing reconstructed human skin in a test tube. Primarily its potential was to help people suffering from skin disease, but it could also be used as an alternative to some animal testing.

As we became more confident, we found new ways to promote our campaign slogans. When we were able to change our bags from high-density polythene film to paper bags made from recycled material, we printed all kinds of messages on them. We questioned the enormous waste of paper used for junk mail, we asked why gas and electricity bills and the like were not printed on recycled paper, and we appealed to customers to use our refill service to reduce waste and save money.

We also tried using bags to recruit members for Survival International, the human rights organization which campaigns on behalf of endangered tribes. The message on the bag said: 'This is a Survival Bag. Use it to Save Lives', and the text explained the plight of the Yanomami tribe in the Brazilian rainforest and why it was facing extinction. On the reverse side was an application form to join Survival International.

Moving Messages

**Till bag for Survival
International, 1989**

On the basis of any flat surface being a viable medium for a message, we turned our delivery trucks into mobile billboards. Each truck had a different quotation painted in enormous white letters on its side. They ranged from 'If you think education is expensive, try ignorance', via Gunther Grass's 'The job of a citizen is to keep his mouth open', to an unnamed Sioux Indian's 'With all beings and all things we shall be as relatives.' To publicize the issue of animal testing we used a quote from the philosopher Jeremy Bentham: 'The question is not, can they reason? Nor, can they talk? But, can they suffer?' My contribution to the truck campaign was the message on the tailgate: 'Education is at the very heart of The Body Shop. We encourage the development of the human spirit as well as the mind. We transmit values as well as knowledge: we want to educate our people to be good citizens.'

'Our people' are our staff, our 'family'. Someone who worked for The Body Shop for many years said to me once, 'I've never felt more responsible, never felt so much part of a family, because everybody's involved. What we're doing is bigger than the products, bigger than the shops.' Gordon and I have always been very, very sane about maintaining the delicate balance between trading and campaigning. His pragmatism is a perfect counterweight to my passion, and if he thinks I am going over the top he will not hesitate to tell me that we cannot afford it, or that it is the wrong thing to do, or that there is another way. But he has always known inherently, too, that I am a great trader and that I could never allow us even to begin to lose our edge in the shops. I am instinctively aware of the danger of people being put off coming into our shops if we go too far and make them feel guilty. I never want them to walk into a Body Shop and think, *Oh no, not another bloody collecting tin shoved under our noses. Not another bloody information leaflet.*

Getting it Right

The way we maintain the balance is to apply our trading principles to our campaigning. I tell the staff never to pressurize customers into buying our products. If the product is good and a visual delight, they will buy it without any sales pressure. Similarly with campaigns: they can buy our message by supporting our campaign, or they can choose not to.

Although I usually make the final decisions on which issues we campaign about, I don't expect staff to follow me like sheep. An essential part of The Body Shop ethos is to *empower* our staff: we encourage debate, encourage employees to speak out and state their views. People who visit us are often astonished at the passion with which every issue is debated, at all levels in the company. During the Gulf War I put a plea for peace on the billboard outside our warehouse in Littlehampton. Some of the staff complained that I was being unpatriotic; I explained that wanting peace was perfectly compatible with patriotism. We each argued our side without giving an inch – that is how I expect it to be.

One of the risks of corporate campaigning is that the staff start to fall in love with doing good and forget about trading. We have got close to that in the past. In 1990, after I had been working abroad for a month, I went into one of our shops in London's Oxford Street and was horrified by what I found. There were balloons for one charity and raffles for another and collecting boxes all over the place. It was almost like a charity shop – you could hardly see any of the products for posters and collecting tins. I thought: *My God, this is a mess.* What really annoyed me was that when I asked what the hell was going on, the staff said they had been trying to stop it but had been told that it was what *I* wanted.

It was a classic case of non-communication, in a company that prides itself on its ability to communicate. What had happened was that some of the management thought I was perfectly happy for every charity and good cause in the land to use The Body Shop as a collecting post. I was not. I got all that extraneous stuff out of the shop in twenty-four hours and told everyone that we would henceforth concentrate on a single campaign, that we would go strong on that campaign and not dilute it with other causes, no matter how worthy, and that nobody was to campaign without company approval. It was not before time: I had even heard of another shop which had put an old lavatory outside with a notice saying: 'Drop your penny in here' in aid of something or other.

The Animal Testing Debate

Now we try to mount two major international campaigns every year, one on a human rights issue, one on the environment. The staff put forward issues which they think we ought to tackle, but the final decision is made by me, Gordon and about half a dozen of our senior executives.

I think at the beginning the media, typically suspicious, believed that our environmental campaigning was no more than a fad, or a gimmick to boost trade, but the fact was the The Body Shop had always embraced the concept of corporate idealism. From the beginning our products had used only natural ingredients which were easily renewable and not scarce or under threat. We leaned heavily on our suppliers to adopt similar ethical and environmental standards to our own, and insisted that they all signed a mandate confirming that none of the ingredients had been tested on animals in the previous five years, either by themselves or by their suppliers.

In 1989 the European Community came up with a new challenge when it issued a draft directive calling for all cosmetics products to be tested on animals. The reasoning behind this piece of lunacy was to ensure that safety procedures throughout the community were 'harmonized'. We would certainly have chosen to go out of business rather than start testing our products on animals, so we mobilized a massive campaign against the directive in our shops and in the media.

To prevent the debate going back and forth like a tennis ball we went on the offensive, calling for all animal testing to be stopped. Alternatively, we asked the EC to require those companies which still tested their products on animals to label them 'TESTED ON ANIMALS'. I knew that would put the cat among the pigeons.

There is absolutely no justification for testing cosmetics products on animals, particularly when there are plenty of alternatives like cell culture tests and computer simulations. I knew we had the support of our customers and the public on this issue, but even so I was surprised at the level of response. More than 5 million people signed our petition calling for the directive to be withdrawn, which eventually it was. I would still very much like to see products tested on animals labelled as such. If we could persuade the EC to introduce *that* directive, I am certain that animal testing would end very rapidly.

You have to go in the opposite direction to everyone else.

From a public relations standpoint, the fact that The Body Shop is serious about social and environmental matters does us no harm at all. While other businesses are only talked about in terms of success or failure, when people talk about The Body Shop they talk about our philosophy, our campaigning, our social and educational policies and the way we have managed to humanize business practices.

What everyone wants to know – and no one seems to be able to work out – is if there is a direct link between the company's values and its success. When people ask us how we do it I tell them it is easy.

- First, you have to have fun.
- Second, you have to put love where your labour is.
- Third, you have to go in the opposite direction to everyone else.

I don't know how many of them understand what we are saying, but the fact is that we are still pretty lonely on our home territory. I would love it if The Body Shop had a few groupies in Britain, but we don't. It's a great pity: personally I would go to the other end of the earth to learn from a company that was trying to make the world a better place.

Nevertheless, there is no doubt that the environmental movement worldwide is having *some* impact on big business. Under pressure from environmentalists, McDonald's are phasing out the polystyrene containers that seem to litter every high street; Tesco, the supermarket chain, is promoting recycling; Guinness is supporting the protection of elephants in Kenya; and Sainsbury's is funding dolphin protection patrols in South China. Prince Charles is also pushing the concept of corporate good citizenship with his Business in the Community programme, so now we find that IBM is getting involved in schools, cultural initiatives and community projects; GrandMet, the international food and drink combine, is spending $20 million on education and welfare projects for the underprivileged: and Arco, the US oil combine, is supporting a voluntary environmental agency. All this is good news, but we have a long way to go in Britain before business in general accepts that success and social responsibility are not incompatible.

Do It Differently

Running in the opposite direction and breaking the rules has always been part of the culture of The Body Shop. I get a real buzz from doing things differently from everyone else. It was breaking all the rules of retailing, for example, to use our windows not to promote a product but an issue we feel strongly about. And we were certainly running in the opposite direction to the yuppie mood throughout the eighties, when greed ruled and success was measured by excess.

I believe that our resources, plus the audience of millions passing by on the pavement and through our shops around the world, have combined against the odds to raise public consciousness, encourage action and educate. In a society in which politicians no longer lead by example, ethical conduct is unfashionable, and the media does not give people real information about what is happening in the world, what fascinates me is the concept of turning our shops into centres of education – a kind of information exchange house for social and environmental issues. While the art of protest is being stifled and apathy reigns, my ambition is for our stores to provide the conduit for a different vocabulary which will continue to irritate, agitate and get things moving. We'll provide an arena for debate and discussion – a chance for people to make their voices heard. We will be a vehicle for challenge and change.

The Body Shop does not claim to be an authority: what we do instead is to humanize issues and popularize concerns by taking them straight to the people in the streets. That's where it matters.

THE *WALL STREET JOURNAL* QUOTED A
HARVARD BUSINESS SCHOOL PROFESSOR
AS SAYING THAT TO SUCCEED IN THE USA
WE WOULD NEED, 'AT MINIMUM', A MAJOR
LAUNCH ADVERTISING CAMPAIGN. WE
REPRINTED THE QUOTE ON A POSTCARD
ALONG WITH MY RESPONSE: 'I'LL NEVER
HIRE ANYBODY FROM HARVARD
BUSINESS SCHOOL.'

6

A FIRST BITE OF THE APPLE

It might seem strange, looking back on it, that we opened a Body Shop in Muscat, Oman, before we opened in New York. We opened in Reykjavik, Iceland, years before we opened in San Diego. We opened in Taiwan before we opened in Washington DC. In fact we had more than two hundred stores in thirty-three countries around the world before the first Body Shop opened in the United States in the summer of 1988.

US launch poster, 1988

Good timing is the essential feature of all successful business. Although the United States represents 30 per cent of the world's consumer market, it has traditionally been the graveyard of British retailers. The roll call of successful British retail businesses which had foundered in the United States was long and daunting. There were many reasons – unfamiliarity with the market, over-confidence, inability to face the competition or sometimes simple lack of preparation; but mostly, however, a lack of understanding as to the higher cost of entry into such an important market. The American market has a huge absorption rate and could easily hold over 2,000 stores. The numbers of franchise and customer enquiries both by phone and by letter is colossal, and Americans are highly demanding as to the extent and accuracy that they require in answering. The bureaucracy and complicated inter-state regulations are difficult to comprehend. Shop buildings in Manhattan vary in complication. From one area to another one has to deal with Italian-based unions or Irish-based unions. There are no short cuts – you do business the American way or not at all. The threat of litigation is time-absorbing, and it is easy to over-react. The exercise requires proper funding and considerable resourcing with regard to the people side of the business. However it was viewed, breaking into the United States consumer market was a formidable challenge for any European company. We had heard, for example, that Marks and Spencer's had maintained a research office in New York for nearly six years before making a decision on whether or not to open stores in the United States.

There are no short cuts – you do business the American way or not at all.

Initially, I was much more enthusiastic than Gordon about going into America. It was the difference in our temperaments: I was always excited by new challenges, always pressing to see how far we could go; Gordon was always more cautious, looking to consolidate the business, to develop our expertise before going on to the next step. One of the reasons I was keen on breaking into the American market was because of the contact I had made through Social Venture Network. It seemed to me that, compared to Britain, there were so many like-minded companies in the United States, so many businesses who shared our values, that The Body Shop would be welcomed with open arms.

Although Gordon agreed that the opportunities in the US market were irresistible, he warned that the initiation costs were huge and the bureaucracy was complex to the point where it was almost obstructive to trade, particularly for foreign companies. It was Gordon's view that, while the United States offered The Body Shop the greatest potential for growth, it also represented the greatest potential for disaster.

Gordon and I could not help being curious to see if The Body Shop, as a retail business, was good enough to compete in the United States. We knew that the American consumer was aggressive, involved and very demanding. We had no doubt that our products were good enough to succeed, but we were unsure whether or not our business skills were sufficiently honed to overcome all the problems.

We had been taught a considerable amount about the US market by our experiences in Canada, where The Body Shop was doing brilliantly and expanding fast. Our first Canadian franchise had opened in Toronto in 1980, and within five years we had more than fifty stores trading in major Canadian cities. We thought we would get an understanding of the American market from Canada and we agreed to wait until we both judged that the time was right to make a move, even though we were under considerable consumer pressure to start up in the United States.

What was happening was that American tourists were visiting Body Shops around the world, buying products, liking them and wondering why there were no Body Shops in the United States. By 1987 we had received nearly ten thousand letters from Americans asking when we were going to start opening stores in America, or enquiring about franchises. This gave us confidence to believe that if we planned it right, if the arithmetic added up and if we had the financial resources to hold in there while we built up the business, we could make a success of The Body Shop in the USA.

We also received a number of approaches from big department stores – Bloomingdale's was one – asking if we would like to put a unit into their stores. We turned them all down. My gut feeling was that it was not the right way to do things, because we would be viewed as just another product line. I also thought that our plain little bottles would never be able to compete if they were put shoulder to shoulder with the glamorous packaging of companies like Estée Lauder or Dior.

Keeping Our Good Name

We had a further, more serious restraint on our ability to trade in America. The trademark for The Body Shop name was not in our possession. For many years we had been aware of two sister companies trading in the USA, owned by the Saunders and Short families, who, in a similar business, held the rights between them for The Body Shop trademark both in the USA and Japan, over 40 per cent of the world's consumer market. It could have presented a serious obstacle to our further expansion plans.

Gordon had been maintaining contact with the two families and negotiating over a period of years, but timing and the comparative financial strength of our business led us to agreeing a $3.5 million price tag for the rights in both countries: an expensive exercise but one that will look cheaper as time goes by. We had crossed the first hurdle.

Hard Lessons Learned

We next faced the quite extraordinary bureaucracy of the United States, the amazing mass of rules and regulations that circumscribe the activities of every company hoping to trade in the Land of the Free. We were very anxious to get it right and not to make any mistakes, so we employed a US-based consultant and we were in more or less permanent contact with the Food and Drugs Administration in Washington. I think we asked them more questions than they had ever been asked in the whole of their history. On the one hand they were a bit irritated by our persistence, but on the other I think they were also encouraged by the fact that we obviously wanted to keep to the rules.

All this was going on while we were hearing horror stories from lawyers about how we could be sued for this and sued for that. They really put the frighteners on us to such an extent that we felt we had to modify our trading practices drastically – practices which we considered to be decent and honourable. We were advised not to put 'Against Animal Testing' on our products because of what the cosmetics industry might do to us. How we were ever seduced into dropping that statement I have no idea. It was a huge moral mistake. We should have showed it loud and clear, but we were warned that the cosmetics industry was so nasty that it would clamp down on us. It was nonsense – now we are trying to redress that error of judgement by conducting huge campaigns against animal testing.

We were also warned never to have a refill bar in any of our shops. It was madness. Refilling was one of our core values and to abandon that core value in the biggest consumer market in the world was a terrible betrayal. It was thought it might present an insuperable insurance problem, but in any event our insurers had no concerns and we went ahead after a lengthy delay.

But to judge from what the lawyers were telling us everyone in America was suing everyone else, and as it was a game which we did not want to play we accepted their advice. It took us about a year to realize that we were certainly being too careful – we were probably the only retailer in the market sticking rigidly to every rule and every regulation. Suddenly we thought: *What the hell are we doing?* We woke up to the fact that we should never have abandoned any of our principles.

We set up an operational base in New Jersey, which I now recognize has made life more difficult, even though we were planning initially to concentrate on opening shops on the east coast. (I thought it would be possible to export the heart and soul of our company intact into the United States.) I thought that our values were global, that everyone would immediately understand and espouse them, that our image and style were so strong that they would be easily transferable across the Atlantic. I was wrong.

We woke up to the fact that we should never have abandoned any of our principles.

Initially we found it very difficult to recruit staff in New Jersey either willing or able to embrace our corporate culture. Most of them came from conventional, moribund jobs and seemed confused by the idea of a company being quirky or zany or contemptuous of mediocrity. I could never seem to get their adrenalin surging. We are a company in which image, design, style and creativity are of paramount importance, but we were unable to find employees who appreciated these qualities.

Walking into our offices in Littlehampton was sometimes like walking into the Folies Bergère. There was a real energy about the place – always something funny going on, lots of kisses and looks. Whenever I went into our offices in New Jersey all I could see were workers bent over their desks and screens everywhere. The atmosphere was completely sterile and, to me, alien. It was as if it was not my company at all and that I had wandered by mistake into the branch office of some heartless multinational.

What I should have done, looking back, was to send out more staff from Littlehampton who would carry our culture with them and have a better chance of establishing it among the locally recruited staff in New Jersey. I did not necessarily want to impose an English style on to our

Littlehampton - Never a dull moment

American operation; what I wanted was for an American style of the same strength and verve to emerge. It might have happened more readily had we set up our headquarters elsewhere in the United States, perhaps San Francisco, Santa Fe, or Boulder – somewhere where there is more spirited new thinking and a stronger sense of creativity.

We made an abnormally high number of recruitment mistakes and radically underestimated the culture gap between the two languages. It is an old cliché, perhaps, but although the words that we say to one another between the two countries sound familiar, the meanings are worlds apart. As the business has grown there has been an improvement in our hit rate on recruitment. We had our first USA franchise meeting in early 1991. The atmosphere was electric and the sense of achievement in opening up thirty-four stores, trading highly successfully with wonderful franchisees, was almost a rerun of the magical early days of our business.

The whole idea of launching a retail enterprise without massive advertising support was considered to be foolhardy at best, suicidal at worst.

Gordon had estimated that initiation costs and building an infrastructure in the United States would probably cost in excess of $3 million over the first three or four years. We thought it would be better to start trading with company-owned shops so that we could iron out the interminable bureaucratic problems before we began franchising. As we had no idea how trade would go, we provided the warehouse in New Jersey with a huge amount of inventory, all shipped from Littlehampton, in order to be able to cope with any eventuality.

A few weeks before we were due to open our first shop, in Manhattan, there was a great deal of speculation in the American business community about whether or not The Body Shop could succeed without advertising. The general view was that it was quite impossible, and the whole idea of launching a retail enterprise without massive advertising support was considered to be foolhardy at best, suicidal at worst.

The *Wall Street Journal* quoted a Harvard Business School professor as saying that to succeed in the USA we would need, 'at minimum', a major launch advertising campaign. We reprinted the quote on a post-card along with my response: 'I'll never hire anybody from Harvard Business School. People are international. Ideas have wings. If we can manage in Chinese-speaking countries and in the Middle East, why do they think America's going to be such a problem?' This postcard was one of a pack we had just designed and distributed to all our shops and our shareholders worldwide to propagate our values and philosophies.

Body Shop Makes First Base

The first Body Shop in the United States opened at Broadway and 8th Street on 1 July 1988. It was a great day for both Gordon and me. The shop was packed out all day, but the moment I relished most was typi-cal New York – a striking woman of about thirty-five arrived on roller skates, slid right the way through the shop, threw up her arms and shouted: 'Hey, hallelujah! You're here at last.' This was pretty much the view of all our first American customers. They loved The Body Shop, loved our values and welcomed us with great warmth and enthu-siasm. All the difficulties we had encountered, all the worries, all the frustration about New Jersey . . . it was all made worthwhile by our reception in New York.

Despite the gloomy scepticism of the experts, we never for a moment considered paying for a single advertisement to launch our US opera-tions. Instead we got incredible support from the media who were intrigued by our values and philosophies. Our opening in New York was covered by all the major television networks and news magazines – more publicity than we could ever have hoped to obtain through adver-tising. The New York shop was an instant success from day one, trading much more profitably than we had anticipated. We opened thirteen more company-owned stores over the next two years, some with less difficulty than others, and our mail-order business built up very rapidly.

Outside the big cities, we had quite a problem at first getting into some shopping malls. Because they said they had never heard of us we

Thanks for the dream Dr King

had to do big presentations to mall owners, attend all the mall conferences and say, in effect: 'Hey listen, we're a top retailer in Europe. Why are you closing the doors on us? Wake up, give us a break!' Often, when we finally got in, we quickly became the top performing store in the mall in terms of turnover per square foot. Once, when we could not persuade a mall outside of Seattle to let us in, we galvanized our customers to campaign on our behalf. Our mail-order department wrote to every customer within a 110-mile radius of the city suggesting they might like to make their views known. The mall owners were absolutely deluged with letters asking why there was no Body Shop there. Within a few months there was.

By the time we were ready to start franchising in 1990, we had received more than 2500 applications from hopeful franchisees. Our first were in Washington DC and were absolutely brilliant, running their stores with skill, love and passion. Despite the fact that we had to employ a member of staff full-time to ensure that we were complying with the book of franchise regulations, we managed to get twenty-three franchises open that first year. Another fifty-plus are scheduled to open in 1991, and probably double that number in 1992.

Although our start-up costs were a little higher than we expected, our sales have also been higher, so we should be trading profitably at some stage in 1991. I believe time will show that we probably arrived in the United States at about the right moment, when Americans really started taking the environmental message seriously and were very sympathetically disposed to a company which demonstrated its concern for environmental and social issues. I also believe that Americans are people with a great sense of fair play. When we were able to explain to them how our business worked, how we attempted to put back what we took out, it immediately struck a chord with them. They warmed to the concept much more quickly and much more readily than in Europe, where we had been shouting our views for more than a decade.

The purchase of the US trademark began to pay even greater dividends in 1990, when we opened our first shop in Tokyo. By the end of 1991 we will be trading in more than twelve outlets in Japan – and that is just the beginning.

'SURELY WE'RE NOT HERE TO *SELL*?' SHE WAILED, AS IF THE NOTION WAS TOO AWFUL TO CONTEMPLATE. 'WE'RE HERE TO HELP PEOPLE, DO GOOD, LOVE THE CUSTOMERS.' *OH JESUS, I THOUGHT, HERE'S A BAD SIGNAL COMING THROUGH.*

7

THE POWER OF LOVE

In The Body Shop the twin ideals of love and care touch everything we do: how we view our responsibilities, how we treat our staff, how we educate and communicate, how we relate to the community and the environment. When we invited our staff to write a charter that would codify our core values, the word 'care' cropped up time and time again.

The object of The Body Shop Charter was to try and set down, as simply as possible, what we were, what we did and what we believed. Getting it written was tied up with our efforts to try and convince our staff, as shareholders, to think of themselves as the true owners of The Body Shop. When it was completed I thought it was probably the closest we would ever come to producing a truly noble document, particularly since it implic-

The Body Shop Charter, May 1990.

itly invited everyone to contribute in turning The Body Shop vision – of making the world a better place – into reality. It is my hope that the Charter will eventually become so much a part of our corporate culture that it can never be eroded.

All of this was curiously and sadly at odds with the prevailing mood of the eighties, the decade of the yuppie and the bulging Filofax, when greed was good (and God!), when corporate brutalism reigned, when success was measured in ludicrous salaries and BMWs. The eighties will go down in history as the decade when, more than ever before, altruism became so alien in business that anyone claiming to be motivated by it was viewed at best as flakey, at worst deeply suspect.

The reaction to the lack of moral and spiritual values in the capitalist blow-out of the eighties was the enlightenment of the so-called New

Age, into which The Body Shop is now firmly slotted. It makes me laugh, since Gordon and I have no doubt at all that our attitudes are tempered not so much by the New Age as by the sixties, when sexual and intellectual liberation set us all free to question and challenge the system. In the sixties we learned about people power, about alternatives, about the futility of war, about challenge as an acceptable form of growth. We learned that femininity and love were no longer dirty words, that financial profit was meaningless without spiritual profit, and that being successful did not necessarily mean being soulless.

The Right Way to Educate

It was because our thinking was forged in the sixties that we took a holistic view of business, one in which we saw ourselves not just as a creator of profits for shareholders, but as a force for good, working for the welfare of our staff, for the community and ultimately for the future of the planet itself.

As early as 1984, under 'Review of the Business and Future Developments' in The Body Shop's first annual report, Gordon noted: 'We propose to concentrate in the immediate future on placing greater emphasis and resources on training both our own staff as well as our franchisees and their staff. Work has begun on the fitting out of a new training school based in central London. We believe that consolidation and communication of company objectives will continue to provide a solid foundation for our future.'

This was not the kind of language either of us would ever use outside the pages of a company report; nevertheless it neatly encapsulated our mutual sentiments. First, we did not want our staff – or our customers, for that matter – to stop learning just because they had started working. Second, if we were going to brag about our goals and values being as important as our products and profits, we had to find a way of propagating those goals and values.

Gordon and I both felt we had missed a great opportunity, in the months before we went public, to educate our staff on the implications of the flotation, the workings of the City and what it meant to be a shareholder. Share-owning was still very much a secret society at that time, and we really should have taken steps to break down the mystique for the people who worked for us. Unfortunately we never did anything about it, and we regret it to this day.

The Body Shop Training School opened in the offices above our shop in Great Marlborough Street, in the West End of London, in the autumn of 1985. As always, we went in the opposite direction to the rest of the retail industry. Ours was a company school like no other, with courses which concentrated on human development and consciousness-raising. Conventional retailers trained for a sale; we trained for knowledge. They trained with an eye on the balance sheet; we trained with an eye on the soul.

Conventional retailers trained for a sale; we trained for knowledge. They trained with an eye on the balance sheet; we trained with eye on the soul.

In fact, training was the wrong word. You can train dogs and you can train horses, but what we wanted to do was *educate* and help people realize their own potential. So we didn't talk about subjects like sales techniques or unique selling points. We ran seminars and workshops on urban survival, drug and alcohol abuse, community action, unemployment and a whole range of environmental issues. We brought in social workers to talk about homelessness, Aids sufferers to talk about their experiences, and elderly people to talk about the problems of ageing in the present-day society. Instead of telling them how to sell our products, we gave them lectures on natural ingredients, their history, how and where they evolved, their present uses and their future potential. We gave them a great fund of information, along with anecdotes and funny stories to pass on to customers. We ran a course on 'management by humour'.

Knowledge is wonderfully seductive, and the staff loved the first courses we ran for them at the Training School. As word spread, we began to get many more people applying than there

Hands-on instruction

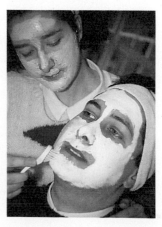

were places; soon we were having to turn down so many applications that we began making plans to move the school into a larger, purpose-built building. Today, two thousand staff go through the school every year.

The closest we came to conventional training for the retail trade was a course on customer care, one of my particular hobby horses. There are shops that I never go into because I feel intimidated by the staff. I hate London's Sloane Street, for example, because the people working in the shops make you feel you are not good enough to buy what they are selling; whereas I am happy to go into Dickins and Jones in Regent Street, for no other reason than that the staff smile at me.

On our customer care course we encouraged staff to treat customers as potential friends, to say hello, smile, make eye contact and to offer advice if it was wanted, to thank them and always to invite them back. I have often thought we could learn a lot from the Americans in this area. The British are cynical and dismissive of American social behaviour, of the constant 'Have a nice day' that follows you wherever you go. Personally, I like it – no matter how evidently insincere, it helps to break down barriers and establishes personal contact, which is more and more important in an increasingly impersonal world.

When I was a teacher I liked to try and promote an entrepreneurial culture among my kids, and at The Body Shop school we held special courses for school-leavers – up to sixty at a time – to give them a grounding in the retail industry and our attitudes towards it. It was not a recruiting exercise *per se*, although I think probably quite a few got fired up by our enthusiasm and ethics and eventually joined us.

I never thought of money spent on staff training as an expenditure; it was an investment. I felt that education was a major responsibility in a company like ours – particularly since retailing was one of the few growth employment areas for women, but one in which educational status was considered less important. All those high street chains were competing with each other to have wonderfully designed shops and yet were forgetting the needs, certainly educational, of their staff. It was an extremely short-sighted policy, since staff were increasingly beginning to look for companies which valued their labour and which espoused principles with which they could empathize. If I was running the retail industry I would make staff training mandatory and require every shop to obtain a licence to show that their staff had received basic training.

Communication on All Fronts

After education, nothing has been more important to The Body Shop's success than our ability to communicate – with our staff at all levels, our customers, the community, the media and the world. I took the view that it did not matter a hoot how much I knew and cared about what The Body Shop stood for and about its role in the community and society at large if I was unable to communicate my views to other people.

How we communicate is gob-smacking. We use every available medium to preach, teach, inspire and stimulate, and in everything we do – whether it is a simple leaflet or a full-length video – our single-minded passion shines through. One of my favourite quotations is from the seventeenth-century French philosopher Descartes: 'The passions are the only advocates which always persuade. The simplest man with passion will be more persuasive than the most eloquent without.'

Wherever you go in The Body Shop organization, throughout all our offices and warehouses you will see informational displays, statements on our philosophy, charts, illustrations, words and images, all designed to propagate our core beliefs and raise the consciousness of our staff. Sometimes we will just blow up a single inspirational quotation: 'It is not enough to make a financial profit, we must make a spiritual profit. If we can say we have given more of ourselves than we have taken from others, we have made a spiritual profit' (Agha Hasan Abedi).

We bombard our staff with information about everything from dirty tricks in the cosmetics industry to the breakdown of communism in the USSR. Every shop has a fax machine, and our communications network includes bulletins which go out to all the staff to keep them up-to-date with new ideas, new developments and new products. In addition, we have a multi-lingual monthly video magazine, *Talking Shop*.

I was anxious to get into video communications early on but I was dismayed by the quality of training videos, particularly those being produced for the retail trade. They were chronically boring and devoted far too much time to talking heads. I thought they were little better than moving wallpaper – largely irrelevant and certainly not motivating.

Do-it-yourself had characterized The Body Shop from the start and so in 1987 we set up Jacaranda Productions, our own independent video production company, with a brief to produce training and weekly TV information, campaigning and documentary programmes specifically for The Body Shop. Basically, Jacaranda Productions came into being for the same reason as The Body Shop – there was a demand which was not being met by anyone else.

Setting up this new company was a major achievement in terms of our communications and unquestionably the most important development in relation to keeping staff in touch with what we were doing. *Talking Shop* is distributed worldwide every month and is seen by every member of staff in every shop, every factory and every office. It features a rich mix of ideas and news, along with items on environmental issues and on subjects which we think will be of general interest.

Jacaranda's multi-lingual output keeps warehouse, office and shop staff informed, intrigued and entertained right round the world, as well as producing a regular stream of training videos. As an example of how our range varies, we recently produced a brilliant training video about customer care called *Smile, Dammit, Smile*, and another about loneliness in our society and the crying, bleeding need to deal with the problem. We are now making plans for wider distribution of our general videos to schools and colleges via cable and satellite.

We communicate with our customers via leaflets and posters and information boards in the shops, and they can communicate with us through the suggestion boxes to be found in every shop. We don't just pay lip service to their views – six members of staff work full-time cataloguing their suggestions and replying to them. In addition we hold regular forums, when we open up a shop from six till nine in the evening and invite customers to come and tell us what they like, what they don't like, and what products they would like to see added to the range. It has always been Body Shop policy to find out what customers want by simply asking them, a concept thought to be eccentric in the retail trade.

SMILE

DAMMIT SMILE!

Anita's 20 second crash course in Customer Care:

Never treat customers as enemies, approach them as potential friends.

Think of customers as guests, make them laugh.

Acknowledge their presence within 30 seconds: smile, make eye contact, say hello.

Talk to them within the first 3 minutes.

Offer product advice where appropriate.

Smile. Always thank customers and invite them back . . .

TREAT CUSTOMERS AS *YOU'D* LIKE TO BE TREATED!

"I think loneliness is a time bomb ticking away in our society, especially in the shopping malls. Anyone who can figure a way of reducing loneliness, either through their stores or their marketing, will have a business that will thrive forever..." Anita Roddick

"Good customer care has to be our top priority: The Body Shop firmly believes that, as we head towards the next century, our survival is based on the fact that we must be special to our customers." Anita Roddick

Democracy at Work – A Scary Thought?

Two general themes ran through all our education and communication programmes when we set them up. The first was that information was power. Staff were constantly invited to challenge the rules, to question the *status quo* and things we took for granted, and never to accept that a manager, simply because he or she was a manager, necessarily knew better. We stressed the importance of the individual and the fact that we wanted to hear from anyone, no matter what their position in the organization, if they thought they had a better way of doing things, of if they had a complaint. We were always saying to them: 'Tell us how we can make things better, how we can ennoble your lives, how we can make your spirits sing.'

We invited contributions from everyone to something we called DODGI – the Department of Damned Good Ideas. Many of the ideas are put into practice. As a result of DODGI, for example, we now have a company lottery with 50 per cent of the money going in prizes and the remainder to charity; we recycle the backing from sticky labels and use it as shred in gift baskets; and we have a new approach to problem solving: if one department cannot come up with a solution, another department will 'brainstorm' it for them.

Gordon and I both did our best to get feedback from the grass roots of the company, to find out what was happening on the shop floor without having it watered down or interpreted through the mouths of managers. We made it our business to walk about everywhere and chat to everyone; we poked our noses into every corner, barged into meetings and made sure everyone knew we were around.

We tried to break down the barriers that isolated work from family activities by holding meetings and presentations at our house in Sussex or at our holiday home in Scotland. We organized dinners for directors and members of staff selected at random to talk about everything and anything. At one of these dinners a guy from the warehouse filling room asked me why they had to wear stupid hats, since everything was automatic and they never even saw the products. I could see his point, so I told him to go in the next day and hide all the hats. His mouth dropped open in amazement. 'Look,' I said, 'if you don't want to wear the hats, don't wear them. But have fun not wearing them.'

Sometimes it was an uphill battle to convince staff not only that they had the right to challenge everything but that they also had the power to effect change. All the shop staff wear uniforms which we change about four times a year, usually to coincide with the launch of a new range or a campaign, when we will put the campaign slogan on their T-shirts. One day I was having a conversation with a group of management staff and they were complaining about the red culottes that they had been given to wear for their current uniform. I said, 'Do you like them?' and they said 'Oh no!', I said, 'Do you feel like nerds wearing them?' and they said 'Yeah!' So I said, 'Then why the fuck are you wearing them?' I told them to parcel all the culottes up and send them to me and I would find someone in the world that did want them, which I eventually did in Romania. Those situations always surprised me. There we were, banging the drum about empowering our staff, encouraging them to speak up whenever they were unhappy about anything, yet they waited until I was around before they said how much they hated those culottes.

Justine: This Year's Model.

It was the same when we introduced a two-way assessment system. Instead of just having the managers assess the staff, we asked the staff to assess the managers as well. This caused endless rumblings and incredulous questions like, 'Do you really expect us to tell you what we think of our manager?' Our answer was an unequivocal, 'Yes.' None of the managers objected; if you are a manager in this company you know the importance of listening to the workforce. When we held an open debate on the subject 'Are the management eroding our values?' we put up posters all over the place inviting people to attend. More than three hundred members of staff turned up.

When it seemed that some were still reluctant to air their grievances, we set up a 'Red Letter' system through which they could bypass management and go straight to one of the directors. It was through a Red Letter that we realized that our maternity benefit scheme was not as good as it should have been – we made substantial improvements.

The Business of Caring

The second major theme we wanted to get across to everyone who worked for The Body Shop was that wherever we traded we were an integral part of that community, with consequent responsibilities and duties that could not be ducked. It had always made me angry that most businesses, big and small, operated in almost total social isolation from their immediate surroundings. I think it is completely immoral for a shop to trade in the middle of a community, to take money and make profits from that community and then ignore the existence of that community, its needs and problems. Many primitive societies would consider such behaviour to be absolutely unacceptable, almost shocking.

Gordon and I had frequently threshed over the need for us to 'give something back' to the community, but we had never got anything organized. I was talking about this one night to a friend of mine, Nicola Lyon, while we were having dinner together at the Chelsea Arts Club. Nicola worked for Save the Children and was a very dynamic woman with lots of ideas and contacts, and we began to discuss the possibility of setting up a special department which would work actively to integrate every Body Shop with the community in which it traded. I remember we sketched out, on a paper tablecloth, the areas of interest and plans of what we thought we might or might not be able to do. In a way the whole notion was no more than an extension of the sense of corporate family which is very strong in The Body Shop .

'We liked the idea of concentrating our energy and resources on the elderly. . .'

We quite liked the idea of concentrating our energy and resources on the elderly, perhaps because bringing groups of aged and infirm people on to our training courses to talk about their problems had been very successful. I thought it would be interesting to spend more time with them, to see what they had to tell us, how we could learn from them and how we could best help them.

By the end of the evening I had hired Nicola to work part-time to evaluate whether our ideas were feasible. Personally I was certain that we would be preaching to a very receptive audience because I was convinced that our staff of mainly young people, mainly female, were in search of a belief system, of values and causes to champion. We had already, at that time, dipped our toe into wider waters with our Greenpeace campaign – so we knew how good you could feel by doing good. It seemed to me that involving the staff in community projects would positively enhance their working lives as well as helping other people.

I have no doubt that wealth is corrosive.

For me, there was also another motivation: I was worried that we were becoming so big and so rich and so powerful that our humanity was at risk. I have no doubt that wealth is corrosive. No matter how sensible I try to be, I think I am corroded by my own wealth, less able to understand the everyday problems faced by most of my staff, probably less sensitive. The other day I went into a shop and got depressed because a couple of the girls were wearing crumpled shirts that had obviously not been ironed. I said to one of them, 'Why don't you come to work looking less of a drudge?' She turned round and snapped, 'You're assuming we all have washing machines and ironing boards, like you.' Christ, I thought, she's right. On a personal level I can deal with incidents like that by recognizing my mistake and asking for all staff rooms to be equipped with irons and ironing boards. On a corporate level, as The Body Shop expanded around the world I felt we had to neutralize the corrupting effect of our wealth by taking positive steps to ensure that we remained a humane and caring company.

We set up the Community Care Department in an office with a computer at the training school, and started making contact with voluntary organizations to explore the potential of what we could do. It was soon obvious that we should not place any restrictions on how or where shops chose to make a contribution – what was important was that they made it. We suggested that every shop should undertake its own community project – do something, commit themselves to a local voluntary organization or a charity or whatever, get out of the shop and into the community. They could choose what it would be, according to local needs, and the company's contribution would be time: the staff could work on their projects during the shop opening hours.

The majority of the franchisees were delighted with the idea and it was received very, very well by the staff, who were tremendously excited and enthused by it. Within a matter of weeks, the Community Care Department had opened up a great well of caring among Body Shop staff worldwide.

People were absolutely astonished that any commercial company would want to do something for nothing.

What was initially depressing was the reaction they got when they first went out into the community, like fervent nuns in the Congo, to offer their services. It was not unusual for them to be greeted with total cynicism. People were absolutely astonished that any commercial company would want to do something for nothing. It all came back to the sad fact that altruism in business is seen as suspect. People would say: 'Why should you want to help? What do you really want? What are you trying to sell us?'

Once we had got across the strange idea that we did not want to sell them anything, that we just wanted to help with no strings attached, the projects started getting underway. Body Shop staff could be found giving talks to local schools, helping in hospitals, assisting the elderly and handicapped, providing work experience for young people and any number of other worthwhile ventures.

The Leicester shop linked up with the Douglas Bader Centre for the Physically Disabled; the Guildford shop sent staff to work in the geriatric department of the local hospital; the Bath franchise got involved with the Avon Wildlife Trust, helping to run an educational training establishment and a demonstration organic farm; in Northampton the shop sponsored a full-time warden for the Northamptonshire Wildlife Trust; in Edinburgh they went into the women's prison as therapists, educators and instigators of fun. In Brighton, where The Body Shop started, we set up a pilot project with the Red Cross to send volunteers into hospitals and day-care centres to give facials and massages. We trained the volunteers and equipped them with a regular supply of Body Shop products which had been rejected because of damaged packaging or incorrect labelling.

There was similar enthusiasm abroad. In Brantford, Canada, staff helped at a school for crippled children. The shop at Kungstorgen in Sweden stayed open after hours for the blind and disabled. In New York our shop participated in the Aids 'Buddy' programme. In Victoria, Australia, staff worked with the homeless and in Melbourne The Body Shop galvanized 500 people to plant 250,000 trees.

It is true to say, of course, that in terms of morale and motivation our staff benefited in parallel with the communities in which they were working. The various projects raised their status and self-esteem by providing them with a role considerably more significant than cashing and wrapping. They loved doing it, we loved them for doing it and they loved us for giving them the chance to do it. Everyone was happy.

Although the Community Care Department provided general guidance and support, we found there was no need to exercise any selective control over the projects because they tended to select themselves. If there was a common thread linking them all up it was care for the elderly, children and the sick and involvement in the whole gamut of environmentalism.

If I had a complaint, it was that they were not imaginative enough. I was surprised that no one was running an illiteracy programme – I would have thought that would have been a wonderful one to do – and there was not much evidence of agitprop. If I had been in charge of the shop in Oxford Street, for example, I would have had my staff cleaning up the pavements and protesting outside the hamburger joints about the amount of garbage they were generating and spreading all over the street. But it was tricky, and probably unwise, for me to interfere. I remember once I went to a management meeting and told them about an idea I had for a community project in a local prison and how brilliant it would be and how we could pass it on to the staff. Gordon was furious with me afterwards and told me off. 'I could see they didn't like it,' he said. 'They thought you were blackmailing them emotionally.'

Balancing Profit and Principles

Although we made it clear that the community projects could be under-taken in the company's time, many girls became so involved and so in love with what they were doing that they spent their evenings too on their projects. That was fine with me. I never wanted it to become a chore. I always told people that it was not piano practice; it had to be existing and they had to feel they were getting something out of it. If they weren't getting anything out of it they should pack it in.

If a shop didn't have a community project and said, in effect, it didn't give a damn about the community, it was usually the franchisee speaking, not the staff. I often found that I could talk that person round, and when they got converted to the idea they were more passionate than any religious convert; they had forgotten what a buzz one gets out of being liked and wanted. But if a franchisee absolutely refused to become involved, there was not much I could do about it – other than to make quite sure they did not get another shop.

As far as I was concerned, there was only one inherent risk in our community care programme: as with campaigning, doing good might get in the way of trading to such an extent that our profitability was affected. By and large we managed to maintain a sensible balance between the two, since most of our staff understood that we could only undertake social welfare work or environmental campaigning by the gift of our profits. But every now and then we had someone who got it all about face and thought her primary job was to love the world rather than to trade. (Sometimes people get us entirely wrong and apply for jobs thinking we are an environmental protection organization or a charity; they are quite taken aback to learn that working in a Body Shop means selling and cashing and wrapping.)

One girl who just lived and breathed The Body Shop told me how worried she was by a memo that had gone round the shops talking about selling some product or other. 'Surely we're not here to *sell*?' she wailed, as if the notion was too awful to contemplate. 'We're here to help people, do good, love the customers.' *Oh Jesus*, I thought, *here's a bad signal coming through.* I explained it to her simply. There were fifteen people working in her shop. If the trading figures went down, there would soon only be fourteen people, then thirteen, then twelve. . . I asked if she realized what that meant. She thought about it for a moment and then said: 'Well, I suppose there will be fewer and fewer of us to do good.' Sometimes it was not easy to get the message across.

The shops embraced community projects with much more enthusiasm than staff in the warehouse or the office, or those in management. What I objected to, and I know Gordon agreed, was the fact that the people we employed were shareholders, making money from the way we were, happily sharing the wealth of the company, yet failing to share our human wealth and spiritual wealth. I didn't see how you could divorce one from the other. The malingerers obviously did.

On Earth Day one year we tried to persuade the staff from the warehouse and offices in Littlehampton to clean up the beach. Only thirteen turned up. I thought it was appalling. What made me even angrier was a cyclist who stopped and said, 'What's all this about, then?' When I told him what we were doing he said, 'Great. I'm really glad someone's doing something.' I suggested that he should get off his bike, grab a bag and help. 'Not on your life,' he yelled over his shoulder as he rode off.

Practising What We Preach

While I was always hustling and cajoling individuals to get involved in what we were doing, it was also imperative that the company itself was seen both to take a lead and to set an example. An opportunity to do both presented itself towards the end of 1987 when I gave a talk in London about our holistic approach to business. Afterwards a young man buttonholed me and introduced himself as a community worker from a place called Easterhouse in Scotland; I had never heard of it. He wanted to know if I really practised what I preached. I assured him that I did. 'OK,' he said, 'will you come and see if you can do anything in Easterhouse, which is a depressed area desperately in need of new employment?' I was not at all sure what, if anything, I could do. But I felt I could hardly refuse and arranged to go up there the following week.

I was absolutely horrified by what I found. Easterhouse was a bleak sprawl of grey council blocks thrown up on barren fields just to the east of Glasgow. The few shops still open were mostly boarded up as a pro-

tection against vandalism, and a couple of depressing pubs provided the only entertainment. The place had been built after the war to house families cleared from the Glasgow slums, but as employment in the shipyards and steelworks dried up, conditions for the people of Easterhouse had grown steadily worse – so bad, in fact, that the area had been described in an EC

Easterhouse, 1988

report as more closely resembling the Third World than the developed west. More than half the men were out of work and solvent abuse among young people was endemic, often leading to tragic deaths. Yet, despite the conditions, it was impossible not to be impressed by the people. They had an unmistakable spirit and an apparent determination not to be crushed by their circumstances. I was very touched by their guts and friendliness.

Back in Littlehampton I described what I had seen to Gordon. I still had no idea how we could help, but I suggested he should go and take a look for himself. He was just as shocked as I had been, but when he got back he had already formulated a plan. We had been talking for some time about manufacturing our own soap; Easterhouse provided the spur to turn words into deeds. 'We're going to put our soap factory up there,' he said, 'and we are not only going to provide employment, but we're going to put 25 per cent of the profits back into the community.' That was it. Done.

Making the decision was easy, but it was far from easy getting the project off the ground. We were dealing with hard-line traditional socialists who had no real enthusiasm for change and suffered from deep-rooted suspicion of capitalism, new ideas and management promises. To convince them of our good intentions we got all the local councillors to come to a meeting at which we just talked and talked – about ourselves, about the company, about what we believed in and about what we thought we could do in Easterhouse. When they asked what we thought about unions I told them straight that it was my view unions were only needed when the management were bastards. That raised a few eyebrows, I can tell you. We tried to explain as best we could that we were not a traditional company, that we did things differently from almost all other companies. When we had problems we resolved them by talking to people, one to one, rather than talking to shop stewards.

It was my view unions were only needed when the management were bastards.

I knew from the start that we would have a hard job persuading them that our motives were entirely honourable, but I also knew that passion, as always, would persuade. In the end after we had positively overwhelmed them with Body Shop facts, figures and philosophies, they fell in with our proposals like lambs.

Within eight months, and with an investment of £1 million, the Soapworks factory was up and running, with a firm commitment to donate 25 per cent of future profits to a charitable trust for the benefit of the local community. By then we already had a community project going and had begun to raise funds for a playground. I was appalled by the lack of facilities for the children of Easterhouse and I had talked about the situation at our International Franchise Meeting a few months earlier. Their response was wonderful: they came up with more than £26,000 from their own pockets to launch the project. Local schools were invited to contribute ideas, and the final result was a magnificent adventure playground designed to encourage exciting and imaginative play for children of all ages, including those with disabilities. The whole scheme cost about £180,000 and factory staff are represented on the management and committee.

With the Soapworks staff

When Soapworks is at its full capacity it will provide more than a third of our total soap requirements for all the shops worldwide. The factory started with just sixteen employees, all of whom were previously

unemployed, and within two years had a payroll of nearly a hundred.

They are wonderful people. When I visited the factory after it had been in production for about a year we all had a great party. Everyone let their hair down and got gloriously tipsy. People kept coming up and saying to me, 'Och hen, but you're so *wee.*' One young guy put his arm round me and confided: 'Anita, we love you, but cannae gi' you a piece of advice? Why don't you do something about your hair?' I thought that was *wonderful.*

When you take the high moral road it is difficult for anyone to object without sounding like a complete fool.

Siting Soapworks in Easterhouse was as much a moral decision as a commercial one, but it was a natural one for us to take since we see business as an integral part of the social fabric of family life. We could have set up the project in a safe suburban industrial park in the south, but we chose to employ the unemployable in Easterhouse rather than the already employed in Sussex. (We were eligible for a government grant, but it was no more or less than we would have received had we gone into any development area.) Not one shareholder complained, perhaps because when you take the high moral road it is difficult for anyone to object without sounding like a complete fool. Notwithstanding the fact that it was Gordon who had the idea, I wonder if the same decisions would have been made in a traditional, male-dominated company.

I also doubt, very much, that many male-dominated companies have considered setting up a day-care centre and child development centre for their staff. Working mothers get no respect in this country, and nowhere is this archaic attitude more brutally exemplified than in Britain's shameful lack of childcare facilities. In the whole of the United Kingdom there are no more than two hundred workplace nurseries. This figure means that only one woman in five thousand can lay claim to a workplace nursery provided by her employer. The state similarly reneges on its responsibility. In Denmark, 45 per cent of children under the age of three have access to day nursery facilities; in the UK less than 2 per cent of children have such access. It is my belief that county councils use out-of-touch statutes to absolve themselves of responsibilities. In West Sussex, for example, where The Body Shop is based, there is not a single nursery. The result is that the UK workforce boasts the lowest level of participation by young mothers, and yet, in an increasingly competitive labour market, it is very important that existing staff can continue to work while raising young families.

In Support of Working Mothers

Since childcare is a family responsibility The Body Shop as a family company, believes it has a duty to share that responsibility by offering parents with young children the option of being able to work without the continual worry of inadequate childcare. In January 1990 The Body Shop Day Centre opened its doors at our head office and warehouse in Littlehampton. Almost two years in the planning, it cost nearly £1 million and is a state-of-the-art facility set in 1.5 acres of landscaped playgrounds, with five full-time staff available to supervise as many as forty-eight children. The Body Shop pays a subsidy for all employees using the centre, and places have been made available to the social services and to workers at other local businesses.

This project is one of many undertaken in our continuing efforts to humanize the workplace. In September 1989, for example, we set up an Education Department to cope with the flood of demands for information from schools and colleges around the UK. One of the packs we send out is titled *Go Bananas!* and is a kind of crash course in environmental activism, aimed at making children aware that, as future consumers, they are powerful people with the ability to bring about change.

'The Body Shop Day Care Centre opened its doors in January 1990'

To broaden the horizons of our staff we have introduced an international job-swapping scheme. Staff can put in for a three-month sabbatical to change their jobs with someone in another shop in another country. We have had girls going out to work in the United Arab Emirates and Arab girls taking their places in the UK; others have arranged UK

– Australia exchanges. As we open more shops in more countries opportunities for job-swapping will increase, creating a network of shared ideas and experiences. The staff pay their own expenses; we guarantee the job. Another idea I am continuing to pursue is the opening of charity franchises. Although we failed to persuade Friends of the Earth to open their own franchise, I was not prepared to let the idea go and we eventually got a charity franchise opened in Brixton, a multi-racial inner city area in South London which had been the scene of devastating riots in the seventies. The franchise is dedicated to Project Full Employ, a group providing job training for minority groups, and is tremendously successful. This is an idea we would like to extend to other deprived inner city areas, both in the UK and abroad.

Our most recent venture was in Romania. With the opening up of communications in eastern Europe I thought I would go mad if I saw another picture of a dying Romanian baby in the newspapers, so in May 1990, I decided to take a trip over there to see if there was anything I could do to help. I was taken to the village of Halaucesti in Moldavia, where there were three orphanages which had so far received no help from the outside world.

From a distance one of them looked like a fairytale castle, made from sugar and spice, with golden turrets reflecting in the sun. But when we eventually arrived at the gates and the door was opened we were almost knocked over by the stench of faeces and urine. I have seen some appalling sights in the Third World, but nothing had prepared me for this. The place was full of children who were never washed, who were covered in scabs and mosquito bites and who slept

Romania, May 1990

on mattresses soaked in urine and crawling with flies. All these little shaven-headed kids came swarming around us and I asked someone how many boys lived in the castle. 'These aren't boys,' was the reply, 'these are girls.' Their heads were shaved because of lice. The second thing that hit me was the total lack of stimulus: nothing to engage the eye, no touching. They simply sat there, in silence or moaning, rocking backwards and forwards. Many of them were banging their heads against the wall or the rusty bars of their iron cots out of sheer boredom.

Back in Littlehampton, I could think of nothing else but the horrors of what I had seen and I made an appeal for volunteers to go out there and help; within six weeks The Body Shop Romania Relief Project was up and running. My daughters Justine and Samantha were involved right from the start, working through a long shopping list of everything that was needed and trying to wheedle the stuff out of manufacturers. In July the first convoy went out and within two weeks had completely renovated the first orphanage. Along with skilled craftsmen, we sent out people just to cuddle, and play with, the children. This project has now extended far beyond the company and has a life of its own, with volunteers providing long-term commitment to the care of the children of Halaucesti. I have been both astonished and inspired by the reaction of our staff and of all the people who have become involved.

'Within two weeks they had completely renovated the first orphanage.'

Cynics, Up Yours!

I know there are still plenty of cynical outsiders who view The Body Shop with suspicion, who believe there must be some ulterior motive, some hidden agenda, in what we do and say. This is not an attitude you will find anywhere within The Body Shop. Our people never become cynical about the values we espouse; on the contrary, people who work for The Body Shop tend to fall in love with the company. I don't necessarily claim that is a good thing – I don't think, for example, that it is a good idea for people to become too dependent on the company – but it gives the lie to the cynics.

The absolute truth is that nothing of what we do in terms of education or communication or staff relations or community care is undertaken with an eye on our 'image', or how it will be viewed in the City, or by our competitors, or by anyone else. If there is a single motivation for what we do it is, in the words of the American writer Ralph Waldo Emerson, 'to put love where our labour is.'

WHEN WE ARRIVED HE WAS STARK NAKED AND COVERED IN ASHES AS PART OF SOME CLEANSING RITUAL. HE WAS ALSO ROARING DRUNK. WITH HIS COARSE AND KNOTTED HAIR (HE WAS NOT MUCH INTERESTED IN BODY SHOP SHAMPOOS) HE LOOKED LIKE A MADMAN. TOWARDS THE END OF OUR MEETING HE BOOZILY OFFERED TO DEMONSTRATE HIS IMMENSE STRENGTH BY BALANCING TWELVE BRICKS ON HIS PENIS.

8

TRADE TALES

I never had any doubt that the Third World needed work rather than handouts. Trade gives people in the Third World the ability to choose their destiny when they meet the pressures of the west, and helps them utilize their resources to the benefit of their own social, cultural and material needs.

Too often development aid is a process by which you collect money from poor people in rich countries and give it to rich people in poor countries. I loathed the psychology of giving aid with no responsibility – of going in somewhere, dumping money and leaving. When I was working for the International Labour Organization in Geneva I had seen the abuse of the system and the waste involved in aid programmes. Part of the reason was that the United Nations was a huge, monolithic organization with no real sense of being held accountable for its actions. Most multinational companies didn't give a damn about the Third World: their only interest in it was as a source of cheap labour and extra profits. We believed that Trade Not Aid was likely to be the most effective way to alleviate suffering and poverty around the world, and over the next few years from 1987 we refined the ground rules into an international trading policy.

The principles behind Trade Not Aid were that:
- we respected all environments, cultures and religions
- we utilized traditional skills and materials
- we created trade links that were not only successful but sustainable
- we traded in replenishable natural materials
- we encouraged small-scale projects that could be easily duplicated
- we provided a long-term commitment to all projects.

For me Trade Not Aid also advanced the possibility that one day we would be able to go to the source for all our products – cut out the middlemen and trade directly with those people thoughout the world who grew or harvested the raw ingredients we needed. That was my ambition. I wanted to be Christobel Columbus, going into little villages in Mexico or Guatemala or Nepal and seeing what they had to trade, instead of going to those boring old trade fairs where everyone buys the same mediocre products year after year.

Too often development aid is a process by which you collect money from poor people in rich countries and give it to rich people in poor countries.

I am astonished that most traders in the west think that the best way to get ideas is to go to a trade fair. I get my ideas on the road, and I believe that going to the source stimulates trading creativity. I always come back from a trip with lots of other ideas, picked up from the locals, for ingredients for skin care products and pot-pourri.

In 1987 we made a deal to buy 'footsie rollers' from a charity in India called the International Boys' Town Trust. I had always been tremendously excited by the prospect of creating trade in the Third World – for me it was quite as exciting, if not more so, as creating trade in the high street – and our deal with Boys' Town was not just a personal goal but an absolutely brilliant start (at least that is what I thought at the time) to what would become our Trade Not Aid policy.

The 'footsie roller' was a little wooden massage device which one of

our franchisees had found in America and which we originally had made for us by a small factory in the Channel Islands. When we learned there was a chance of getting them made in India by a charity that provided a home for destitute boys and taught them a trade, Gordon and I flew out to investigate.

Indian Love Call

I had never been to India before and I was slightly apprehensive about the trip because I was worried about how I would handle the poverty, which everyone told me was terribly oppressive. The poverty *was* dreadful, but the sights and sounds and smells and colours were captivating; I fell in love with India and with its people, its history, its culture and its art.

Tirumangalum, which was where the International Boys' Town Trust was based, was a small, scruffy town clustered alongside a railway track in the province of Tamil Nadu in southern India. The daily train from Madras, wheezing and clanking and belching steam, scattered chickens and goats and children as it rolled into town.

More than half the 40 million inhabitants in the province of Tamil Nadu live below the official poverty line, but the poverty was less overwhelming than I had imagined – although I still found it very hard to cope with the begging, and the tugging at your sleeve everywhere you went. What was very striking about the people was that they were very friendly and curious; everywhere we went they would stare openly at us, never averting their eyes like people in the west do when they have been caught staring.

By then the Boys' Town Trust was running seven Boys' Towns and two Girls' Towns and was providing hundreds of poor children with a decent start in life. They came from all round the region. Sometimes they just showed up alone, destitute and half-starved; sometimes they were brought in by families who were too poor to care for them adequately. All the children got a basic education and learned a trade – things like farming, printing, weaving or carpentry. They were paid for their work, and when they returned to their villages they usually had enough money saved to buy a couple of buffalo, or a flock of sheep, or an ox and cart. They took back with them the skills to become valued members of their own developing communities.

We stayed in the guest house at the biggest Boys' Town, which was startlingly perfect; paradise unfolded. There were little groups of houses with whitewashed walls separated by clumps of flowering rhododendrons and azaleas. There was a play area and a pool for the boys to swim in. It was very simple, very primitive, but in excellent order. I was surprised by how clean and tidy everything was. The workshops and the farm buildings and cattle pens were pin-neat; it reminded me a little of the kibbutz where I had worked as a student in the sixties.

The boys themselves were a delight. Every morning as I went around the place they would greet me with, 'Good morning, sister' and a big smile. It was like having a surrogate family. They all attended school in the mornings and worked in the afternoons. In addition, each of them was allotted a daily task to keep the community going – it could be cleaning or polishing, washing, preparing, cooking or serving food. Everyone, no matter how small, was expected to pitch in.

We had been warned that it might take about four months to train boys in the carpentry workshops to make our footsie rollers. In fact, it only took them about four weeks and when we arrived they were all

ready to start production. We were very curious to see how they would make them. A long line of primitive lathes had been set up, each one driven by a band from a drum on a central revolving spindle. The boys squatted on the floor, jammed a piece of acacia wood into the lathe and then just carved the grooves by hand with a chisel. How they did it so evenly, I don't know. To finish it off they took a piece of string larded with honey wax and ran it through the grooves, very fast.

Perfecting the footsie roller

And there it was – a perfect footsie roller.

We placed our first formal order on the spot, I think for a thousand. Our only stipulation was that we would expect quality, and that anything not up to our rigorous standards would be rejected (actually the standard of their production was excellent right from the start). It was a heart-warming sight to see trays of footsie rollers being carried out of the workshops and loaded on to an ox cart on the first stage of their journey to Body Shops around the world.

With the footsie roller contract agreed, we were obviously keen to explore what other things they might do for us. Before we left England we had anticipated that the boys might be able to grow on their farm herbs and plants which we could use in our products, but it turned out that neither the climate nor the conditions were suitable. However, they had a number of other manufacturing projects which we felt we could adapt. They were already making little embroidered flags for Rotary Clubs and printing very nice Christmas cards, which they silkscreened on recycled paper. Before the end of our trip we had placed two additional orders, one for Christmas cards, which were a great success, and another for shop uniforms, which were not.

Finished product

As the local cotton was wonderful in India and as the girls in the Girls' Town appeared to be able to make anything on their little sewing machines, we asked them to make several hundred baggy trouser suits in white cotton with The Body Shop logo sewn on the back. I thought our girls would look great in them. I was wrong. First, they were much too sexy. The cotton was so thin that you could see their knickers and their bras, and if they didn't wear bras – and most of them didn't – you could see their nipples. Secondly, working in a shop can be a pretty messy occupation, and because the uniforms were white they looked grubby in a couple of hours. I should have realized that, but I think I got carried away by being in India where young women wafted around in beautiful light-coloured saris which always seemed to be spotless, no matter how filthy their surroundings. So the uniforms were a disaster – one of our little experiments that did not work. I think most of the girls ended up using them as pyjamas because they were very comfortable and cool to sleep in.

A big advantage of the Boys' Town deal was that we could agree, with a clear conscience, to pay them what we were paying to have the footsie rollers made in the Channel Islands. The boys working the lathes in Tirumangalum earned more than adult farm labourers, but the money did not screw up the local economy because it went straight into the Boys' Town Trust and was used to support its charitable work.

In fact we never viewed Boys' Town as a charity. Our involvement was an expression of an attitude that was, above all, intensely practical. We simply considered Boys' Town to be our trading partners. What they wanted was work; what they did *not* want was to be patronized.

Our part of the bargain was to use our expertise to market the products, although I have to confess we made a hash of it at first. We were so excited about the genesis of the exercise that we lost sight of one of the things we do best – selling. Basically, we failed to explain to our customers what we were doing. We just shoved the footsie rollers into the shops and thought the world would buy them because we knew so much about them and we loved them and they had a little label attached saying 'Made by our Boys' Town project'. It was sheer arrogance on our part, and the world did not buy them.

Whenever we wanted to persuade our staff to support a particular project we always tried to break their hearts.

It was some time before we woke up to the fact that we needed to get up off our arses and really sell the footsie rollers. We had to tell customers where and how they were made, to give them the whole story of Boys' Town and explain our Trade Not Aid policy in detail with leaflets and posters. When we did get round to doing it, we did it brilliantly and the footsie roller became one of our best-selling lines.

I am not ashamed to admit that I was completely and utterly enchanted by Boys' Town. When Gordon and I got back from our first trip we were full of plans to organize sponsorship of the boys and to set up another Boys' Town totally funded by The Body Shop. We wasted no time in getting the message across. Whenever we wanted to persuade our staff to support a particular project we always tried to break their hearts. At the next franchise holders' meeting we put on a real tear-jerking audio-visual presentation, with wonderful slides of the children against a background of Willie Nelson's version of 'Bridge Over Troubled Water'. And to enable members of staff to experience what we had experienced, the next edition of *Talking Shop*, the monthly video distributed throughout the Body Shop organization, was devoted to Boys' Town and what we could do there. The response was a joy. Everyone wanted to get involved in raising money and sponsoring boys, and from that moment onwards the International Boys' Town Trust more or less became an integral part of The Body Shop's extended family.

In 1988, Gordon and I went back out to India to open The Body Shop Boys' Town, which had been built with money raised entirely by the company, its franchise holders, employees and customers. Four hours' drive from Tirumangalum, it was a delight. At the entrance was a low white wall with our logo painted on it in dark green. Beyond was a semi-circle of single-storey dormitories fronting on to a courtyard, behind which was a farm and a magnificent backdrop of mountains. There were palm trees all around the compound and they had planted bougainvillea everywhere because they knew I was crazy about it.

We stayed in the guest house, which was clean and very simple. There was no electricity, although there was a great shower that worked by pulling on a rope. I thought it was just lovely – an incredibly peaceful place. There was no pressure on either Gordon or myself, no telephones ringing, no one knocking on our door.

Our boys – we thought of them as 'our' boys because all eighty-five of them were sponsored by The Body Shop – were already in residence by the time we got there. They were at school all day but it was great to spend time with them afterwards – to play with them, to help them with their work, to go for walks holding hands, simply to love them and be loved by them in return. Gordon and I stayed a week, but it was such a happy time for us.

A Cruel Deception

I am always ready to put my faith in people and I am rarely burned. When I am, it hurts – and it never hurt more than when I discovered our first Trade Not Aid project had gone terribly wrong.

It was some months before the first warning bells started to ring. Because of our close involvement, Body Shop people were going backwards and forwards to Tirumangalum quite frequently and they were coming back with rumours that things didn't seem to be right, or that the welfare of the boys wasn't being properly safeguarded, or that our contracts were not being honoured. I was arrogant: I would not listen. I had seen it all with my own eyes; I *knew* everything was all right and that it was paradise out there. The fact is that I simply could not countenance the possibility that I might have been taken in.

But the rumours would not go away, and in the end one of our franchisees who had become a director of Boys' Town Trust brought allegations of serious financial mismanagement and other, as yet unsubstantiated, allegations. This report was devastating to me personally, because it made it clear that I had been totally duped and that my trust had been betrayed. We discovered, among other things, that the footsie rollers weren't being made by the boys at all, but in local sweatshops around Tirumangalum at a price far below what we were paying.

We obviously couldn't continue to sell them to our customers as being made by Boys' Town, and so we immediately severed our connection with the Trust. Maybe we will support it again one day – I don't know. Meanwhile, we have made arrangements for the footsie rollers to be manufactured in local workshops and we are paying 20 per cent of the profits into a welfare fund to improve working conditions and provide health care and education. In addition, we are looking at other projects in the Tamil Nadu area in the hope of expanding our Trade not Aid activities. Even though I was very shaken by what had happened in Boys' Town, I remained totally committed to the notion that Trade Not Aid was a workable and basically honourable concept.

High on the Himalayas

Our second Trade Not Aid project, based in Nepal, was largely the inspiration of an extraordinary woman called Mara Amats, the mother of my daughter Sam's best friend at school. For us it was not an unusual connection. We have always, in The Body Shop, been happy to employ family, neighbours, friends, or friends of friends; I have never understood the arguments against doing so. We have dozens of employees who have brought in husbands and wives, brothers and sisters, uncles and aunts, friends and neighbours.

Early in 1988 our Environmental Department made a decision that we should use recycled paper throughout all our operations. That was fine with me – but I wanted to use brilliant, beautiful, aesthetic recycled paper, and at that time you could not find such quality for less than about £10 a sheet. One evening I was moaning over dinner about how difficult it was to find a decent recycled paper when Sam suddenly said: 'You've got to meet Mara. She knows a lot about paper.'

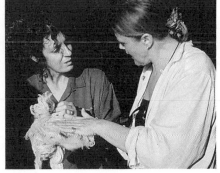

Mara Amats was one of those special women who turn their lives into non-stop adventure. She was Jewish, a Canadian resident in Britain who considered herself to be a political refugee. She had worked for many years in Ethiopia, where she had had a room in Emperor Haile Selassie's palace; she had lived with monks in Paris; she was a world-renowned expert on restoring icons; she had directed various overseas development projects in the Caribbean, in Africa and India; and she had recently turned her multitude of talents towards the art of papermaking. Several exhibitions had already been devoted to her work.

'Mara Amats is one of those special women who turn their lives into non-stop adventure'

I hit it off with Mara the moment we met; there was an instant chemistry between us, and I soon persuaded her to come and work for us as a consultant on Trade Not Aid projects. The first problem I wanted to solve was to find a supply of acceptable paper. What she did not know about papermaking was not worth knowing, and she suggested that instead of looking for recycled paper we should consider paper made from materials other than wood pulp. The place to go, she said, was Nepal, which had a long history of papermaking dating from the eleventh century and, as one of the ten poorest countries in the world, was desperately in need of trade.

Mara was soon on her way out there. I think she was surprised at how quickly we made decisions; she had been used to working for the United Nations where it took about eighteen months to approve a three-month project. Samantha had just finished school and was very keen to be involved, so she went with Mara as her assistant. They rapidly started making contacts and through a local women's group they got an introduction to the Queen, which opened lots of doors.

Within a couple of weeks they reported back that they had found a tiny family-run factory just outside the capital, Kathmandu, which seemed to have potential for our purposes. The art of papermaking by hand had declined rapidly in Nepal because of a shortage of the basic raw ingredient, the fibrous bark of the daphna shrub, called lokta. Deforestation had destroyed the forests in which the shrub grew to such an extent that the Nepalese government had put a limit on how much daphna could be used for papermaking, virtually destroying the industry overnight.

Mara knew all this, of course, and began investigating the use of alternative raw materials, including hemp, bamboo and banana fibre. One of the most promising sources of environment-friendly paper initially was the water hyacinth which, despite its attractive name, was a truly dreadful weed. It had been introduced into India in Victorian times by an Englishwoman who liked its pretty flowers and had no idea what devastation it would bring about. The water hyacinth flourished mightily in the tropical climate and spread rapidly throughout Asia. Growing at an astonishing rate, it was soon choking vital internal waterways and killing all other marine life. Finding a purpose for the otherwise useless water hyacinth offered an economic way of keeping the rivers and waterways clear, so we thought that using it to make paper would be doubly beneficial.

Street trading in Kathmandu

I had made arrangements to join Sam and Mara in Nepal and could hardly wait to get out there, to find out for myself what they were doing and what the prospects were for another Trade Not Aid deal. In the week before I left, telephone callers to The Body Shop in Littlehampton who were put on hold were entertained with a tape of Bob Seager's 'Kat-Kat-Kathmandu, I'm Going Off to Kathmandu'.

It will be impossible ever to forget my first glimpse of the Himalayas, from a window of the aircraft, as we approached Kathmandu. Whenever I saw parts of the world which I had only previously seen in photographs it reminded me of how rapidly the globe was shrinking in our age of supersonic travel, and of the pressing need for us all to think of ourselves as global citizens. Staring out at the majesty of the Himalayas, my passport ready in my hand, I fervently wished that the day would come when I would never need such a silly document to travel around the world.

Mara and Sam were waiting to meet me at the airport, but even if they had not been there I would have pretended that they were. It is my technique for getting through foreign airports quickly. I can't bear to hang around in queues, particularly in airports; it drives me nuts. So I grab my bag as quickly as I can, fix my cyes on a distant point on the other side of the barriers and barge through, smiling and waving at a (sometimes non-existent) friend. Getting quickly through an airport is the only time I ever knowingly lie.

Paper Worth

As we were driving into the centre I was surprised to find that Kathmandu was a bustling, thriving little city. There were battered, honking taxis scooting about everywhere and people thronging the streets. It had little of the serenity that I had expected to find in such a romantic and ancient mountain kingdom. Only the glorious purple jacaranda trees, which were in full bloom everywhere, hinted of the peace and beauty which had once prevailed.

Mara had booked a room for me in a boarding house full of aid workers. (Everyone is an aid worker in Kathmandu; it's bloody aid city.) Next day we drove out in a terrible old car to visit the paper-making factory which Mara had discovered in the back streets of the city. As we approached it seemed as if there were walls leaning up against the house, but I realized as we got closer that they were aluminium sheets on which the paper was hung out to dry.

This tiny factory, run by a young man called Milahn Battahria and his family, was one of the few still in business making beautiful paper

Nepalese paper drying in the sun

by hand. How they did it was extraordinary. First they boiled the lokta fibre for several hours with ash or caustic soda to soften it; then it was beaten by hand and fed into a kind of mangle. After this it was mixed

Making pulp for paper, Nepal

with water to form a slurry – and dyes, flowers or perfumes were added to the mixture as required. Finally it was spread out to dry into paper over a fine mesh frame.

Mara had suggested to the family that they experiment with different raw ingredients, notably banana fibre and water hyacinth, and the results were really spectacular. We sat around the courtyard inside the factory, drinking endless bottles of Coca-Cola and looking at the various samples they had produced. There were papers in dozens of different qualities – for writing letters, for envelopes, for bags, for wrapping products, for making gift boxes; for all the needs of our business, in fact.

I was delighted with the stuff and gave them an order for £25,000 worth of different paper products – mostly bags, notebooks, wallets for pot-pourri and scented drawer liners. It represented the factory's entire production for the next four months. Was it a sensible business decision for me to take? Absolutely not! It was loony tunes. But we are a company getting bigger and bigger and I was convinced that it was imperative to make such decisions in order to keep our soul. If we were not willing to get involved in these ventures we would have all our managers running around and getting incredibly excited about our profits, or the annual report, and forgetting that business is not just about performance but also about staying human. It was my belief that for as long as we, as an emerging multinational company, could concern ourselves with these micro-enterprises in the Third World, they would help to protect us from the perils of giantism and the inhumanity of big business. I felt it was these wacky little deals that kept us alive, kept the adrenalin running.

I count myself as being very fortunate to be in a position to make such snap decisions, but if I was not around to do it there would be someone else standing in my shoes. I am going to make sure of that over the next few years by looking for the young people in The Body Shop who will be the custodians of our culture, who will preserve and protect our core values with the fervour that I preserve and protect them. I am not worried that it will all disappear after Gordon and I have gone. We have our Charter and we have a whole lot of young people who live and breathe The Body Shop, who will provide our moral backbone in the future and who will be able to take over from me. Maybe Sam will be the one – she will certainly never let our ideals be diminished – but if not her, there will be others who will keep this company bubbling, enthusiastic, motivated and challenging.

Actually, our papermaking project was a classic Trade Not Aid success story and probably the most rewarding example of The Body Shop's relationship with the Third World. The first order generated future orders that enabled the family to wire their factory into the local electricity supply – a great luxury by their standards. In June 1989 they were able to buy a tract of land just outside Kathmandu to put up another papermaking factory which eventually created employment for fourteen men and twenty-three women, giving the women a novel sense of self-empowerment in a society in which they had long been repressed. A proportion of the money earned was capitalized for use as seed money for other projects, with the aim of creating a new-found independence among the local community.

Was it a sensible business decision for me to take? Absolutely not! It was loony tunes.

As for the environment, the use of water hyacinths for papermaking assisted in the clearing of Nepal's waterways and rivers; and the planting of banana palms, also used for paper, helped turn the tide on the problem of soil erosion as well as providing food for malnourished children. Finally, the residue from the papermaking process was used to make organic pots for the planting and transplanting of much-needed trees in the locality.

In this way we forged real links. They were happy because we were helping to expand the horizons of a traditional industry; we were happy because we were purchasing a product we knew we could sell. I loved the way these deals connected up – the way the sale of a product made from water hyacinth and banana fibre paper, on a high street in England, had a direct impact on the prosperity of a family business in Nepal, six thousand miles away. That purchase, and every purchase like it, assisted a community that few of our customers would ever meet

and helped to protect an environment that few of them would ever see.

While I was in Kathmandu on that first trip the Nepal Women's Association, which had been set up to support women in rural communities and help them produce craft goods which would be marketable in the west, helped us investigate other trade prospects. These included woven materials produced by Tibetan refugees and extraordinary knitted scarves in brilliant colours using a lustrous form of cashmere from the pachmina goat.

I had hoped that we would get some cooperation from people in the British Embassy there, but they turned out to be completely ineffectual. Before I left England I had

Introducing a new customer to The Body Shop.

gone to the Foreign Office they were very nice and promised that they would give me all the help they could. But it was only promises, promises. In Kathmandu I went to the Embassy, introduced myself and told them I was there to create trade. I heard that there was a disused paper-processing plant somewhere in Nepal that had been put in by some Japanese and had never been used, and I asked them if they could help me to locate it. They shrugged their shoulders and rolled their eyes, as if it was the most difficult request in the world. Then I asked them if they could supply me with a jeep to go up-country. They said they couldn't get hold of one. It was amazing to me. Every aid worker in Nepal has a jeep; they've got jeeps up to their eyeballs.

When I had given Milahn my order, I went back to the Embassy to ask them to help transfer the money. I was hoping to find a way of paying the family direct, instead of lodging the money with the government and allowing them to sit on it for months. Once again, our so-called diplomats were hopeless. In the end I gave them up as a bad job. I thought it was bloody stupid. What the hell are they doing there if they are not trying to encourage trade? I am sure if they had been at all interested in what we were doing they could have put Mara in contact with Milahn straight away; instead she had to waste weeks ferreting him out for herself. Our dealings with the Embassy only proved the truth of the adage that if you want to get something done, do it yourself.

Following Trade Routes

While we were setting up these first Trade Not Aid deals, The Body Shop agreed to be the major corporate sponsor for *Millennium*, a Canadian-produced ten-part television series which aimed to record the wisdom and culture of endangered tribes around the world. I had always regarded these people as the natural caretakers of the earth and I was more than happy, where possible, to combine my Trade Not Aid trips with reconnaissance for *Millennium*. It was in this context that I returned to Nepal in the summer of 1989.

On this occasion I travelled with a television crew up into the Humla, the most remote mountain region of Nepal, to visit the Nyinba tribe, which practises fraternal polyandry (where the woman not only marries her husband but his brothers as well) and is virtually untouched by western civilization. We had to trek with backpacks to between 17,000 and 18,000 feet to reach the Nyinba and I remember stopping on the way up, gasping for breath in the thin air, and seeing a man dressed in rags working in a field just below where I was standing. He was digging in the earth with a knife. He did not have a plough, he did not have a spade, he had a *knife*.

It was the first of a sequence of humbling experiences. The Nyinba rarely washed their clothes, simply because washing wore them out. I have always been fussy about being clean and so I thought this was pretty awful at first, but after a few days I began to be aware that I had always equated being clean with being somehow superior. It was as if I lived by the tenet 'I am clean, therefore I am better.' But I did not have to stay long with the Nyinba to realize what nonsense that was. By the end of the trip we all had amoebic dysentery, I had shit stains on my skirt and we were as dirty as everyone else. It was an

I get my ideas on the road

extraordinary lesson – having to reassess yourself because of the simple fact that you could not wash your clothes.

Eight bricks on his penis!

One of the highlights of our visit was an audience with Pagali Baba, a holy man known as a *sadhu*. Pagali Baba turned out to be a bit of a character. When we arrived he was stark naked and covered in ashes as part of some cleansing ritual. He was also roaring drunk. With his coarse and knotted hair (he was not much interested in Body Shop shampoos) he looked like a madman. Towards the end of our meeting he boozily offered to demonstrate his immense strength by balancing twelve bricks on his penis. Fearing he would do himself some damage, we negotiated through an interpreter and in the end he agreed – somewhat reluctantly – to perform the feat with only eight bricks. I have a photograph to prove it.

During that same trip I also visited the ancient city of Bhaktapur, to the east of Kathmandu. The remains of medieval Nepal are still to be found, perfectly preserved, in an extraordinary palace in the centre of Bhaktapur, but I was more interested in a papermaking venture that had been set up in the city under the auspices of UNICEF. It was one of the most enlightened projects that I had ever seen and was all the more impressive because of its UNICEF backing. It was offering good employment to poor families from all around the area, it had a creche facility for mothers, and it was producing the most wonderful range of coloured and scented papers and little notebooks and bags and cards. I was pleased to be able to give them a fillip, with an order from The Body Shop, and forge another link in our Trade Not Aid programme.

In all of these deals it is the trading that excites me. I am not rushing around the world as some kind of loony do-gooder; first and foremost I am a trader looking for trade. When I went to visit our shops in Saudi Arabia they took me to see the *souk* and I was absolutely knocked out by the hurly-burly and the wonderful little shops and the incredibly dynamic trading atmosphere. I immediately thought, *Why aren't we here?* Why didn't we load up a little waggonette with our products and trundle it into the *souk* and start haggling with everyone else?

Travelling either directly or indirectly on behalf of Trade Not Aid is now an integral part of my life and one which I welcome. Apart from the personal rewards to be obtained by the experience of visiting other cultures and societies as far afield as Africa, China, Lapland and South America, the search for trade can also be combined with a constant search for new ideas for products, new ingredients and new (to us) methods of body care. After every trip I dump a knapsack full of herbs and aromatic plants and oils in our Research and Development Department – the smell there is usually redolent of the last country I visited.

I am not rushing around the world as some kind of loony do-gooder; first and foremost I am a trader looking for trade.

Accompanied by an interpreter and sometimes an anthropologist, I am happy to go anywhere in the world to look for trade and to talk to women about what they use – and what their mothers and grandmothers used – to polish and cleanse and protect their skin. What I have learned is that it is better to *share* than to give or to receive. That is why all our Trade Not Aid projects are partnerships. I have learned that the poorest people are anything but helpless when given the slightest opportunity to help themselves. I have also learned the pure joy that is to be obtained from mixing with simple people whose lives are untainted by what we have laughably described as 'progress'.

African Odyssey

On another recce for *Millennium* I spent two weeks in the Sahara Desert with the Wodaabe people, an amazing nomadic tribe which has survived in the desert for more than two thousand years despite living constantly on the brink of starvation. To meet these people and see how they survive with such dignity against all the odds was incredible and very nourishing for the soul. As is so often the case with primitive peoples, they were incredibly hospitable and willing to share their rations with us – however meagre. We were all given Wodaabe names; I was christened Jalbedo, which means ripe, delicious fruit. I was very flattered.

The Wodaabe are known, for good reason, as the 'tribe of taboos'. Some are very bizarre. Women are never allowed to speak to their first-born child and usually give the baby away to relatives. After the birth, the mother is not allowed to have sex for two years and wears a talisman around her neck to show that she must not be touched. Wodaabe men, who are tall and thin and strikingly handsome, are allowed four wives. The first wife is chosen for him at birth and he acquires the others by abduction in the dead of night. If he can smuggle a woman away from her husband, carry her across the calf-rope which divides the male and female areas of the camp, and slaughter a sheep before anyone finds out, he can keep her. Quite often it goes wrong: the husband finds out, and then the two men fight a duel.

With the Wodaabe, July 1990

Amadou, a travelling medicine man, visited the Wodaabe while I was with them. Although he was a cripple, he managed to walk hundreds of miles across the desert selling dinky little items like severed chicken claws to make camels run faster and a whole range of potions which he claimed would cure everything from itching to impotency. I was hoping I might be able to trade with him – exchange a few Body Shop products I had with me for some of his secrets – but he had other ideas. He said he wanted to 'honour my beauty' and drew geometric patterns on my face with a charcoal pencil, finally sketching feather whiskers from my lips. Somehow it was incredibly soothing and I was purring like a kitten by the time he had finished. All I needed was a bowl of milk and I would have fallen asleep in his lap. I thought it was ironic, though, to travel thousands of miles to find myself in the middle of a baking desert with a man who was in the cosmetics business.

Before I left the Wodaabe I asked them if I could see some tribal dancing. The reaction was absolutely incredible. You only have to mention dancing to these guys and within a few hours dozens of them have arrived from miles around, on camel or on foot. The young men of the tribe put on fabulous head-dresses made of ostrich feathers, paint their faces, whiten their teeth and eyes and then dance to try to attract a woman. It was one of the most spectacular shows I have ever seen,

beginning at eight in the evening and continuing until about four o'clock the next morning. Occasionally a girl would sidle round to a man she fancied and gently scratch his back, meaning that she wanted to join him under the blanket afterwards.

The Wodaabe dance

With continuing devastating droughts, probably exacerbated by the Greenhouse Effect, and pressure from the military government of Niger to settle into fixed communities so that they can be made to pay taxes, the future of the Wodaabe people is in doubt. But if courage, ingenuity and fortitude count for anything, they will survive.

Sometimes my travels have led me into hilarious situations. Once, in Oman, I was trying to wheedle the formula of a heady perfume from a group of Bedouin women. They were very shy at first, but we soon got friendly and they made it clear they were very curious about my hair. The women of this particular tribe shaved all their body hair so they had never seen anyone like me, with a great frizzy black shock of the stuff. We were sitting in a tent giggling and talking and in the end they said they would tell me how they made their perfume if I would show them my pubic hair. 'Great,' I said, 'it's a deal.' I dropped my drawers and just stood there while they stared at me and hooted with laughter.

I have never been embarrassed by things like that. When I was in Japan, where nearly all women are flat-chested, I was with a group of women pearl divers who seemed to be fascinated by my boobs. In the end, as a joke, I asked them if they would like to have a squeeze. The interpreter solemnly translated my offer and they all started nodding, so I had to stand there while they lined up to take it in turns.

Only once, to date, have I been faced with a situation I could not handle. In Mexico City an anthropologist friend took me to the Restaurante Meson de Alonso, which was apparently the place to go for pre-Columbian food. What I did not know was that the speciality of the house was insects, which were a great source of protein for the Aztecs. The bar snacks were *chapulines*, which my friend told me were grasshoppers, and the menu was full of dishes based on beetles, cockroaches and fly eggs, with armadillo meatballs for the faint-hearted.

The most prized delicacy, I was assured, was a taco stuffed with live bugs which sometimes escaped and crawled across the diner's face. When I heard that, I fled. Thank God, there was a market nearby, selling the most delicious strawberries.

Although we are actively pursuing Trade Not Aid projects in Somalia, Burkina Faso, Malaysia, the Philippines and Kenya, not all of our Third World ventures have worked – although we do better than the United Nations, which only has a 10 per cent success rate. We tried to set up a project in Bangladesh and sent out a textile designer for three months to work with women's groups and the homeless to make simple cosmetics bags. It seemed like a good idea, but we couldn't get it right without having someone permanently *in situ* and so we had to abandon it. Another project in southern Turkey, where we were the major purchaser of sponges, aborted because the sponges started getting diseased. I went out there to find what was going wrong and the fishermen told me it was due to fall-out from Chernobyl, although I was never able to establish whether or not that was the real reason.

Small is Beautiful – And Fruitful

Fundamentally what we have learned is that the art of giving is not simply the act of doling out money; neither is it dishing out things we assume people want. It is the ability to work with them, and to figure out what they truly need. By the same token, the art of development is not a process of entering a country and inflicting some blueprint, some master plan, on the population. It is the process of helping people find the right tools, and the right approach, to develop themselves.

Large-scale aid is not going to go away, and I do not say that it should. It may be awkward and often inefficient, but it has its place. Highways and dams do have to be built, and huge efforts like malaria eradication are beyond the abilities of companies like ours.

My point is that if someone is willing to donate millions of dollars to some vast project – and never see where the money goes or get an accounting for it – why not earmark a tiny percentage of that figure for small-scale projects. Because the most wonderful aspect of simple, small-scale projects in the Third World, and dealing with people, is that they *work*.

SUDDENLY WE HEARD THEM CHANTING OUTSIDE – AN EXTRAORDINARY, LOW, PULSATING NOISE BETWEEN A HUM AND A GROWL. IT WAS AN ELECTRIFYING MOMENT; MY ARMS PRICKLED WITH GOOSE PIMPLES AND MY THROAT WENT DRY. THEN THE FIRST LINE OF WARRIORS APPEARED, TEN ABREAST, AND MARCHED SLOWLY INTO THE STADIUM WITH GREAT DIGNITY TO TAKE THEIR PLACES.

9

RAINFOREST GATHERING

It is hard to know which of our campaigns have been the most success-ful – how do you measure success? – but in terms of empowering and motivating the staff, instilling in them a belief that they are the most powerful people on the planet, Stop the Burning, our campaign to save the rainforest, probably had most impact. It was an issue that captured everyone's imagination, involved the whole of my personal family and the whole of The Body Shop family, and will certainly continue to involve us for years to come.

Towards the end of 1988 I was invited to speak to the Business Network, a group of successful business men and women who feel that business should be run in a more holistic way. They get together once a month in London, at the School of Alternative Medicine in Port-land Square. A lot of them are idealistic, New Age thinkers, who are basically concerned to effect change and I was happy to support them.

It was through a member of Business Network that I learned about the Rainforest Peoples' Association and its plans to organize a major protest meeting at Altamira, in north-west Brazil, where there were proposals to build a

Logging the life out of the rainforest

£6 billion dam system which would flood 15 million acres of the Amazon's most ecologically and culturally rich territory, the home of thirty-five thousand Indians.

The general situation in the Amazonian rainforest was immensely depressing. Millions of acres had already been destroyed in 'develop-ment' projects – logging, road-building, mining, damming and ranch-ing – financed by US, European and Japanese banks. The rainforest Indians, the true custodians of the forest, had taken the brunt of this destruction. They had been thrown off their land, murdered, decimated by diseases against which they had no immunity, and used as cheap labour. The loss of plant and animal life was incalculable – the rainforests provide the sole habitat for half the species of the earth, many of which still wait to be discovered.

The idea of the Forest Peoples' Gathering was to bring together the various different Indian tribal leaders with ecologists and environmentalists, to bear witness to what was happening and report back to the rest of the world. One of the problems in promoting joint action had always been that many of the Indian tribes were very warlike and tended to hack off each other's heads when they got together, but the organizers believed they had at last got across the urgent need for the rival tribes to cooperate to try and ensure their survival.

A couple of months before the gathering was due to take place, we were asked to contribute funds towards the cost of transporting tribal leaders from their villages to Altamira; and then, out of the blue, someone suggested that I should attend the gathering myself. I had not thought of it before, but I realized it would be a wonderful opportunity to talk to many of the world's leading ecologists and environmentalists, as well as to learn about the problems of the rainforest at first hand.

Justine was by then working in America, helping to open up new stores; but Sam, my younger daughter, was at home and looking for a cause and so we decided to go together. Since it was a first for both of us – neither of us had been to Brazil and neither of us could speak any Portuguese – I thought we might need some back-up. I heard that David Mayberry Lewis, the anthropologist who runs Cultural Survival in Boston, was sending his son, Bjorn, to the gathering. Bjorn could not only speak fluent Portuguese but he also knew that area well, so we hired him as a guide and interpreter.

We met up in Rio and flew from there to Altamira, which turned out to be like something from a very bad Western. On the Xingu river, about a hundred miles south of the Amazon, it was a dingy sprawl of shambling single-storey buildings, many of which appeared to be bordellos, with flea-bitten horses tied up outside. The streets were ankle-deep in mud; most of the locals carried guns and looked as if they would be delighted at an excuse to use them. The place was already packed with people who were to attend the gathering, but we managed to find a small room in a seedy establishment that claimed to be Altamira's hotel. We were told that nearly a thousand Indians, many of whom had travelled hundreds of miles by canoe, bus, plane or whatever means of transport they could find, were camped at a mission just outside the town. As the rainforest is virtually inpenetrable, it was a considerable logistical feat to get them there.

The meeting was due to start next day in an indoor sports stadium on the outskirts of Altamira. Sam and I got there early and found seats on the mezzanine floor looking down into the stadium. Around the edges were benches packed with white people who had a vested interest in supporting the dam development; and in the centre of the floor was a large space carpeted with palm leaves which had been reserved for the Indians, who had not yet arrived.

The gathering of the tribes at Altamira

Suddenly we heard them chanting outside – an extraordinary, low, pulsating noise between a hum and a growl. It was an electrifying moment; my arms prickled with goose pimples and my throat went dry. Then the first line of warriors appeared, ten abreast, and marched slowly into the stadium with great dignity to take their places, squatting on the palm leaves. Their faces were painted with red geometric patterns, their chests and arms were draped with beads and their bodies were smeared with a mulch of jackfruit and ash. Most of them wore shorts, their only concession to western modesty. Line after line of them followed – it was an amazing sight, all these wonderful men with their body paint and gaudy headdresses of yellow, red and green parrot feathers, each of them carrying a spear.

A Meeting of Minds

The gathering was nothing less than four days of absolute emotionalism. We were thrilled by the oratory, thrilled to be in their company, thrilled by the good sense of what was said. The Indians had extraordi-

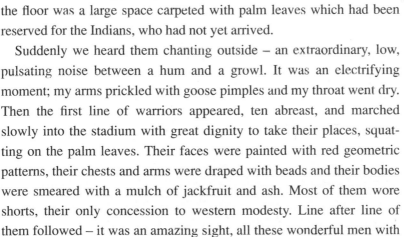

nary presence: they spoke from the heart with stunning eloquence, and their wisdom was evident to us all. It was impossible not to be moved by what they had to say. They told us, in no uncertain terms, to leave them and their forest alone. One bent old woman hobbled up to the microphone, completely unawed by the occasion, and said: 'I have children and grandchildren. These are our lands and our waters and our forests. Listen, white man, you've already got plenty of land. We, the Indians, have only a little left and we want to live with our children on our land in peace.' Their pleas were supported by environmentalists, who warned that the senseless destruction of the rainforest not only threatened the Indians' culture and way of life, but destroyed many plant species valuable in medicine and threatened the whole world by contributing to the Greenhouse Effect.

Paulinho Paiakan, a leader of the Kayapo

Paulinho Paiakan, a leader of the Kayapo, was the most impressive of all the speakers, with a natural gift for oratory. His words sent a shiver down my spine: 'We are fighting to defend the forest because the forest is what makes us, and what makes our hearts go. Because without the forest we won't be able to breathe and our hearts will stop and we will die.' Paiakan was an extraordinary man. While he was still very much a leader in his tribe, he also had a foot in the west, as he had travelled extensively to publicize the plight of the rainforest people and to inform the world of what was happening. He had talked to the World Bank and the US Senate and Members of the UK Parliament, and had been awarded the Reght Livelihood Award, which is presented in the Swedish Parliament on the day before the Nobel Prize.

It was wonderful just to be there, to be able to talk to all those people every day and every evening, to bond with international environmentalists, ecologists, ethno-biologists and anthropologists and all the rest. It was like walking through a Who's Who of the Green movement. That was the value for me, getting to meet the people who mattered in the environmental movement. One of them was an extraordinary woman called Elaine Elisabetsky, who was looking at medicinal plants and pharmacological ingredients found in the rainforest. We agreed to meet later to talk about the possibility of one of the tribes with whom she was working cultivating plants for The Body Shop.

I was the only representative of a commercial company at the gathering and I meant absolutely nothing to any of them. It was only when they began to realize that we actively wanted to help and to be involved, and that we actually *could* help, that they began to take any notice of me. I don't blame them – it must have struck them as odd that someone from a cosmetics company would want to attend such a function. What they didn't know is that I would never in a million years waste my time by attending a conference run by the cosmetics industry.

Losing the collected wisdom of the rainforest tribes would be like burning every library in the world without bothering to look what was on the shelves.

On the last day I learned from a mutual woman friend that Paiakan's life has been threatened by the same group that just a few months earlier had murdered the activist Chico Mendes, who had been campaigning against deforestation on behalf of impoverished rubber tappers. She arranged for me to meet Paiakan, secretly, on the roof of our hotel, to talk to him about how we might be able to help. It was the first opportunity I had had of close contact with him and I was deeply moved by what he had to say. Even after translation, it was poetry that was pouring from his mouth. 'Paiakan says.' said the translator, 'that the tears are rolling down his face. His people are dying and he does not know why.' Up there on the roof of that crummy hotel I knew I was in the presence of a 'somebody'; he reminded me a little of Gandhi. He had no idea who I was or what I did; I was introduced to him as someone who might be able to help.

What his friends were asking for was financial help to get him away to safety, up to Canada, until the heat died down. By then I knew the problem was so big that I could not make an arbitrary decision and say

Altamira, 1988

'Right, the company is going to fund him to look after him.' But I promised that I would try and raise some money at our international franchise holders' meeting, which was due to take place in England in a few days' time.

Altamira, my first front-line exposure to an environmental problem, was an important experience for me. It was the first time I had had a true understanding of what was happening to the rainforest. To hear and see for myself the testimony of the rainforest peoples, to meet Paiakan, to see members of the Yanomami tribe carrying banners saying 'Stop the Killing of the Yanomami' – these were experiences that do not easily slip out of the brain cells. I read somewhere that losing the collected wisdom of the rainforest tribes would be like burning every library in the world without bothering to look at what was on the shelves.

A Message from the Heart

Having Sam with me was also an important factor. Adults can argue and debate and be reasonable and pragmatic, but young people react straightforwardly from the gut and the heart. I always look to see how kids react to things, and I could see how moved Sam was by what she had observed and everything she had heard Paiakan say. She saw things in his gestures and in his eyes that made her say over and over again, 'We have to do something, we must do something.' Since it is the young people who are going to inherit the problem, their reaction can't be ignored.

Littlehampton seemed rather more than a world away from Altamira when we got back, but I was looking forward to the international franchise holders' meeting, without quite knowing what to expect in terms of fund raising. As it turned out, I didn't have to do a thing. Sam, my wild seventeen-year-old daughter, just got up and gave a five-minute speech about what she had seen, what she felt and what she thought we should be doing. It was all straight from the heart and it was like an elegy – one of the most beautiful things I have ever heard. This is part of what she said:

" *My trip to Brazil has changed my life. I learned more there than I have ever learned in my whole life, and as my awareness grows I feel that I have to pass my passion to others and tell people, especially of my age, what really is happening out there and what we can do about it.*

I was lucky enough to take part in a historical event, for it was the first time the Amazon Indians had had a chance to voice their views and demonstrate about what is happening to them and their forest.

It is vital that we save these people, not only for moral reasons, but also because they hold incredible knowledge and wisdom of what the forest holds. In one day, I learned that there was a plant which can cure epilepsy, thousands of plants which can cure all kinds of cancer, roots for backache, rheumatism . . . one scientist even claimed he was seriously looking at the possibility of a cure for Aids – and these are only a few examples. These people are our only link to saving the forest.

It has been said that the rainforest will be totally destoyed in a little over twenty-five years and the effect it will have on the rest of the world is worse than a nuclear war. So really what we are in is a race against time.

I could go on all day spilling out these amazing and horrific facts, but first of all let me tell you how I was affected by these people and what I experienced out there.

I didn't know what to expect or what part I was going to play in the gathering: all I can say is that I went out a tourist and came back an environmentalist. I was silent the first three days and I cried for the last three.

Watching and listening to the Indians speak was an eye-opening experience, because we had to throw out of the window all western presumptions of what they want and need. They not only talked about their suffering and struggle to survive, but also of the poor white Brazilians who took up their fight for justice as well. They talked about what progress was. Was it the town of Altamira, where there are slums, no schools or hospitals, dirt and disease everywhere? They didn't seem to think so. They said they want to progress on their own terms, not ours. And you saw in some strange way that they were already way ahead of us in humanity. Maybe all of us ought to ask ourselves, once in a while, who are the savages and who are the innocent?

Sam: speaking from the heart

What does it take to make people realize what is really happening out there? What does it take for people to realize that they have a responsibility to the planet and the people?

If half of us in this room decide not to take part in making a change then it will take twice as long to put a stop to this, and other kinds of butchery. But if all of us make a small effort, if we all contribute, whether it is eating brazil nuts or not eating hamburgers, working out there or passing the message on, then we can change the world. We can save it. I really believe this, because I am not prepared to sit back and watch it all happen.' "

By the time she had finished, nearly everyone in the room was weeping. One of the oldest franchisees got a black eye – he was crying so much that when he got up he walked straight into a pillar.

We always introduced an environmental issue at the international franchise meeting. The way it was planned was that the first part of the day was devoted to retailing – new ideas, new products, new developments and so on – and then the afternoon is given over to education, with workshops all over the place and guest speakers and lots of videos. On this occasion the rainforest issue took over, emotionally, and became the primary topic of the day.

In the evening we held a crazy auction to set the fund-raising ball rolling. I offered to go to any country in the world to do public relations in return for a £5,000 contribution, and people started getting their chequebooks out. There was some grumbling that we were blackmailing the franchise holders without giving them enough information, but mostly they were caught up by the spirit of Sam's speech and by the videos that we had shown them of the Altamira gathering. Gordon and I gave money, the company gave money and the staff gave money. I had thought that if we were able to raise around £10,000 we would be doing very well indeed. In fact, everyone got so fired by the idea of helping that when we counted up the cheques at the end of the day we had collected more than £200,000.

Active Aid for the Indians

Then we had the problem of what to do with the money. In April we invited all the major non-governmental organizations, like Cultural Survival and Friends of the Earth and Greenpeace, to a meeting at our offices and said to them: 'Look, we've got all this money. Tell us what to do with it.' Their reactions were incredible, as if we had no business to be raising money and whatever we did with it would be sure to cause trouble. I came away with the strong impression that Survival International, for example, was only interested in keeping the Indians as they were, whereas I knew from my own contacts at Altamira that most tribes were ready to accept change, as long as it was at their own pace.

In the end, as usual, we trusted our own instinct. Paiakan had asked

Who says we don't have a marketing department?

for a light aircraft to provide communication between the Kayapo villages and to act as an air ambulance. So we allocated a first chunk of money – £70,000 – to buy a second-hand aeroplane and to hire the pilots and maintenance back-up needed to keep it flying.

Then Gordon and Dr Jason Clay of Cultural Survival went out to Brazil to talk to key non-governmental organizations campaigning for Forest Peoples' rights. They set up a three-year support programme for four groups: the Ecumenical Centre for Documentation and Information, which was documenting the prevailing situation of 180 Indian nations throughout Brazil; the Union of Indian Nations, which was working to ensure the voice of the forest peoples was heard; the Nucleus for Indigenous Rights, which was pushing forward with test cases to establish pro-Indian legal precedents; and the Rubber Tappers' Movement, which was spearheading moves to bring the murderers of Chico Mendes to trial.

We also arranged for four members of the Yanomami tribe to meet government officials in Brasilia to protest about the invasion of their land by gold miners, who were pillaging the forest and massacring the Indians. That was quite an experience. The Yanomami are the largest group of American Indians surviving in the rainforest untouched and untainted by 'civilization'. The four we brought to Brasilia had never left their village before, had never seen glass and had certainly never been in an aeroplane. There was a tragically poignant moment at the meeting when they were shown a map of their tribal area. They studied it for a long time and then asked: 'Where are our villages?' Their tribal settlements had been removed from the map as being no longer of interest or relevant – all the government cared about were the gold miners' camps and the airstrips they were carving all over the place.

Not long afterwards a report by the Brazilian Committee for Citizenship Action warned that the Yanomami people – all 9000 of them – were facing imminent extinction from epidemics, massacres and mercury poisoning. The good news, such as it was, was that as a result of the Altamira gathering the World Bank funding for the dam project had been put on hold, despite objections from the electricity and the mining companies and all those people who could see fat profits from it.

In January 1989 120 branches of The Body Shop had displayed rain-forest posters produced by Friends of the Earth, but soon after the Altamira gathering I began planning a major rainforest campaign to be mounted by The Body Shop and spread over four years. In the first year we would educate ourselves about the problems and possible solutions; in the following two years we would campaign for the rights of indigenous tribes; and in the last year I wanted to have a look at reafforestation and the management of sustainable resources.

Stop the Burning

The most immediate way in which I felt we could help was to motivate public opinion to try to stop the annual burning of the rainforest. Every year, during the dry season between July and September, thousands of acres were set ablaze to clear the land for cattle ranching, primarily to provide meat for the United States' insatiable demand for hamburgers. Apart from the devastating effect on the Indian tribes, wildlife and plants, carbon dioxide released by the burning forest accelerated the Greenhouse Effect, which scientists were predicting would bring about major climatic changes. In the 1988 burning season, 300,000 square kilometres – an area larger than the whole of Britain – went up in smoke. It was the biggest fire in the earth's recent history.

The first thing we did was look at the images and colours of political protest and make a decision that all the visual material for the campaign would be in red, yellow and black. Our art department came up with two brilliant posters, one showing a skeletal nut tree against a background of flames with the copyline 'The Future of the Planet is Going up in Smoke' and another very strong graphic design with a quarter of the globe on fire. These posters went out to 135 shops in the UK and another 315 abroad, including twenty in the United States.

Then we had Stop the Burning T-shirts printed for all the staff, along with educational videos which went out to all the shops explaining the problem and what we were trying to do about it. Experience had taught us by then that it was vital to the success of any campaign to ensure that the staff were well briefed – that they understood the rationale and were enthused by what we were doing.

We explained the gravity of the threat in simple terms: if the destruction continued, most of the Amazonian rainforest would be gone in twelve years. If it disappeared, so would the home for two-thirds of the world's plant and animal species. A four-square-mile area of rainforest can contain up to 1500 species of flowering plants – as many as in the whole of Britain. Burning the forests brought short-term profits to a few wealthy farmers, but long-term, devastating loss to the forest dwellers, who were left homeless and destitute.

The aim of the campaign, we explained, was to heighten concern over rainforest destruction, to educate people as to what they could do to protest and to encourage active participation in the move towards the protection of land rights for the Brazilian Indians.

Our Stop the Burning campaign was launched in July. Over one weekend every shop was transformed into a rainforest campaign base, with posters and leaflets and protest letters addressed to the President of Brazil for people to sign. We urged customers to check that their banks were not funding destructive projects in the rainforest, to boycott tropical hardwoods and meat originating from Brazil, and to make their views known to the government. All our bags were printed with campaign slogans and our delivery trucks rolled out with a new message on their sides: 'The Indians are the custodians of the rainforest. The rainforests are the lungs of the world. If they die, we all die.'

Outside the Brazilian Embassy, May 1989

That July was gloriously hot and many of the staff took the campaign out into the street, setting up tables outside the shops, getting housewives and policemen and all kinds of people to sign up. I went around the stores in those first three weeks and saw the tremendous effect it had on the staff. They were high as kites, charged with a real sense of power and purpose and a belief that they could effect change. I think everybody felt good about what they were doing. We even ran a competition to see which shop could collect most signatures, and publicized the results in our internal newsletter.

In the first two weeks of the campaign we collected half a million signatures – and this was at a time when we only had 135 outlets in Britain. Even as a campaigning company, I think it is hard not to be impressed by figures like that. In the second two weeks we collected another half a million. No environmental organization anywhere in the world had ever achieved such a result.

Then, of course, we had to decide what to do with them. We had one million signed letters addressed to President José Sarney saying:

Dear President Sarney,

I know we are all polluters of this planet, and I know that we must do all we can to save it. But we need you to act on everyone's behalf to save the forests of Brazil, and especially to STOP THE BURNING this year . . . . We hear that there is much you can do to halt the destruction: abolish the tax incentives that encourage the destruction of forest for profit, implement land reform to tackle the root causes of agrarian violence; support sustainable development through long-term projects that incorporate the knowledge and methods of the traditional forest peoples.

Please act. There is much at stake: the life of the plants, animals and the people within the forest is threatened.

They could be lost forever. The balance of nature is being disturbed by the destruction: the weather patterns of the world are being altered. The future of all our children and their children is in danger. The future of the planet is in doubt.

So please – STOP THE BURNING and save the forests before it is too late. The whole world looks to you for action.

Yours sincerely . . .

I did not want simply to package up all these letters and ship them off to President Sarney because I wanted to get maximum publicity out of them, particularly in Brazil. I decided the best thing to do would be to deliver them, *en masse*, to the Brazilian Embassy in London. We alerted the international news media and gathered together 250 staff, all wearing their Stop the Burning T-shirts, to make the delivery. So the press and the television cameras were waiting when our fleet of coaches pulled up outside the Embassy and we started unloading sacks printed with the Stop The Burning slogan in Portuguese. Some of us carried placards and all of us were chanting 'Stop the burning, stop the burning . . .' at the tops of our voices. Whoever it was who answered the door took one terrified look at what was going on, said, 'We're not taking them' and slammed the door in our faces.

When it became obvious that we were intent on dumping the sacks on the doorstep someone called the police to shoo us away. But the police realized that we were very peaceful and organized, and they were very sympathetic to what we were doing. In fact when a sack split open, spilling the letters out on to the pavement, one of the policemen started pushing them through the Embassy letterbox with the comment that his wife worked for Friends of the Earth! We left the sacks piled up in the doorway, with a couple of protest placards thrown on top. All this took place in front of television cameras broadcasting the protest, live by satellite, to Brazil. That was what I really wanted to achieve – coverage in the country where the decisions would have to be made to save the rainforest from further destruction.

A few of our franchise holders were worried by all the publicity – one wrote to ask if we were going into the 'rent-a-mob' business – but the very great majority supported what we were doing and we had fantastic messages of congratulation from other environmental groups around the world. The Brazilian ecological movement sent us a telegram saying: 'Thank God. What you are saying is what we want to hear.' Even the Italian branch of Friends of the Earth faxed us a simple message: 'Wonderful. More, more.'

With the Kayapo

In August I was invited back to Brazil to meet the rainforest tribal leaders and explore the possibility of trade. It was Paiakan's idea. He was back with his tribe and he knew that I was keen to set up direct trading links, if it was possible, with his people. For his part, he wanted to find somebody to trade with who he could trust, who would not pressurize him, who would move at his pace and who would preach the just cause of his people.

We had already done some preliminary research into what marketable products might be available in the forest. A professor at the Royal Botanical Gardens in Kew, returning from a field trip in Brazil, had brought us back a suitcase full of plants and roots and tropical powders, all culled from sustainably managed sources, some of which had potential. In addition we had two projects of our own in Brazil. One was at the university in Belem, at the mouth of the Amazon, which was studying seeds and plants for pot-pourri and aromatic oils. The other was to try to persuade Indian tribes to harvest brazil nuts.

Brazil nuts

I knew that brazil nuts could produce oil and that we could do something with it, but there was a multitude of problems – not least the effect that trade with the outside world would have on their culture and way of life. I was well aware that you couldn't just march into an environment like the rainforest, make a deal with the locals, then bring in plant and machinery to start processing brazil nut oil willy-nilly. But at the same time I did not buy the argument that well-meaning groups like us should leave the rainforest people alone. By leaving them alone we had left them at the mercy of racketeers and they were dying like flies. I was convinced that we had to look for ways to make the rainforest economically viable, with an internationally acceptable strategy for trade that was based on conservation and husbandry. If the controlled extraction of sustainably managed plant materials could provide a permanent livelihood for the rainforest peoples, it was my view that the people themselves should decide how much change they wanted to accept, how much they wanted to be 'culturalized'.

All this, and much more, I wanted to discuss with Paiakan. We met in the little township of Aukre, from where we flew out to the Kayapo tribal area in the Body Shop aircraft. It was about an hour's flight to Paiakan's village. From the air the rainforest looks like a green tufted carpet, so thick that it seems completely impenetrable. You only know where the Indians are when you see a copse of slightly different trees, indicating that some tribe has been busy with agro-forestry.

Most of the village was there to greet us when the aircraft touched down on a little dusty airstrip of packed red earth. It is customary to greet someone returning to the village by keening – crying real tears. They cry for the time they have been separated from you, and so there was a lot of keening at Paiakan's return.

As we were walking into the village a group of young girls, virtually naked except for strings of beads worn like crossed bandoliers, came

A Kayapo chorus line

towards us. They have a way of holding each other across their backs and walking in a kind of sideways goose step; they are very tactile and hold and scratch each other a lot, although they don't kiss. One of them took my backpack and I linked arms with them, making them laugh by jostling and winking at them and they tried to teach me to sing one of their songs as we started off down the track. I thought it was a wonderful way to be welcomed to the village; in fact everyone was charming to me – I think because Paiakan had confirmed my credentials.

My first impression was of astonishment at how clean it was. There was a huge hut in the centre of the village, known as the men's hut, which was the meeting place and debating chamber; all the sleeping huts were arranged in a semi-circle around it. In the middle of an open area at the edge of the village was an 80-foot deep pit into which they put all their refuse. There was another small hut over a hole in the ground, which was the lavatory.

What was also remarkable was how little variety of colour there was all around. There were any number of shades of green, but hardly any other colours at all except when a parrot appeared through the trees and shocked the eye with its gaudy blue, yellow and red plumage. It is easy to understand why the parrot is the only art symbol of the Kayapo, and why all their beadwork and body painting is in the same bright, primary colours.

I was allocated a hut with a hammock near the river, and on the morning of my first full day the whole village gathered in the meeting hut so that I could show them some of the Body Shop products and explain how we might be able to trade. Usually the meeting house is reserved for men only, but Paiakan managed to get all the women and kids in as well. I realized immediately that I had made a major boob as I had only brought about thirty bars of soap and everyone wanted a bit, so we had to cut each bar into half, and then into quarters, to make sure it went round.

Paiakan had brought in eight Indian leaders to talk about the possibility of trade, and I had come prepared with samples of raw materials to demonstrate the process of turning natural ingredients into skin and hair care products that sold in faraway countries that most of them had never heard of. They had a wonderful form of spontaneous debate where each man in turn would stand up and say his piece, often acting out his oratory, then sit down and let the next one take the stage. I showed them how bananas were made into shampoo and how pineapple was used for a facial wash and how oils could be extracted from roots and nuts. Then I asked them to show me what forest plants they used on their own skin and hair.

In the end it seemed that brazil nuts still offered the greatest potential for our use; and when I asked them if they were interested in gathering nuts for The Body Shop, Paiakan assured me they were. It is interesting that the Kayapo are entirely responsible for planting brazil nuts in the rainforest. People tend to think they grow everywhere, but they don't – only the Kayapo know how and where to plant them.

We did not even begin to discuss how we might pay for them, because I was not at all sure that handing over money was the right solution. Out there in the middle of the Xingu, you are stepping back in time; I had to think in terms of how Christopher Columbus would have traded with them, and he would certainly have done it by barter. I wanted to be able to reward the Kayapo, as primary producers, but I did not want to disrupt their culture or their environment. Primarily, I was satisfied simply to establish that they were interested and willing to trade with us.

It was funny next morning when I went down to the river to wash. There I found half the village happily lathering themselves with Body Shop soap, so that the whole area reeked of our corporate aroma. It was extraordinary – like walking into a Body Shop eight thousand miles away in Europe.

The Love of the Jungle

Living with the Kayapo was, for me, paradise. The clear river at the end of a path leading out of the village was where we bathed and played and drank. The Kayapo eat a lot of yams, sweet potatoes and fish, but I ate mainly fruit – there was a lemon tree nearby with fruit the size of grapefruit, and I squirted it on a slice of mango for breakfast. In the evening I would sometimes grill fish over an open fire, or just eat bananas.

At nights I slept in a hammock slung in one of the sleeping huts, and by day I spent all my time learning from the Indians. What absolutely knocked me for six was their innate wisdom. There was a rhyme, a reason, a rationale for everything they did. They knew which plants grew happily together; they knew that if they planted a certain shrub it would attract butterflies which attracted bees which ate ants which ate their plants. Each family in the tribe was allocated a species of plant which they 'owned' and which was their responsibility to nurture and protect.

The forest was actually very different from what I anticipated. First, it was much lighter under the leaf canopy than I thought it would be, and wherever the light shone through there were little shoots growing almost in front of your eyes. But you quickly became aware of how fragile it all was. The trees looked enormous, but the moment you scraped away the ground foliage you could see that there was nothing there but sand. The Brazilian forest is not like European forests, with deep layers of humus and soil and that is why the burning policy was so terrible. The cleared rainforest cannot sustain pasture for more than a couple of years, and all that cleared ground will quickly become a barren, desert waste.

I often went into the forest with the village medicine man, who was an extraordinary character. He claimed that every illness encountered in the villages had a remedy in the forest. He had identified 230 different forms of dysentery and a plant cure for each one. He had catalogued bees in a way that had never been thought of in the west, and had discovered nine different strains of bee with no sting. I labelled all the potentially useful plants that he showed me. It was worth it. The Kayapo use red beads from the urukum shrub for body painting; The

Body Shop now uses the same beads, gathered by the Kayapo, as colouring for our mango body butter.

One day when I was in the forest with the medicine man he asked me how old I was and if I would like to get pregnant again. I said I wouldn't mind, and so he said he would show me how. I wondered quite what was coming next, but I needn't have worried. He took me down to the river, told me to strip off to the waist and stroked my back, very gently, with some kind of leaf. Then he mixed up a drink with water and shavings from the bark of a tree and tied a vine around my waist. He told me to wear the vine for three days, after which I would be pregnant with a female child.

The trees looked enormous, but the moment you scraped away the ground foliage you could see there was nothing there but sand.

Now I knew that you needed sperm to be pregnant, but I was also in awe of the rainforest people and their wisdom. Supposing I did get pregnant by the rainforest method? I would know how it had happened and so would the Indians, but no one else would believe me. Certainly I think Gordon would have found it a bit hard. I worried about it so much that I went back to the medicine man and asked for an antidote. He gave me another kind of vine, which I had to wear around my wrist, and told me it would act as a contraceptive.

There was a cultural reason for this pregnancy ritual. There was no kind of marriage ceremony within the tribe and many of the young women seemed to have attachments to a number of different men; they called them 'women who were friends of many'. Presumably if, when they became pregnant, they could say they had been impregnated by the forest, it avoided all kinds of problems with rivals claiming paternity.

It was already clear that one of the major problems about trading with the Kayapo would be shipping. The Indians were obviously keen to gather brazil nuts for us, and I was pleased about that, but how were we going to get several tons of nuts out of an area where the only means of communication was by light aircraft? There was apparently a primitive road that stretched to within fifty kilometres of Paiakan's village, but I knew that those people concerned with the preservation of the rainforest were unhappy about extending roads into the forest.

It seemed that the river probably offered the best means of transport, if it was navigable, and I resolved to take a look at it when the time came for me to leave. I was genuinely sorry to say goodbye to the Kayapo people, who I thought epitomized both the dignity and the tragedy of the rainforest tribes. The knowledge that their future was in terrible danger was truly shocking.

Most of the village came to see me off at the airstrip; I felt as if I were leaving old friends. As soon as we were airborne, I asked the pilot to fly low along the course of the river so I could take a look at it; I discovered there were at least half a dozen huge waterfalls within the first twenty or thirty miles. There was no question of shipping our brazil nuts out of the forest that way.

On the way out of the rainforest we stopped at another village that was an object lesson in how contact with the outside world can be completely destructive, even if well-intentioned. The headman of this village was an extraordinary old guy called Pomba. A few years back he had agreed to lease part of his tribe's reserve to gold miners for a substantial annual rent. Unusually, this particular mining company did not try and exploit the Indians and paid the rent, every year, on the nail.

Pomba set about 'improving' his village. He replaced all the nice old palm frond huts, which had soft, warm dirt floors, with concrete huts. It was not until the new huts were built that Pomba discovered that none of the Indians liked them. They were uncomfortable, unpleasant to live in and the women found they got a vaginal discharge from sitting on the concrete. He had a big storehouse built in the centre of the village and stocked it with food, but he had to employ a poor Brazilian (not an Indian) to guard and ration it out. None of the men had to bother with their traditional skills of hunting and gathering. The village quickly lost its soul as it became more and more westernized, and Pomba soon realized that he had made a terrible mistake. When I met him he was talking about trying to put everything back as it was, and rebuild a replica of the original village. I thought he should certainly do it.

Tribal Technology

Back in England, the obvious solution to transporting the brazil nuts was to cut down the weight; and the obvious way to do it was to process the nuts *in situ*, and extract the oil before shipping. I went to the International Labour Organization, explained the problem and asked them if they could lend me some old bit of Heath Robinson machinery that might do the job. They eventually came up with an ancient crushing machine which worked with a handle. We tried it out in our warehouse, but it was so ineffectual and labour-intensive that I just couldn't see these rainforest warriors being prepared to sit all day feeding one nut after another into it, just to extract a few drops of oil.

Then we found another machine which was much lighter, much faster and much more efficient, and we have shipped that out to Paiakan's village to see how they get on with it. ICI (Brazil) have cooperated with us by working out a method for oil extraction and training two Kayapo to work the machine. We eventually hope to be able to harvest some 20 tons of brazil nuts every year, which will produce 1500 kilos of oil for a brazil nut conditioner.

'If video cameras help the Indians to preserve their culture, they're a good idea.'

I am working on a lot of other ideas, both independently and with groups like Cultural Survival. One of the things I would like to be able to do is to give every village a video camera – I have already been talking to Sony about fitting video cameras with solar-powered batteries – so that the Indians could record all their collected customs, legends and wisdom about the rainforest, its animals and plants. The medicine man in Paiakan's village knew so much, but there must be many other medicine men in many other villages who know even more. It would be just incredible if all the knowledge of the rainforest tribes could be gathered by the Indians themselves on videotape and catalogued in some educational library.

The Indians would love it, too. When I visited Paiakan's village I showed them a videotape I had with me of Indians dancing and singing at the Altamira gathering and they thought it was magical. They would adore to be able to watch themselves on video. Some people have said there is a danger that they'll just sit out there in the rainforest and watch television all day. I think that's ridiculous. As far as I am concerned, if video cameras help them to preserve their culture they're a good idea. It was interesting that, after seeing themselves on video, the women stopped wearing the little bits and pieces of western clothing they had acquired; they suddenly realized they looked strange and reverted to their original, naked state.

'The Kayapo women make wonderful necklaces, bracelets and rings . . .'

Another project we have been pursuing is to set up a Trade Not Aid deal under which The Body Shop could act as the trading arm to sell Indian beadwork. Beads are fundamental to the way of life of the Kayapo in terms of art, leisure, pleasure and wealth. The women make wonderful necklaces, bracelets and rings for themselves, their menfolk and their children, and we felt there was a market for them abroad. We offered to give them 100 kilos of coloured glass beads to get the project going . If it is successful, the project will provide the Kayapo with an income of up to $20,000 a year from work that will not greatly intrude on their daily lives.

In addition, Paiakan is very keen for us to investigate and analyse all the plant material in the Xingu river region to assess what applications might be viable in the west. We have our own product development team working intensively to explore how rainforest products can be adapted for our use and we have a brilliant project set up with the Kaxinawa tribe, who are planting and cropping ten ingredients that they have used for centuries for their own skin and hair care. These are being sent to Elaine Elisabetsky at Belem University, where they are freeze-dried, mixed into oil or alcohol solutions and sent to us in Britain for further study.

My ultimate aim is to launch a 'rainforest range' of Body Shop products, but it is not going to be easy. We won't ever be able to guarantee a regular supply of raw ingredients, so we are going to have to be

flexible – perhaps put the range into some shops and not others, or just sell it as and when the ingredients are available. There is no point in saying we've got to have 5000 tons of this or that before we can launch the range, because we will probably never get to that stage. It is an absolutely crazy way of trading, by ordinary standards, but there it is – it is the only way it can be done.

It is an absolutely crazy way of trading, by ordinary standards, but there it is – it is the only way it can be done.

In October 1990 Gordon and I went back to visit the Kayapo together, to check on the progress of our projects. It was wonderful to see that things were happening. There were fifty-eight women already involved in making bead belts, bracelets and necklaces, and we packed the first thousand samples into our bags to bring home with us. Then we had a grand counting-out ceremony in the meeting hut, at which I made sure everyone could see we were paying the women for their efforts. Gordon sat down with some of the chiefs to explain how the business would work and how to organize a simple cash flow; they seemed to understand and to be quite happy with what we were doing.

Harvesting of brazil nuts had not yet started, but we arranged for the processing hut to be reroofed with woven palm leaves and for a drying hut to be built nearby. We also advanced the cash needed to equip the harvesting expedition with an outboard motor, fuel, mosquito nets, machetes, sharpening stones, blankets and medicines. Gordon again worked out a simple business plan with them, indicating a potential profit for the community of around $50,000 in the first year.

It was a great trip and it was wonderful to do it with Gordon. Some of the chiefs took us trekking through the forest – this was quite an honour – and in the village we bantered with the women and played with the kids as if we were old friends. One day they painted our faces and bodies, which gave us a good laugh, and when the time came for us to go the son of one of the chiefs shyly presented Gordon with a full Kayapo head-dress as a leaving present.

I don't feel, after getting to know the Kayapo, that we will ever be able to abandon them. If these projects don't work, we will always try others. What I would ultimately like to be able to do is to set up a perfect example of honest trading with a fragile community and make it a benchmark of how we should conduct such trade in future. The rules are pretty simple. First, we have to be invited in. Second, we must not mess with the environment or the culture. Third, we must reward the primary producers.

It would also be useful if our projects helped to change the attitude of people in the industrial world, to make them sensitive to the issues and enable them to realize how far their responsibility extends. I do not believe that what we are doing carries any inherent dangers for the rainforest people and I don't think I am interfering. If I thought that, I would pack it in straightaway. If, by collecting brazil nuts, they can help safeguard their future and improve the quality of their lives, that's fine by me. They decide what those improvements might be. It is hard to put yourself in the shoes of a person whose culture is so different that they don't even wear shoes; but one thing I am certain of – they are far from persuaded that our ways are the best. They made that clear at Altamira, when one of them stood up, pointed to the town and said, 'Do not think that this is what we want. We want to hear the sound of the birds, not the sound of trucks.'

The rainforest and the rainforest people are still in dire peril, but their situation has improved very slightly. There has been some movement away from mega-development projects; the new government seems more enlightened and has ordered a 70 per cent cutback on burning.

For us, what was initially viewed as a four-year project is now a total lifetime commitment which we will never abandon. No species faces extinction without a fight, even if that battle is against the massed might of western consumerism. Our job now is to show that there *is* an alternative and it's so incredibly simple. It is just a basic exchange of resources carried out in the traditional manner – as a token of friendship and respect.

YOU HAVE TO LOOK AT LEADERSHIP THROUGH THE EYES OF THE FOLLOWERS AND YOU HAVE TO LIVE THE MESSAGE. WHAT I HAVE LEARNED IS THAT PEOPLE BECOME MOTIVATED WHEN YOU GUIDE THEM TO THE SOURCE OF THEIR OWN POWER AND WHEN YOU MAKE HEROES OUT OF EMPLOYEES WHO PERSONIFY WHAT YOU WANT TO SEE IN THE ORGANIZATION.

10

LEADER OF THE PACK

No one has yet told me, to my face, that I am a pain in the butt, but it would not in the least surprise me if this was a view nurtured in some quarters, particularly in the City. When you have a big mouth and you're not frightened to speak your mind, you make enemies. I have never made any secret of my disdain for the financial community. What are they contributing to the greater good? Why are business people lauded for making money rather than making things?

Neither do I have much respect for traditional businessmen. When, in November 1987, The Body Shop was named as Company of the Year by the Confederation of British Industries, I should have been incredibly thankful and proud (which I was) and servile at the award presentation. Instead, I decided at the last minute to speak out. The newspapers next day described my speech as a 'blistering attack' on traditional business values.

Celebrating our
Queen's Award for
Export

All I said was the truth as I perceived it: that the world of retailing had taught me nothing, that it was populated by tired executives working tired systems, that huge corporations were dying of boredom caused by the inertia of giantism and that I had not come across a single British company that provided a vision for their workers by incorporating the pursuit of honest profits with a sense of social awareness. They may well be out there, but I have never found them.

When I was invited to address the Marketing Society I told them that I thought marketing departments primarily provided camouflage for lazy or worn-out executives. When the advertising agency J Walter Thompson asked me to give a speech to their major accounts, I bartered and got them to agree to design a series of posters for one of our environmental campaigns. Then I delivered a speech entitled 'Why I would never use an advertising agency'. That was fun: I loved them for allowing me to do it. So all these high-powered advertising people and their clients sat with fixed smiles while I told them that I didn't think succeeding in business without advertising was any big deal.

A Woman's Place

None of these statements, particularly coming from a woman, was calculated to win me many friends. Despite the great strides that women have made in recent years, we are still second-class citizens in many areas of business and the top echelons of industry are still closed to women. How many women are there in senior positions in engineering or the petrochemical industry? How many women bank managers are there? Precious few.

With more media interest and more media exposure it might seem, superficially, that women in business are rapidly achieving true equality. But I do not believe women have a chance in hell of achieving their deserved status and power in business within the foreseeable future. My daughters might see it, but I won't.

The reason is that corporations are largely created by men, for men, often influenced by military or public school models. Hierarchical structures built on authority remain unchanged, and many men find it difficult to accept the rise of women to top management positions – perhaps because they have never learned to deal with women other than as secretaries, wives, girlfriends, mothers or adjuncts to themselves.

Male-dominated cultures set up difficult hurdles for women. Much business is conducted in formal and informal clubs, from which women are usually excluded, and criteria for promotion are based on male values. Women have to keep proving themselves by a process of constant education, whereas men can still earn a living in their fifties on skills acquired in their early twenties. It is little wonder that women become frustrated, particularly when they can claim credit for many innovations like flexitime, cafeteria benefit plans, creches and day care, not to mention the general humanization of the workplace.

Why are we always called naïve and innocent; why aren't we just right? There are those men who tend to view The Body Shop as nothing more than an ephemeral business phenomenon, a flash in the commercial pan that will collapse and disappear even more quickly than it mushroomed around the world. They patronize our proselytizing, our environmental campaigning, our social welfare policies, our constant talk of putting love where our labour is. The big mistake they make is to equate our feminine values with weakness and inefficiency. What they do not realize is that while The Body Shop is founded on principles generally alien to mainstream business, it none the less operates according to strict criteria in terms of marketing and customer care and motivation and all the other elements that combine to make a successful retail business. The public perception of The Body Shop is that we are a bit loony; the perception within the company is that we are cautious and responsible, particularly in controlling our growth.

I do not believe women have a chance in hell of achieving their deserved status and power in business within the foreseeable future. My daughters might see it, but I won't.

It always amazes me that anyone can believe that The Body Shop can have grown from one shop to more than six hundred shops around the world in less than fifteen years without being an efficient and well-run business. The fact that we have grown with compassion, love and a sense of fun does not negate our business efficiency, neither does the fact that we have never employed anyone from Harvard business school or Procter and Gamble, have never had a marketing department and have never paid for a single product-based advertisement. We are not a bunch of bleeding hearts who have somehow stumbled into a successful business. We know how to run a business. OK, we do it differently, but we do it well.

We might not advertise, but we market our products brilliantly, whether it is through striking store window promotions, by linking products to political and social messages, or by taking a high profile in the community. From the day when I opened the first store in Brighton,

we have used the power of the press to promote The Body Shop. It's only because I'm always available to the media for interviews; at a conservative estimate, we probably rack up about £2 million worth of free publicity a year from editorial coverage. We are like kids in school, always putting up our hand and saying listen to us, we have something to say, we've got a viewpoint.

A handle on the headlines

We do our research ourselves, we know the market we are in and we don't diversify. We don't necessarily want to have a shop on every high street, like Benetton, and we want to retain our sense of fun. Customers can never actually predict what they will find in the windows of The Body Shop – it might be a funny promotion for one of our products or a

No one – not even our most cynical critics – can deny that we are passionate in everything we say and do.

picture of a devastated tribe in the rainforest. We talk with our customers rather than at them. By creating conversation instead of branding, we let our customers spread our message by word of mouth with their friends and neighbours. It is they who do our advertising for us. As to our passion, no one – not even our most cynical critics – can deny that we are passionate in everything we say and do: The Body Shop positively radiates passion. I can't bear to be around people who are bland or bored or uninterested (or to employ them). The kind of brain-dead, gum-chewing assistants you find in so many shops drive me wild. I want everyone who works for us to feel the same excitement that I feel; to share my passion for education and customer care and communication and motivation and to put it into practice.

Rapping and Wrapping

We want people in our shops who care, who are enthusiastic, who like trading, who enjoy rapping and don't mind wrapping. Working in a Body Shop is a bit like being in a show – it's a performance, and so we want people who are actors and actresses and like to perform. These are the values I admire. Working with us is also like being part of a family. Despite our size we have desperately tried to maintain a sense of family within the company, a sense that we are all in it together, that it is ours, that we have all helped to make it. They want the family to survive so they don't abuse the system, and try desperately to do a good job.

I don't want to have to tell people why it is important to keep the shops clean, to display products well, to treat customers courteously and to know the answers to their questions. I want them to accept all these requirements as a natural part of their working lives. We know about customer care in The Body Shop because we are all customers. We know how we want to be treated when we go into a shop, so that's how we treat our customers. You don't need any expertise, there isn't any secret and no skill required. It's really very, very simple.

What thrills me when I go into a shop – any shop, it doesn't have to be mine – is first to be acknowledged. I was in a department store at Christmas and there were some Australian part-timers working there and it was a joy to be served by them. They were polite, amusing and attentive; nothing was too much trouble and they knew about the merchandise. What more could any customer ask? I've never met an Australian shop assistant who wasn't perfect.

I might be the managing director of The Body Shop, but I am also every customer. Every time I go into one of my stores I want to be thrilled by what I see and by the people I meet. I want to be delighted and surprised, and not bored. When I go into someone else's store I want to be treated as I would be in my own store. I want to be acknowledged, I want the place to be meticulously clean, I want the staff to be friendly and helpful and knowledgeable. I think every customer is like me. If you lose sight of that, you lose sight of a basic trading principle.

Our customers are generally classless, mostly female and mostly under thirty-five. An enormous number are in the under-seventeen age bracket and they are probably our strongest and most loyal group. They not only stick with us, but they introduce their mothers to Body Shop products, perhaps weaning them away from the big brand-name cos-

metics. The customers we definitely do not see are those women who want to spend £50 for an ounce of moisture cream in the mistaken belief that they will be made young again.

Customer care is the number one priority in the retail trade. If you make your product good and you make your store a pleasant place to be in, people won't object to paying your prices. But above all you have got to have staff who

A view of the future

know about customer care. If the customer is pleased, the staff are pleased, I am pleased and we are all happy. It's all a question of service.

The Green Machine

On top of all that, we believe that consumers are increasingly saying they want more than just honest products – they want to feel sympathy with the company trading in those products. In response, many trading companies are now fighting to clamber aboard the green bandwagon and are loudly proclaiming their brand-new, shining green products and policies. I would be happier if I thought they were motivated by real concern for the environment rather than, as I suspect, a desire to increase sales.

I was not in the least surprised by the upsurge of the Green movement in the eighties. What surprised me was how long it took for the media and politicians to cotton on to it. Women who had gone through the war knew all about recycling, refilling and keeping their costs down. Everybody's mum did it all the time.

When the environmental movement started shouting the same thing, at first the media and the politicians did not listen and categorized environmentalists as brown rice and sandal freaks with a screw loose. They sneered at them. Not until they got a word they could lock on to, an expression they understood, like 'Green consumer', did their brain cells slip out of neutral.

The Body Shop is, and always has been, an unashamedly Green company, but for us it was never in any sense a bandwagon; it was a simple expression of our core values and beliefs, values that are constantly policed by our customers and staff more diligently than any other organization I know.

I was not in the least surprised by the upsurge of the Green movement in the eighties. What surprised me was how long it took for the media and politicians to cotton on to it.

Apart from all the moral arguments, the great advantage for a company with values is that your staff will love you for it. When we get together now and talk about the 'early days', we swap endless do-you-remember stories like a Darby and Joan Club reunion, even though the early days were only ten or twelve years ago. Story-telling about the first campaigns and the first community projects intermingled with trading is now part of our culture.

However, we mustn't be complacent. What worries me now is that within the company there is an umbrella of corporate goodness which some people are hiding under, saying I work for The Body Shop, therefore I am sincere, good, caring, humane and so on. It really depresses me. The mere fact of working for The Body Shop is not enough; what counts is what else you do while you are working for us.

It is, of course, the luxury of our healthy earnings that allows us to pursue an aggressive policy of social and environmental activism. Although both Gordon and I wholeheartedly support all our campaigning we would never sanction any of it if we could not afford it, or if it somehow endangered the future prosperity of the company. Our core values, of course, are unaffected: whether or not we have high or low earnings, we would still be a humane and caring company.

In fact, we do not lash out money left, right and centre; in some ways the very reverse is true. I have a really tight-fisted sense of housekeeping, which is even more acute during the current recession. When you start something off yourself you are more likely to be worried about waste than are those staff who were not there at the beginning, when you were struggling to survive. Gordon and I have never lost the sense of outrage we felt at the beginning when we thought we were being misused, or our time and money were being wasted. I get really pissed off when staff don't care about things like turning lights off. Cutting down waste is no more than good housekeeping. I'll suddenly have a blitzkrieg on paper wastage or office furniture. I stormed into the Sundries Department like a virago one day because they were not printing brochures on both sides of the paper and they were using plastic folders instead of ordinary cardboard. Gordon is now talking about running the company without an office, just a chair which will move from department to department.

We are also obsessive about cleanliness and I am very bugged by carelessness – by people doing things like spilling coffee on the carpet at new offices. Coffee stains do not rank high on my list of global concerns, but it is a symbol, a metaphor, for a whole way of thinking, a lack of housekeeping and a lack of care. We talk about being lean and Green, but I can see a fat cat mentality creeping in: the paper is wasted, the lights left on after meetings. What it comes down to is arrogance. We have to keep an eye out for that soft, smug attitude which says we think we're so brilliant, so successful, that anything we do is all right – that really infuriates me.

One of the problems in the retail trade is that until recently sales staff had a very low status. Before the war it was different: it was a high-status, quite snooty, occupation; you had to be firmly middle class to work in a store like Harrods. The end of the apprenticeship system, falling standards and low pay all combined to change the status of sales staff after the war. The fact that the retail trade largely employed women and was part of the service industry, which had never really valued labour, also contributed to a lowering of esteem.

Only when the nature of the high street began to change from serving everyday needs, with tobacconists, grocers, butchers and bakers, to feeding the needs of fashion-conscious young people with money to spend, did the status of retail selling begin to change. The consumer boom hastened the process by which the brand names and chains pushed the traditional shops out of the high street and it became more attractive as a workplace – but not necessarily as a place to shop.

Staff meeting

If you have a company with itsy-bitsy vision you have an itsy-bitsy company.

In The Body Shop we have, proportionately, more university graduates among our shop staff than in our top management. We don't attract people who are just 'cash and wraps' any more; if we do, they don't last. Personally what I am looking for is people like me, because I know that if they're like me then I've got to keep them entertained, keep them informed, keep their minds so exercised that they want to stay. That is my responsibility to them.

They are looking for leadership that has vision. If you have a company with itsy-bitsy vision you have an itsy-bitsy company. You have to look at leadership through the eyes of the followers and you have to live the message. What I have learned is that people become motivated when you guide them to the source of their own power and when you make heroes out of employees who best personify what you want to see in the organization.

Ninety per cent of the people running our shops have no formal business training whatsoever, yet they are brilliant business people and brilliant retailers because they don't think that business is about sitting behind a desk pushing paper. Actually, the day I realized my employees did their jobs better than I could was the day I began to carve out a new role for myself in the company.

I couldn't run one of our shops now the way I did when I started in

1976. Now you have got to be computer-literate, you have got to be able to look after fourteen or fifteen staff, you have to be a mother-figure to them and you have got to know how to motivate them. In addition to all that you have got to keep the shop looking pristine, you have to know enough about all the products to answer the most extraordinary questions from customers, and you have to be involved in our campaiging on social and environmental issues.

This happy franchisee started out as a shop staffer

When we are looking for staff we don't take much account of scholastic background (although many of them *are* high academic achievers). We want to know *who* they are, what kind of people they are, rather than how many pieces of paper they have. We hope they have got some GCSEs, but it is more important to us to know the kind of music they like, or the books they read, or how they spend their spare time. We can tell far more about people that way than we can from their academic qualifications. The one stipulation is that they have got to love us and what we do, and so they have got to know more about us than that we sell skin and hair care products and don't test on animals.

There is a similarly rigorous selection procedure for franchise holders. It includes a personality test, a home visit and a series of interviews and assessments to establish the candidate's business acumen and attitudes towards people and environmental issues.

Energise!

You have got to have energy to work with us and you have got to have a sense of curiosity, but what I particularly like is to find people who are bright enough to want more, who can see that there are ways of getting more within the company, who can learn and grow and be somebody, who take all the information and education we give them and run with it and challenge the management. We have always believed in widening the window of opportunity for everyone who works for us, whether they are making paper in Nepal or packing in the Littlehampton warehouse. Self-empowerment is the aim.

I have always been baffled by the tendency of many big companies to treat their workforce like children. Outside the workplace they are responsible citizens – they are husbands and wives and parents and house-owners. But the minute they get to work they are treated as irresponsible kids who have to be constantly supervised and cajoled.

The one aspect of recruitment which is absolutely vital in an entrepreneurial organization, and doesn't receive anything like enough attention, is to learn to love the person who irritates you. Tap the energy of the anarchist and he will be the one to push your company ahead. I believe they will be the future custodians of the culture of this company. I don't think they are going to be found among the ranks of managers and executives – the custodians of our culture will be found among the young kids who are joining us now for reasons beyond just wanting a job.

'Self-empowerment is the aim'

'If you employ people with small thinking and small ideas, you become a company of dwarves.' David Ogilvy said this and how right he is. If an organization's response to new ideas is encouraging, appreciative and supportive, that keeps the workforce interested and innovative better than any material rewards would. If new ideas are constantly turned down, it turns people off: they stop generating ideas, no matter how much you pay them. An organization needs commitment to common goals and shared values, and must be built on communication and shared responsibility, but it also needs innovation.

Leading from Behind

I believe that one of our major strengths – leadership – is one of the major weaknesses in other companies. Leadership is not commandership – it is about managing the future. The principal forces which motivate a leader are an incredibly high need for personal achievement and a different vision of the world – one who marches to a different drumbeat, who does not see himself as part of the mainstream, is essentially an outsider. You don't necessarily have to be charismatic, you just have to believe in what you are doing so strongly that it becomes a reality.

A fundamental shortcoming in much of business today is that the leadership lacks vision and passion – the two most important ingredients to inspire and motivate. In The Body Shop we have both in abundance and we possess, in addition, a further secret ingredient: an extraordinary level of optimism, almost amounting to euphoria, which permeates the whole company. We are incurable optimists – and incurable optimists believe they can do anything.

Leaders in the business world should aspire to be true planetary citizens. They have global responsibilities since their decisions affect not just the world of business, but world problems of poverty, national security and the environment. Many, sad to say, duck these responsibilities, because their vision is material rather than moral.

Authority to lead should be founded on a moral vision rather than a desire to create the biggest or the richest company in the world. I don't understand how anybody can be a leader without a clearly defined moral vision. If your ambitions and interests do not extend beyond the role of making money or expanding your business, as far as I am concerned you are morally bankrupt.

I think the leadership of a company should encourage the next generation not just to follow, but to overtake.

In The Body Shop our obsessive vision since 1984, when we went on to the stock market, has been to act as a force for social change. We are embarked, essentially, on an experiment designed to prove that a successful business can take on board a whole slew of social responsibilities, that it can divert energy and resources to areas completely divorced from its principal trading activity, and yet can still be extraordinarily successful and satisfy its shareholders.

Although we have now become a global brand and a global business, it is my view that this experiment will have been a failure if we start to resemble, in any way, the other global brands and global businesses, most particularly those soulless and faceless multinational giants. We do not want to follow them; we want them to follow us and to realize, above all, that a social conscience is not incompatible with profit.

I don't think leaders gain respect by artificial status, by fancy titles, by having parking spaces allotted closest to the factory door or by having their own luxurious dining room.

I think the leadership of a company should encourage the next generation not just to follow, but to overtake. The duty of leadership is to put forward ideas, symbols and metaphors of the way it should be done, so that the next generation can work out new and better ways of doing the job. The complaint Gordon and I have is that we are not being overtaken by our staff. We would like to be able to say, 'We can't keep up with you guys', but it is not happening. They should be annoying us, irritating us, questioning us.

One of the greatest failings in most organizations is that there is no one to tell the emperor he has no clothes. Leaders must develop mechanisms that provide dissonant information and surround decision-makers with people who can operate effectively in the role of devil's advocate. One of the most effective ways of doing this is to encourage *lèse-majesté* from your staff, by hollering and hooting, by what you wear, by the language you use, by taking the symbols of authority and challenging them all the time.

In The Body Shop you don't get noticed by being a stuffed shirt or by being over-polite. You get noticed by being funny or passionate or working your buns off. I don't think leaders gain respect by artificial status, by fancy titles, by having parking spaces allotted closest to the factory door or by having their own luxurious dining room.

Leaders should not be 'holier than thou': they should have flair and a sense of fun, but most of all they should be a Pandora's Box of ideas, offering others the means of taking an idea, opening a door and going through by themselves. Leaders who are also entrepreneurs create new rules, throw out stereotypes, succeed for themselves. Three components make up an entrepreneur: the person, the idea and the resources to make it happen. It is the quality of the person and the integrity of the idea that matters most. For an entrepreneur the most important thing is his vision of something new and his determination to see how far that vision or idea will go. He is both a dreamer and a doer, and he welcomes change because he recognizes that constant change provides constant new opportunities.

In The Body Shop we believe that everything is subject to change and we have learned to love change. Personally, I love to find new ideas. I stay in to the 'alternative' business grapevine to find out what is going on, and I will go anywhere to talk to people who say they are doing things in a better way, in case we can adopt or adapt it. I am a courier of ideas and information for my staff, always rushing back and bursting into meetings to say I have seen the most amazing new management system or the most incredible new training method.

Follow My Bliss

The bliss of my job is networking – finding people with visions similar to mine, or even greater. Through an organization called the Foresight Group, which promotes new business ideas, I recently came across a Brazilian businessman called Ricardo Semler who has turned the management structure of his company upside-down. Semler is the president of Brazil's largest marine and food-processing machinery manufacturer. His basic theory is that staff should be treated like responsible adults and not like children. The vast majority of his eight hundred workers set their own hours and hire their managers, who in turn set their own salaries and bonuses.

I gave Gordon a tape of a lecture by Semler. He played it in his car on his way to work and told me later that he almost drove off the road because he was laughing so much. What he was saying fitted so perfectly with our feelings about business. But he realized at the same time that some of Semler's ideas made a lot of sense and we are now experimenting with some of them, primarily reducing the pyramid of our organization into a much flatter structure with only three layers – the heads of departments, managers and shop floor. All new managers and supervisors will be interviewed by those who will be working under them, so that they will never be in a situation of arriving for work on Monday saying 'Who is this guy who has been put in charge of us?'

I can never understand why, when a idea pops out of my head, it cannot materialize immediately.

What is frustrating, and consistently astonishing to me, is how slow everything is and how long it takes to action a new idea, even in The Body Shop. I can never understand why, when an idea pops out of my head, it cannot materialize immediately. It is in my nature to want to get things done straightaway, I hate to wait for anything, whether it is a bus or the introduction of a new management strategy. It is the same when I travel. I never take time to acclimatize, no matter how long the journey or how many time zones I cross. I plan every flight so that there is just enough time to get to wherever I have to go. Then I do what I have to do and move on without hanging about. It is the only reason I travel first-class: I know that when I arrive at any destination I'm going to go straight to work, so I need to arrive in reasonable shape.

Another way I protect myself is with music. I think the Walkman was one of the great inventions of the eighties, and it certainly helped me to rediscover the joy of music on long-haul flights. It has not only brought me an enormous amount of pleasure, but it helps me relax.

I spend at least five months of the year travelling, visiting shops, trading, searching for new ideas and ingredients, but when I am at home many people would think my life is pretty routine and uneventful. Gordon and I live in a village about ten minutes' drive from our head office in Littlehampton. We have had the same house for more than ten years and it is comfortable rather than luxurious. In the evenings we often have people round to talk business over dinner; if it is just Gordon and me at home then dinner is of the 'twenty things to do with a can of tunafish' variety. Our social life really revolves around our family and the same friends – many of them now work in the company – we have had for years. We *never* go to so-called celebrity events. What I most like to do is to talk, to gather together twenty of thirty interesting people – painters, musicians, writers, anthropologists or whatever – and get a lively discussion going over a few bottles of wine. For me, that's bliss.

When Gordon and I are both in England we drive in to work together, always arriving by nine o'clock. We have completely separate offices because our responsibilities are so different. They're at separate ends of one part of the building, and the corridor between is often the scene of discussions, meetings, arguments – all conducted on the

move. I spend most of my time on staff and press relations and product development. I am a great spreader-outer, organizing everything into piles which I then edit ruthlessly. I have two assistants who organize my diary and fill every minute of the day, mostly with one meeting after another. I love to be busy, but I do think we all spend too much time in meetings – that's something I would like to change if it was possible. Very little of what I do is in isolation, and there is a whole cabal of people close to me in the company whom I can call in to bounce ideas off or to solicit their opinion.

Lunch is always a sandwich and an apple in my office, and we rarely leave before about seven or eight. I am the worst person in the world when it comes to looking after myself – I never diet and never take exercise, although I am aware that I am overweight. I tend to think that any time I spend on myself is wasted, so I'd never go to a beauty parlour or take up meditation – it would drive me crazy. I might go to a hairdresser to have my roots done, but that's about it – and even then I'll want them to work fast.

People often ask me if I only use my own products. It always amuses me. Of *course* – how could I sell skin and hair care products that I did not use myself? It would be completely dishonest.

Apart from movies, which I adore, I don't really have any compelling interests outside the business. It doesn't bother me; I am completely fulfilled by my work. Gordon is mad about polo and plays almost every weekend when he can; it is his one indulgence. Sometimes I'll go along to watch; I don't mind it in small doses, but I'm not a rider myself. I think my legs are too short to get them over a horse.

As a family we're not extravagant – we don't hanker after jewels or fur coats or fancy cars or yachts or foreign villas – and I watch the housekeeping and keep an eye on the bills. Justine and Samantha have got their own flat and their own lives, but they spend quite a bit of time with us at weekends. We've got a holiday house in Scotland which in some ways we think of as our real home. It's a wonderful old turreted place and we get up there whenever we can – whenever we feel we need a break. Gordon rides and I explore on a bicycle and cook huge Italian meals, particularly if we have invited friends to stay.

When I am in England I always work on Sundays. I love to go into the office when there is no one else there and snoop into every department, seeing what is going on. In the winter it is always freezing cold because the heating is switched off, but it never bothers me. I wrap up in a thick coat and scarf, make myself a big mug of steaming coffee and walk around the place with my nose getting redder and redder.

The thought that every day might be my last, and the desire to make the most of every moment, drives me on.

I have always said that I would rather wear out than rust to death and, thank God, I still seem to have as much energy now as when I started the first shop in 1976. I think the older you get the more you realize that this is no dress rehearsal, so you feel you want to put more into life. I am always astonished and grateful, when I wake up in the morning, to be alive. The thought that every day might be my last, and the desire to make the most of every moment, drives me on.

Ever since I was a small girl I have always had an abhorrence of death. I am not of the Buddhist school of thought which says that death is a passage to another life. I want to know what is happening in this world, not the next. Balancing a fear of death with living life as if you have only got one day left certainly concentrates the mind.

Public, Face, Private Foibles

Another dilemma for me, a really personal dilemma, is that I am always seen as a strong character. Yet the truth is that behind that façade I am a bloody wobbly individual, full of neuroses and fears. I don't think I get loved enough, not at all; when you are constantly told that the world loves you, you start to ask yourself who really loves you. I feel as if I am surrounded by a lot of detached admiration, detached curiosity and detached fear. I am also terrified of flying; even though I fly thousands of miles every year it never gets any easier. If there is a bump or an unexplained noise I'm a complete mumbling mess. Maybe it's God's way of punishing me for my past sins.

When I went to Romania, for instance, and witnessed the suffering of children and helpless people, I was devastated, both emotionally and physically. I get emotionally strung up about the fate of indigenous peoples, such as the Yanomamis and Kayapo in Brazil – I've seen their innocence and worth at first hand, and I've also seen the forces ranged against them. Against all this, I get impatient when comfortable, employed people bleat on about 'stress'.

Although we are a paternalistic and caring company, we don't keep anybody who isn't doing a proper day's work. That would be stupid. However, I think that probably the most frequent mistake Gordon and I make is that we tend to keep people longer than we should, constantly trying to find somewhere for them to fit in. Gordon is much more generous-spirited than I am. If someone is not working or is downright lazy I'll say to him, 'Look, it's not worth keeping this guy. He's got to go', but he'll say, 'Well, hang on, let's make sure he's just not in the wrong job. . . ' Sometimes it is entirely our own fault. We bring someone in on an idea and they don't run with it, or the idea doesn't materialize, or it is too soon, too far ahead of its time.

As far as my job is concerned, I think the only real stress is living up to the expectations of my staff. I am supposed to be a role model and a breath of fresh air; I am supposed to be able to make them feel they can do anything in their lives, that they can learn in business, grow and be somebody. The fact that I was just a teacher and I started The Body

Shop from scratch with no business experience makes the concept of success very accessible to them. But it is quite something to live up to.

In The Body Shop 75 per cent of the staff is under thirty and female. To run a company with a young, predominantly female staff trading in the tactile business of skin and hair care needs leadership that goes beyond just being there – it needs hands-on, heart-engaged, operational leadership. One of the problems is that everyone wants me to visit their shop, but now that we've got nearly six hundred round the world it is physically impossible to get round to every one. An assistant came up to me the other day and said, 'Look, I work in Brent Cross. Isn't it about time you came to see us?' Certainly it was, but there is a limit to the time I can spend visiting shops, even those close to home.

We are now making an in-house weekly video series called *Body Shop TV*, which will go out to all the stores and keep everyone in touch with what is going on in the company. In the future I foresee us definitely going into satellite television as a means of communication. If we have got two thousand stores around the world in the next century, it is the natural route to take.

Going Visiting

When I do visit a store it is quite a ritual, very well planned and orchestrated. The staff are all alerted and asked to think about the questions they want to put to me. Then I get a package of information about the store – how long it has been open, background about the manager, remarkable things the store has done, any quirky little events or personal snippets of information associated with it. For the visit itself I always look exactly as they expect me to look: I never disappoint them – or at least I hope I don't. I'm usually in jeans, always look a mess, always carry a knapsack and certainly don't look like a managing director. They take me round and I listen to their ideas and tell them about what is coming up, products in the pipeline, things that even the product development department have not told them about. It is chat chat chat, lots of stories and jokes, lots of laughter and lots of anecdotes.

My favourite products

Then I take them off into a room on their own and ask them a whole series of probing questions. Have we failed you? Are you embarrassed

The Body Shop's yin and yang

by any of the things we do? Are you comfortable with some of the social messages we are putting across? What about education? Do you feel we are challenging you enough? Have we missed the boat on anything? Are we kind to you? What more can we do for you?

After that, we turn it round and they can ask me any questions they like. The things they often want to hear about are stories from my travels, the things that embarrass me – the time I had to pull my pants down to show the Arab women my pubic hair, when I had to sit naked in a hut with Japanese pearl divers. So I tell them all these things and after a bit they are all speechless with laughter. They want to know about the next projects, the upcoming campaigns, what happened in Brazil and what happened when we went to Romania. I usually try to get them on to things that they can chat about among themselves.

If there are problems, it is invariably the management or the franchise who are at fault. If I can, I deal with them on the spot. If that is not possible, I tell them to get hold of the area manager and insist on getting some answers. I tell them to grab him by his lapels and say, 'What the hell's going on here?' We have a very good support system of area managers – people going in to talk, to check what is going on, to pass on information and motivate the staff. Sometimes, if a shop isn't right, we'll send in a whole team to redesign it and get it working.

Gordon rarely accompanies me on shop visits because we are each more comfortable in our own chosen roles of high profile and low profile. Outsiders often think of Gordon as a shadowy figure but that is certainly not how he is viewed within The Body Shop. He is well known to everyone, much loved and deeply respected as the real strength of the company. Our relationship bequeathed a very distinct management style to the company – loosely structured, collaborative, imaginative and improvisatory, rather than by the book – which matured as the company expanded. I think Gordon provides a sense of constancy and continuity while I bounce around breaking the rules, pushing back the boundaries of possibility and shooting off my mouth. We rarely argue, and if we do it is never about values. He sometimes finds my style too loud and strident, but I think I have toned down a bit because he hasn't complained for some time. Although Gordon makes what I mouth about happen, he only does so when he deems it to be a sensible course of action for the company. His calm presence and enormous influence are rarely taken into account by critics, who see The Body Shop as a flaky organization led by a madwoman with frizzy hair.

'Do you feel we are challenging you enough?'

The Heart of the Matter

I do sometimes think that I am rather isolated within the business community. I *love* retailing, I *love* trading, I salivate at the prospect of knocking on the door of like-minded companies – Patagonia, or Rhino Records, or Ben and Jerry's – and talking trading, talking ideas, I love that. But the business aspect, the science of finance doesn't grab me. When the analysts come to lunch they have to drag me there – I'm like a kid, sulking. But I give my show, I perform and then clear off.

I never want to be psychoanalysed because I have a horror that if I start annotating and scientifically dissecting what I do I'll lose everything that goes with a sense of instinct – the ideas, the sense of not knowing how big this company is or not wanting to know. Ever since I had an instinctive feeling when I was a child that my 'uncle' was my father I have learned to trust that instinct; when you go through something like that nothing budges you from clinging to your instinct.

People often say you're a businesswoman, by the tenets of that you should know exactly what the price-earnings ratio of your shares is. I say I haven't a clue, because I'm not interested. I am also not interested in my salary; I am forty-eight years old and I am honestly not sure how much I earn – nor do I really care. Why is it that success is measured in terms of wealth? If you're successful and wealthy you can end up like a baby having your backside wiped for you. I never want to be like that. I think there is a kind of survival instinct that protects me from understanding the nuts and bolts of business information. It seems to me that if you're not interested in profits and price – earnings ratios, your mind can expand towards hundreds of other things.

I love what I am doing now. It is like a dream come true, but I can't believe how easy it has been. I can't understand what's so hot-shit about putting up products that are good and visually exciting and effective and having staff well trained and loving the product. I can't see why it should be such a problem. Justine said to me the other day, 'Mum, what's so different about what you're doing? It's so obvious.' That's true. It's not extraordinary – it's obvious.

YOU EDUCATE PEOPLE, ESPECIALLY YOUNG PEOPLE, BY STIRRING THEIR PASSIONS. SO YOU TAKE EVERY OPPORTUNITY TO GRAB THE IMAGINATION OF YOUR EMPLOYEES, YOU GET THEM TO FEEL THEY ARE DOING SOMETHING IMPORTANT, THAT THEY ARE NOT A LONE VOICE, THAT THEY ARE THE MOST POWERFUL AND POTENT PEOPLE ON THE PLANET.

11

TOWARDS THE NEW AGE?

Despite the world's considerable problems, I look forward to the last decade of this century with some optimism. I do so particularly when its promise is viewed against the bleak moral and spiritual landscape of the eighties, the age of aggressive avarice, when greed was good and productive labour was epitomized by the sight of a man in shirtsleeves sitting in front of a television screen moving billions of dollars from London to Tokyo. For me, the depressing clarion call of the decade was perfectly articulated by Milton Friedman, when he decreed that the only social responsibility of business was to make profits for its shareholders. This dictum, from a Nobel Prize winner and the most influential economist since John Maynard Keynes and arguably since Marx, was enthusiastically embraced by corporate managers, business schools, the business press and the financial community.

In this barren environment, the concept of doing good was perceived as incredibly wimpish and somehow incompatible with success. The notion of making a moral decision rather than an economic one was risible. The idea that values might matter at least as much as, if not more than, the bottom line was perceived to be positively ludicrous.

In some ways none of this was surprising, because the eighties represented a backlash against the dross of the seventies, when there was nothing much to look forward to and the backdrop of daily life was unremittingly depressing, with recession, unemployment, the three-day week and nuclear fears dominating our lives. All those evenings sitting listening to Johnny Rotten droning 'No Future' took their toll.

The eighties opened, as I recall, notably low on thrill, unless it was the emergence of 'gimme' capitalism and the supposition that the first duty of business was to look after Number One. As the decade pro-

The ideas I stand for are not mine. I borrowed them from Mahatma Gandhi. I swiped them from Ralph Nader. I stole them from Walt Whitman. I captured them from Martin Luther King. And I put some of them in this book. If you don't like their rules, whose would you use?

(with acknowledgement to Dale Carnegie)

gressed, it became more and more evident that the new brutalism of the capitalist system was excluding more and more people from sharing in its benefits. New words – aids, glasnost, yuppie, Filofax – were added to our lexicon; old words – crack, greenhouse, solidarity – were given new meanings. We discovered, in the world atlas, the whereabouts of places like Bhopal, Chernobyl and Tiananmen Square. It was a decade in which Ethiopia and Sudan turned browner, while developed countries turned greener. And then, as the eighties drew to a close, we sat transfixed in front of our televisions and witnessed events that our political leaders said would never happen in our lifetime.

Veracity vs. Voracity

Throughout this turbulent period there were a few businesses – The Body Shop was one – swimming against the tide of institutionalized self-interest. These corporate non-conformists clung tenaciously to the belief that there was a better, gentler, kinder way of conducting business, that their responsibilities extended far beyond making profits. Their paradigm was enlightened capitalism, with people inherent in the process rather than excluded from it.

One of our duties was to ask questions. Why does a tree have value when it is chopped down and not when it is sending, giving us oxygen? Why is it considered productive labour for a man to sit in front of a computer screen moving money around the world, while it is considered unproductive for a woman in the rainforest to fetch wood, gather wild vegetables and prepare food? Why, with the melting of the cold war, are international arms dealers stepping up their marketing efforts in Third World countries – countries which desperately need to develop trade.

The corporate non-conformists proselytized vigorously to put idealism back on the agenda, but at first no one listened. One problem was that the media, with its tendency to trivialize everything, was not interested in our message. The media worshipped wealth to such an extent that there was something mildly obscene about it. Corporate raiders were sexy and interesting to the media, junk bonds and robber barons were sexy, the Donald Trumps of the world were sexy...but companies that actually strived to do good were considered boring. Throwing five hundred people out of work was news; helping five hundred people in a community care project was no news.

My great bone of contention with the media was that it was possible to make the activities of the few corporate do-gooders both interesting and entertaining. I believed they had a responsibility to report the fact that there were alternative ways to run a business. The media disagreed.

I was constantly baffled by the fact that I would be considered a newsworthy entrepreneur if I behaved in ways which I thought immoral – like most of the robber barons of the eighties – yet I was viewed with suspicion because I was always rabbiting about values and altruism and social responsibility and doing things differently. They seemed to believe that there was some hidden agenda and that our real motive was to increase sales.

We were stuck up on some sort of pedestal, either to be ridiculed or admired – but rarely, alas, copied.

I was similarly baffled by our isolation. I had set up a business which was clearly successful, which showed that people could actually be happy in their work, which operated on caring principles and made excellent profits. I thought people would flock to our door to find out how we did it, so they could introduce similar ideas in their own companies. It did not happen. Instead, we were stuck up on some sort of pedestal, either to be ridiculed or admired – but rarely, alas, copied. Individuals listened to what we were saying and applauded; companies generally did not bother.

None the less, towards the end of the decade we began at last to sense that a change was coming, belated but still welcome. The loadsamoney culture was slowly but inexorably replaced by an emerging culture of conscience as the fashionable totems and icons of the eighties – power-dressing and Porsches, champagne-swilling yuppies and money brokers – became subjects of ridicule rather than envy.

The marketplace recognized that something was happening, that we were perhaps approaching a new age of enlightenment, the last great gasp of the century. I personally felt, at the end of the decade, that a base had been built for something big to happen in the nineties, a revival of social activism coupled with an increased level of concern for the environment. It seemed to me that the angry protestors of the sixties had metamorphosed into the concerned citizens of the nineties, with a vision of the future and a passion for the moment.

I am convinced that environmentalism will develop into a major political movement.

The realisation dawned that the future of the planet was at stake and that warnings from environmentalists were chapters in the greatest suspense story ever told – whether or not the human species would survive. I am convinced that environmentalism will develop into a major political movement, just as conservatism and liberalism did in the past, and that it will grow into a force that will make the civil rights, anti-war and women's movements look minuscule and insignificant by comparison.

Business must play its part. In The Body Shop we believe, more fervently than any other company or multinational of which I am aware, that environmentalism will be the most important issue for business in the nineties. The principle of environmental performance must be a major priority for every business, big or small, if for no other reason than that it is impossible to make a more tangible stake in the future.

Renewable resources have always been a company lodestone at The Body Shop, and we have run recycling and energy conservation schemes for years. But in 1989 we took an important step to keep our own back yard in order by commissioning an environmental audit of all the company's practices, focusing in particular on packaging, waste and effluents.

The development of new technologies means that constant monitoring is needed to ensure that the company stays abreast of the times. For example, we began using bio-degradable carrier bags at a time when it was thought to be the answer to the massive problem of non-degradable synthetic waste. We now know it was the right question, but the wrong answer. Using plastic rendered degradable did nothing to solve the problem of litter and only encouraged people to discard energy-rich materials. The audit enabled us to identify a waste material from our own manufacturing process, which formerly cost money to dispose of, and turn it into a resource: now Body Shop bags are made from recycled polyethylene, which can be reused or recycled again and again. We also introduced non-chlorine bleached cotton bags stamped with the word 'refillable' to encourage customers not to use carrier bags at all.

As a result of the audit, in 1990 The Body Shop became the first UK retailer to recycle its own post-consumer plastic waste. So far we manage to recover about a tonne of plastic bottles every month – a 40-foot lorry filled to the brim with plastic bottles – which are recycled instead of being thrown into a waste tip and using up precious land.

Recycled paper is used throughout the company – from letterheads to lavatory rolls – and we have a multitude of paper-saving schemes. All office staff are encouraged to write on both sides of the paper, and paper only used on one side is bound and turned into notepads. Facilities are provided for staff to recycle their newspapers, which are first made into bedding for horses and then turned into an excellent garden manure.

It is through dozens of schemes like this, continually monitored and updated, that we strive to limit our impact on the environment and also to set an example to our staff, our customers and other companies. We believe it is not enough, not nearly enough, to abide by existing environmental legislation – for the sake of future generations, business must take a lead.

Status Symbols Clash

One area in which it has been difficult to make progress is the thorny subject of company cars. I did not feel we could be the strongest environmental company and still use company cars as status symbols. I wanted it to be a status symbol in our company not to have a car, or to have a company bicycle, but every time I raised the subject it caused an outcry.

My argument was that people know about The Body Shop, they know what we stand for and what we believe, and if they come to work for us they have to share our values. If they are so anxious to have a company car then they can go and work for someone else. The other directors argued that if we introduced a no company car policy we would lose people. I said they were being paid enough to buy their own cars if they wanted to.

My feeling was that if we were so heavily environmental, why were we not doing something about the product that was causing most damage to the environment – the car? The motor industry, more than any other, has proved itself virtually useless at research and development to protect the environment.

I don't give a damn about cars, and for me it was a personal bandwagon, but there was a lot of resistance from the other directors; it was a real male ego reaction. When they said they lived so far from the office that they had to drive, I suggested that they should move. Even Gordon was opposed to my anti-car arguments at the beginning, although he came round eventually and started saying the same thing.

In the end, we compromised. While we encourage staff to use public transport or bicycles, we provide modest cars, mostly Volkswagen Golf Umwelts, which are the most energy-conscious, for employees who can demonstrate a real business need. All our company cars run on lead-free petrol and are capable of a minimum of 35 miles per gallon in urban areas. Gordon's company car is a Volkswagen, which I share. The first bit of advice I would give to any other company which expressed an interest in green issues would be to sell all the Jaguars and Daimlers driven by their directors.

As a result of our in-house campaigning on the car issue, more than 90 per cent of the staff working at our head office in Littlehampton and who live within a fifteen-mile radius arrive on foot, by bicycle or by public transport. Lobbying for improved public transport will be a major campaigning objective for the company in the future.

Making Global Corrections

In 1990 The Body Shop became the first cosmetics company in the world to employ an anthropologist in residence. Her remit is to research and catalogue disappearing tribes and collect social information on traditional methods of skin and hair care before the knowledge vanishes off the face of the earth.

In addition to collating a glossary of folkloric information on natural ingredients, we will be establishing links with anthropologists, ethnobotanists and indigenous tribal leaders throughout the world. If we save the planet's environmental diversity without preserving the rich diversity of cultures, we will have lost not only vital members of the human community but also a part of ourselves. By communicating the vanishing voices of endangered peoples, we can act to lobby governments, international organizations and oil and mineral companies so as to protect the global village. When governments like those of Brazil, Paraguay and China make it clear that they value economic development over the human rights of their indigenous peoples, something has got to be done to change their views – and soon.

I see businesses like ours becoming more involved politically. As The Body Shop grows, so will our influence. We are already challenging government decrees, lobbying for policy changes and mounting campaigns which are increasingly political. In the mid-1980s we were not political, but it was an easy, and perhaps inevitable, step to take from being a socially aware company to a political one. More than one observer of our operations has noted that the loyalty and commitment of our staff is more akin to that found among members of a political party than on the payroll of a corporation. We would never get that kind of motivation if we were just selling shampoo and body lotion.

By the end of 1990 The Body Shop had over 600 shops trading in 38 countries and in 18 languages; 1800 staff were directly employed, with a further 3500 employed by franchisees. In 1989 we manufactured 2.5 million kilos of products; in 1990 it was 4.6 million kilos. Our Training School ran 41 courses with just over 5000 delegates attending. We had a bigger presence abroad than any other British retailer, our overseas earnings more than doubled in the space of two years, and we were the

Companies I admire:

fastest-growing company in the UK personal care market. Applicants for franchises were beating down our door throughout the year.

To date, no other company offers us any serious competition. We get more serious irritation than serious competition because we are constantly having to go to court to protect our company and our name from being traduced by imitators. We are like a mother lion protecting its cubs when it comes to protecting our name, and we have a whole legal department which spends most of it time fighting copycats.

I see businesses like ours becoming more involved politically.

There are three or four companies which have clearly copied our products and our trading style, but they don't really offer us any competition because they are all so dull. The innovation just isn't there. Sometimes I get our Research and Development Department to nuke our imitators by simply changing the texture of our products – adding a new ingredient that no one else would think of adding. We look at these small copycat businesses very much as an irritation, but they present no threat in terms of taking over our position in the marketplace.

By any criteria The Body Shop is already a large and powerful organization, partly because we resisted all temptations to diversify, which spelled the death knell for so many businesses in the eighties. We do not have any dreams to build empires or to take over the UK retail industry, but there is no doubt that our growth in the eighties will be nothing compared to what will happen in the nineties, since we have barely begun to tap the overseas potential and we still do not know where the ceiling is. The United States could accommodate two thousand stores easily, while most European countries could probably sustain 350 stores each. We opened our first shop in Japan in 1990 – Tea Rose Shower Gel was the best-seller – and a minimum of forty further shops will open in that country before 1995. We certainly believe we are capable of sustaining a growth rate of 40–50 per cent per annum for perhaps the next five or ten years. By the end of the millenuium I believe there will be at least a thousand shops worldwide, all campaigning on social and environmental issues, all pressing for social change.

The Counter Revolution

It is my conviction that businesses and consumers, in tandem, can become a formidable engine of social change if their power is leveraged to focus on certain issues. Consumers have real power to effect change, by asking questions about source and manufacture, by demanding information and ultimately by the use of their feet and their wallets and shopping elsewhere. It really works. No matter how huge or distant the problem may seem, consumers can play a part in the solution of it if they act collectively. One person writing a protest letter might not achieve much; one hundred thousand people writing protest letters demand attention and action.

Some 28 million people, a very considerable consumer force, pass by our stores around the world every month, and we use our shop windows to educate and inform. Our shop windows are our only form of advertising – when we put a product in the window the sales rocket. But we have made a moral decision to use our social or environmental issues.

Our policy is to encourage our customers to use their power responsibly, to ask questions and be more critical in their purchasing habits. If we educate our customers, give them information about the source and effect of our products, they will make decisions more sensibly. If they learn about the efficacy of natural ingredients, products made from chemicals will seem less appealing. If they are made aware of the cruelty and pointlessness of testing on animals, they will seek products not tested on animals. If they realize the connection between certain products and major issues like the destruction of the rainforest, global pollution or the threat to primitive cultures, they will avoid those products.

Unfortunately, too many people are still bystanders. There are many reasons why they think they cannot make a difference, but usually it boils down to the fact that they are either not aware of their responsibilities or they simply don't know how to act. I personally believe that

Britain has failed to educate its citizens on their duties and their opportunities for participation; democracy is not, after all, a spectator sport and the citizen's role is to keep his, or her, mouth open.

Undoubtedly, the route to empowering the consumer is through education. Without being given the information the consumer cannot make responsible decisions, yet there are still too few companies making any real attempt to educate consumers; they only do so spuriously, by advertising, which is designed to create demand rather than provide information with which a customer can make a judgement. Advertising is, in any case, a monologue; in The Body Shop we prefer dialogue.

Society at the moment nurtures an economy in which the sellers work overtime to control their customers through advertising of ingenious complexity, rather than providing comparable information that nourishes rational choice. We, on the other hand, make everything explicit, from our ingredients to our values, so that our customers and investors are able to make informed decisions about whether or not they want to do business with us.

One of the liabilities of a free market economy is that plastic needs frequently overshadow real needs, so that the market is flooded with gadgets and gewgaws and daft inventions like electric toothbrushes. It is my belief that Green consumers will be less susceptible in the nineties to the temptations dangled by an industry dedicated to creating artificial needs and products to fill those needs.

The Mainstream Goes Green

Green consumers have already been prominent in forcing many companies to mend their ways, and they are going to be increasingly prominent in the New Age of the nineties. They will be looking for products which hurt no one, which damage nothing and which are produced by companies espousing the gentler values that they themselves espouse. Aware of the knock-on effect of what we are doing to others, to the environment, to the Third World and to the planet itself, they will demand information, want to know the story behind what they buy, how it was made, where and by whom. They want to feel sympathy not just with the product but with the process supporting it, how it is manufactured, presented and sold.

The groundswell of Green consumers has been gathering pace for some years, but it has yet to be matched by the growth of Green manufacturers and Green retailers. Their number is growing – they are, after all, meeting a demand – but let's hope that the 'greening' of the companies is permanent and heartfelt, and not just a commercial response to the marketplace. The Body Shop still stands largely alone in its support of Green issues, although I certainly never set out to attract Green consumers. They did not exist, at least not by that name, when I started The Body Shop, so it was not so much a marketing strategy on my part as initial desire to sell the kind of products I wanted to buy and then to offer my customers what they wanted in the form they wanted it.

They want to feel sympathy not just with the product but with the process supporting it, how it is manufactured, presented and sold.

I think we at The Body Shop have got more vocal in the last few years because we feel we are a role model and are confused as to why other companies do not seem to be getting our message. It is one that can be clearly stated. There is a better way. You can rewrite the book on business. You can trade ethically, be committed to social and global responsibility. You can empower your employees. It is OK to have fun.

I believe that people employed by most big corporations are hyped out and that the conventional carrots designed to inspire the workforce – compensation packages and motivational seminars and training programmes and all the rest of it – don't work any more. It does not matter how much companies insist they are committed to staff welfare, the staff don't believe it. Employees simply don't buy the argument that companies are in business to make their lives better.

How do you resolve this problem? Well, you educate people, especially young people, by stirring their passions. So you take every opportunity to grab the imagination of your employees, you get them to feel they are doing something important, that they are not a lone

Artists that inspire me:

Robert Doiseneau
Botticelli
Hieronymous Bosch
Pablo Picasso
Frank Auerbach
Paul Gauguin
Andy Warhol
Leonardo da Vinci
Van Gogh
Elizabeth Blackadder
David Hockney
Don McCullin
Howard Hodgkin
Robert Mapplethorpe
Walt Disney
Norman Rockwell
Tom Phillips
René Magritte
Yuri Leonov
Henri Cartier-Bresson
Magnum photographers
Eugene Smith
Dorothea Lange
Ansel Adams
Gillian Ayres
Lee Miller
Man Ray
Auguste Rodin
Russian Constructivists
Joseph Cornell
Joseph Beuys
Fra Angelico
Diego Rivera
Tamara di Lempicka

voice, that they are the most powerful and potent people on the planet. It is finding a way of bonding with the company and producing a sense of passion that you would never find in Selfridge's or Bloomingdale's.

Staying on Track

What is imperative is to create a style so forceful that it becomes a culture. Imposed culture is a cult; real culture is built from pacing and leading – it is a living organism which moves and changes. You have to work to preserve a sense of being different, otherwise the time will come when everyone who works for us will say that The Body Shop is like every other big company. This is going to be such a huge company in a few years that we have to ensure we don't wind up like an ordinary company, but remain part of that global community which believes that business should do more than just make money and create jobs and sell good products – that it should help and solve major social problems and fight environmental causes.

We also have to stay quirky, keep raising eyebrows in the business world and err on the side of eccentricity. In fact the bigger we get the more quirkier we have got to be be: I keep telling Gordon we need a department of surprises.

It is going to be difficult to cope with this monolithic company, to balance growth with the need to love and care, but we have learned a lot; what we are good at, what our strengths are. We know we are brilliant at trading and sensational at campaigning. We know, instinctively, when it is necessary to change course; we know when to act.

We will compromise on almost anything, but not on our values, or our aesthetics, or our idealism, or our sense of curiosity. These are qualities drawn from the very core of our being and they are what keep us human in an alienating business environment.

We will compromise on almost anything, but not on our values, or our aesthetics, or our idealism, or our sense of curiosity.

The Body Shop is not just what it sells. Our shops successfully combine the warmth and friendliness of the old corner store with informative and effective presentation. The people who come to work for us stay with us because of the way we operate, because our values are their values. They often talk about how difficult it would be to go back and work for an 'ordinary' company. It takes about six months to re-educate recruits to the company from other businesses – it takes them that long to get over their amazement that they can spend an entire business meeting discussing everything but profits.

One of our main responsibilities is to allow our employees to grow, to give them a chance of fulfilling themselves and enhancing the world around them. Nevertheless, we still have within our company many people who believe that working for an honourable employer and doing a good job for a good day's pay is enough. It is not. It negates the mutual responsibilities of the employer and the employee: I educate you, you educate me; I help you, you help me; together we help others. We want our employees to be empowered to make their voices heard in the running of the company, to be involved in everything we do.

I have often heard businessmen mouth aphorisms like 'people are our greatest asset', and I have always thought it to be a completely asinine comment. People are not merely an asset, they are the company. I believe that people, rather than things, will be the focus of business in the future; it will be individuals who herald change in the business world.

Traditionally the role of the individual was to conform to the organization. In the future the organization will have to conform to the needs of the individual, both inside and outside the company. From being mindless and soul-less bureaucracies, large corporations will now have to take a look at the growth of human potential, of education, of making the workplace a social centre, of taking the drudgery out of work.

So called 'scientific management', whose god was the stopwatch, has progressively given way to humanistic management. Instead of forcing management and workers to operate as authority demands, companies must seek to harness people's own motivation to that of the

Magazines I love
and learn from:

organization. Staff are saying, 'Don't make me an adjunct to the process, make me inherent in the process.'

It is the individual who is forcing change. He or she is looking not just for the right job, but for the right working atmosphere. People regard the old values of the business world – the robber baron, get-rich-quick mentality – as selfish and outdated; they are less willing to work for them.

Counting Accountability

I have said for years that the responsibility of business is not to create profits but to create live, vibrant, honourable organizations with a real commitment to the community. To do this, business has to become a major educator and nourisher of staff, customers and shareholders.

By our proselytizing we are putting these notions in the minds of the workforce and the consumer. In response, they are asking for manufacturers and retailers to be held accountable for their actions. Social accountability is more than a numbers game – it is a philosophy. And if the primary objective of a company is to maximize profits, how much social accountability can we realistically expect?

I would love it if every shareholder of every company wrote a letter every time they received a company's annual report and accounts. I would like them to say something like, 'OK, that's fine, very good. But where are the details of your *environmental* audit? Where are the details of your accounting to the community? Where is your *social* audit? How can I measure the worth of your company without knowing what you are contributing to the community or doing to help protect the planet?'

I certainly believe that companies should not be evaluated solely on their annual report and accounts. If I bought stocks and shares, I would want the company to relate to me on a personal level – I would want to know what better things they did this year than they did last year. Along with the profit and loss sheets, I would want to know about the profit and loss for the environment, or the community or the Third World. That is the way I would like to look at a company and I don't understand why companies are not routinely checked like that.

Along with the profit and loss sheets, I would want to know about the profit and loss for the environment, or the community or the Third World.

Even though things are changing, I am very frustrated at the slow pace of change. The appearance of ethical funds has been very encouraging. It would have been considered totally nutty ten years ago to have ethical shares; the very name would have been unacceptably wacky. There is more talk of empowering staff, of humanizing the workplace with childcare facilities, flexi hours and job-sharing. Staff education and training are more wide ranging, more adventurous, and include personal development programmes and Outward Bound courses.

But these are little, little drops in the ocean: the institution of business remains resolutely old-fashioned. If you go into the City most things have not changed at all – you could be stepping back fifty years in time.

I cannot understand why people revere the traditions of business when they are so obviously stultified, self-satisfied and selfish. I am convinced it is the constant search for a better way that gives my company its moral strength and sense of purpose.

People talk of The Body Shop as a multinational company because we trade in thirty-eight countries. I prefer to describe us as global. The magic of that word is that it is responsible, it is multi-cultural, it has an anthropological and spiritual tone. Global companies have values; multinationals just trade, make money and gobble up other companies.

Growth and the pursuit of profits are only bad when they become an end in themselves. Growth's reward is a number on a piece of paper or a flicker on a screen and, in either form, of little lasting comfort. Tomorrow, who will care how fast you grew? Isn't it more important to know what you are building with your growth, and why?

As a trader, I want to provide my customers with the goods and services they need. The reward for that effort is profit. But that profit should not then be viewed as the means to improve my standard of living or that of my fellow directors. We don't use our profits to improve

Music to shop by:

Peter Gabriel
Real World
Van Morrison
Neville Brothers
Paul Simon
Sting
Cajun
Miles Davis
Mark Isham
Gabriel Yared
Nina Simone
Keith Jarrett
Pat Metheny
Motown
Otis Redding
Percy Sledge
Chris Isaak
Baroque
Beach Boys
Joni Mitchell
George Formby
k.d. lang
Bob Marley
Vangelis
Everything But
the Girl
Elvis Presley
The Travelling
Wilburys
U2
J Geils Band
Chambers
Pet Shop Boys

the lifestyle of people already well off; we use our profits for higher ends than the purchase of limousines, motor yachts or Van Goghs.

People say to me, 'God, isn't it amazing what has happened to The Body Shop?' I never thought of it like that – in fact I rarely thought of it at all. It is like when you are a parent you need an outsider to tell you how wonderful your kids are – you are so busy telling them what to do that you don't see it yourself. So people kept saying how remarkable we were, and we kept saying we were only doing what came naturally. We never saw what good we were doing or what remarkable things we had achieved.

To me, The Body Shop is still small in human scale. Our shops are like village shops; our offices and warehouses are open plan and informal, everyone knows everyone else by their Christian name, everyone is valued and invited to contribute ideas. The term 'small is beautiful' is essentially shorthand for a new aesthetic and moral view of the world, a return to simpler values and simpler products – and by simpler I mean more personally and aesthetically satisfying.

I never think of myself as the managing director of an enormous company. I am frightened of grandiose thinking, of being thought a bossy boots, or a know-all. I am petrified by that kind of arrogance – petrified that we will lose touch with the sense of joyful amateurism with which we started. I don't spend time worrying that in ten years' time we are going to have a thousand shops and twenty thousand employees and need an Olympic stadium to have our conferences. I prefer to think of the company as a network of interlinked ventures, each one small enough in scale to be intensely personal. What is important is that growth will never be allowed to compromise our values.

What Next?

Gordon and I both hope that our daughters will join us in the business, although at the moment both of them are adamant that they won't. I would be truly disappointed if they didn't. I just think that together they make a great team. Sam has a perfect sense of empathy with the wider issues – she thinks on a grand scale. She wants to save the planet and the cosmos. Justine has a real sense of local care, caring for the family unit and the community spirit. Justine has a great sense of design, while Sam has a great sense of fun. Together they could do great things in the company, but at the moment they are desperate to prove themselves in other areas, which is fine by me.

Justine, who is now twenty-two, still wants her freedom. She works for us intermittently in order to earn enough money to travel, which is her way of educating herself. Neither of the girls has gone to university. We sent them to a good liberal boarding school with a fine reputation for drama, debate and the arts, where they made lots of joyful friends and learned to be curious. It bothered me a lot at first that they were not destined for university, but then I realized we were placing too much emphasis on academic qualifications, which were not really relevant unless they wanted to be brain surgeons or nuclear physicists.

Sam, who is twenty, is one of the team running the Romania project. She has been involved from the start and they have made it into an incredible success, quite independent of The Body Shop. We have donated office and warehouse space, but they run the whole show themselves, raising funds, organizing visits and deciding what needs to be done out there. Their average age is just twenty-two.

One of the reasons I am particularly proud of both Justine and Samantha is that they are not rich kids and they don't want to be. Neither of them will inherit our financial interest in the company. Gordon and I have no intention or desire to stack up a pile of accumulated wealth which goes on and on, *ad infinitum*, for generation after generation. We believe it would be obscene to die rich and we intend to ensure we die poor by giving away all our personal wealth, through a foundation of some kind.

I am such a tramp, such a nomad. The accumulation of wealth has no meaning for me; neither has the acquisition of material riches. I believe we impoverish ourselves by our tendency to undervalue all the other riches that come from our life experiences – the ones that can't be bought. This leads us to avoid pursuits such as leisure that don't yield measurable rewards, and to keep us at work for all the wrong reasons. It is the old story of people acquiring assets for status, to indicate their success. It comes to the point where the gold pen they write with is taken to be more revealing than what they might scrawl.

I think the value of money is the spontaneity it gives you. There are too many exciting things to do with it right now to bother about piling it up, and in any case it is ennobling to give it away. It makes you feel better, and if you feel better you are better, spiritually. Make no mistake about it – I'm doing this for me.

People often ask how much we spend on philanthropy of one sort or another, and the truth is I don't know. Actually, many of our projects that appear to be philanthropic are in fact designed to end up being self-financing and so we are not making long-term financial commitments. Other projects result in enormous media coverage and so could legitimately be costed as public relations. More significant than money, I think, is the substantial time that Gordon and I devote to social and environmental matters.

My hope for the future of The Body Shop is primarily vested in those people who will be the custodians of our culture and our values.

I believe that young people of my daughters' age, the children of the hippies, are going to come forward with a moral code, with a passion, a zest for the moment, and prove to be the true planetary citizens, the ones who will keep this planet alive. My generation has certainly not done much to keep it going.

Business can make a contribution by facing up to moral choices about profits and responsibilities. In The Body Shop we intend to continue to proselytize our values in the hope that one day the cosmetics industry will wake up and realize that the potential threat of The Body Shop is not so much economic as simply the threat – if that it can be called – of good example.

Make no mistake about it – I'm doing this for me.

Anita x

Mother's Day

ONCE IS NOT ENOUGH

MOSTLY MEN

STIFFY

AVE LIVES

OPLE FACING EXTINCTION:
VES OF THE YANOMAMI ARE HANGING IN THE BALANCE

U CAN TIP THE SCALES

Mama
MOTHER AND BABY RANGE

1991
RE-EXAMINE
ALL YOU HAVE
BEEN TOLD
...DISMISS
WHAT INSULTS
YOUR SOUL

BANANAS IN TRANSIT

I'm Dreaming of a
Green Christmas

PASSION
fruit

CLEANSING GEL

Turn your armpits into
CHARMPITS

ANIMAL TESTING
& COSMETICS

CRUEL/UNNECESSARY/REJECTED BY THE BODY SHOP

GRAPEFRU

WASH
SHAMPOO

At last . . .

The Hairspray

STIFFY

AGAINST
ANIMAL
TESTING

DEWBERRY

RANGE

Art